The **Marshall** Story

College Football's Greatest Comeback

Publisher	Henry S. Beers
Associate Publisher	Richard J. Hutto
Executive Vice President	Robert G. Aldrich
Chief Operations Manager	Gary G. Pulliam
Editor-in-Chief	Joni Woolf
Art Director/Designer	Julianne Gleaton
Designer	Daniel Emerson
Director of Marketing and Public Relations	Mary D. Robinson

Printed in U.S.A.

Library of Congress Control Nmber: 2006933195

ISBN: (10 Digit) 0-9776711-9-4   ISBN: (13 Digit) 978-0-9776711-9-9

Henchard Press, Ltd. books are available at quantity discounts with bulk purchase for educational, business, or sales promotional use.

For information, please write to:
Henchard Press, Ltd. • SunTrust Bank Building • 435 Second St. • Suite 320 • Macon, GA 31201, or call toll free 866-311-9578.

www.henchardpress.com

Dedicated to the 75 Marshall players, coaches, athletic department staff, fans and aircraft crew members who perished November 14, 1970, in Huntington, West Virginia.

Prologue

A blessed Son of Marshall

"We are the sons of Marshall,
Sons of the great John Marshall,
Year after year we go to Marshall U.,
Cheering for the team and gaining knowledge, too.

Proudly we wear our colors,
Love and loyalty to pledge,
Sure from far and near you always hear
'The Wearin' of the Green,'
But it's the Green and White of Marshall U."

"Sons of Marshall" is the Marshall University fight song. That song is one of two that strikes a special chord in my heart and stirs my emotions. The other is the U.S. Marine Corps hymn. When I hear either I can count on a chill going up my spine and goose bumps on my arms. The thoughts that come to mind are those of absent companions.

I remember distinctly the moment I forever became a son of the great John Marshall, former Chief Justice of the United States Supreme Court. It was on a chilly morning on November 15, 1970, in Raleigh, North Carolina, while waiting to be seated for breakfast. I was contemplating a hearty meal before beginning a long, grinding drive home to Huntington, West Virginia, with Shirley, my wife of five years, and the mother of our two daughters.

We were in Raleigh because the day before I had covered the Marshall-East Carolina football game in Greenville for The (Huntington) Herald-Dispatch where I was the beat writer for Thundering Herd football. It was only when I glanced at one of the two newspapers I had purchased, the Winston-Salem Journal, I discovered what the world already knew: the Marshall football team had been killed in a plane crash the night before as it flew home from the game.

Shirley and I didn't know about the tragedy because after I had filed my story for Sunday's newspaper we had driven to Raleigh to spend the night. We had the radio on an FM station, and there were no news break-ins to announce the disaster. Tired, we went straight to bed unaware of how our world had changed.

Marshall head coach Rick Tolley's photo was just above the fold of the paper and it caught my attention. My words to Shirley were, "the SOB took the Virginia Tech job and he gave the story to the Winston-Salem paper!" Tolley had come to Marshall the year before from Wake Forest University where he had been an assistant coach. Tolley's name had circulated as a possible replacement for soon-to-be-released Jerry Claiborne, for whom Tolley played at Virginia Tech. Tolley had told me if anything concrete ever developed with him and the job, he'd give me the story.

About the same time that thought ran through my mind, I saw a photo of the wreckage of a crashed airplane. I knew without reading the headline what had happened. At the same moment, Shirley was scanning the front page of The Charlotte Observer and saw the same story. Crying and unable to utter a word to the hostess we simply turned and returned to our room.

Upon reaching our room, the first person I called was my boss at the newspaper, Executive Sports Editor Ernie Salvatore. He had an unlisted number which I could not remember and the operator would not put the call through.

Then I called my mother, Eva Brown. I'll never forget her first words: "Oh, you sound so near."

The Marshall football team, athletic administrators and fans were dead. It was unbelievable then. It is unbelievable now. We both knew without saying that my wife had narrowly avoided being a widow and, even worse, our children could have been orphans.

I was scheduled to fly to the game with the team, and on Wednesday I called Athletic Director Charlie Kautz to cancel out on the flight, explaining I was driving so I could take my wife. Kautz responded by inviting Shirley to fly with the team on its Southern Airways charter.

"She can come as our guest," Kautz said. "We've got plenty of seats."

Chilling words to this day. I thanked him for the offer, but told him we'd drive to Greenville since we had to go through Beckley, West Virginia, to drop off the girls at my mother's home. I would much rather have flown, but fate intervened.

My wife and I are alive today because my mother couldn't come to Huntington to stay with the children. I'm alive because my wife consented to travel with me to the game. I had asked Shirley a couple of times if she wanted to attend the game with me. She was reluctant because of the kids.

Our daughters, Eva Carol and Katie, were ages three years and three months, respectively, and we knew no one in Huntington with whom we could leave them for the weekend. My selling point to Shirley was that in two weeks basketball season would start and I wouldn't have a free weekend until March. Plus, I thought she needed a break from the kids.

At the beginning of the week, Shirley decided she would go if my mother could baby sit. My father had passed away the previous year, and I still had siblings at home. Mom said she would keep the girls, but couldn't do it in Huntington. After hearing that, I called Kautz to cancel my seat on the plane. Ironically, my mother, in effect, gave me life twice. At birth and again 28 years later when she agreed to take care of my children for a weekend.

Because of that diversion, I'm the only member of the West Virginia media contingent to have covered the game who is still alive. All the others perished in the crash.

There are many stories about why people were or weren't on the plane. One involved nothing more than the luck of the draw with Lowell Cade, my counterpart on "The Huntington Advertiser," the city's afternoon paper until it merged with The Herald-Dispatch in 1979.

Cade covered the Herd for the afternoon paper, and he and I split the roadtrips during the season since the city's newspapers combined staffs for the Sunday paper. I was originally penciled in to cover a game at Bowling Green with Cade going to East Carolina. We swapped assignments because he had a close friend who lived near Bowling Green and he wanted to pay him a visit. No problem for me. It gets cold at Bowling Green. I preferred a game in warmer weather. Cade definitely would have flown with the team.

I was an avid sports fan growing up in the coalfields of Raleigh County, West Virginia. But I had no interest in Marshall. I was a West Virginia University and West Virginia Tech guy. The Mountaineers of my youth had Sam Huff and Jerry West while at Tech the Golden Bears of coach Neal Baisi became the first team — college or pro — to average more than 100 points per game in basketball. Marshall was not on the radar screen.

I came to Huntington and Marshall simply because of a job opportunity. I had kicked around some after high school. I had been in the Marine Corps and was working in Beckley when then Herald-Dispatch sports editor George Rorrer, who also happened to be the executive officer of my USMC Reserve unit, hired me. About the only thing I knew of Marshall was that Scott Jarrell and Jim Farley, a couple of guys from my high school, Marsh Fork, had gone to school there. And, I knew its football program wasn't very good.

I was still a Marshall student at the time of the crash, but I was working full-time and had a family. I would hang out at the old Shawkey Student Union where I would shoot pool and play cards. And, honestly, from the time I enrolled until I got my degree, I can only recall being in the Marshall library one time, and then it was only a cursory visit. A good grade point average was not a priority, just the degree.

When I heard the Marshall fight song it was always at a sporting event and it was something I came to take as a perfunctory act, much like the playing of "The Star Spangled Banner."

When I was first assigned the Marshall football beat I wasn't thrilled. I was covering the top high school teams in our circulation area and for three years had been covering Ohio State, West Virginia and Kentucky football on Saturdays. I felt I was taking a step backwards.

But, I took the assignment and, to be honest, by the time we got to the East Carolina game I had fallen in love with Tolley and the "Thin Green." When the plane crashed it hit hard. That was when it finally hit me: This was MY school, MY team, and I knew my life had changed forever.

Marshall lost to East Carolina 17-14. There are things from that day and that game that still stand out and come to mind every time I go into a locker room.

Tolley, his coaches and the players were outraged — and rightfully so — after the game. There had been an intentional grounding call on quarterback Ted Shoebridge which pushed the team out of field goal range with just seconds remaining. Running back Art Harris Jr., caught the pass from the scrambling Shoebridge on the first bounce, but the officials saw it differently.

It was a game Marshall entered expecting to win. The victory turned out to be the Pirates' lone win of the season. Victories against East Carolina and Ohio in the following week's season finale would have enabled Marshall to finish 5-5, quite an accomplishment for a team that the previous season had snapped a 27-game non-winning streak.

Tolley had coached the 1969 season on an interim basis in the wake of a recruiting scandal that led to the dismissal of coach Perry Moss, the school's expulsion from the Mid-American Conference and NCAA probation. Tolley was given the job permanently after winning three of the final four games of the '69 season.

On the basis of that finish with seasoned returning players and a freshman team that went undefeated against the likes of Kentucky and Ohio the Herd entered the 1970 season with high hopes. Despite the disappointing loss to ECU, there was no question that Tolley had the program going in the right direction.

At only age 30, Tolley's future was filled with promise. He was destined to land a big-time job like the one that possibly awaited in the coming weeks at Virginia Tech.

As I was walking back to the press box to write my story, Marshall sports information director Gene Morehouse, who also did the radio play-by-play, and Ken Jones, who was the sports director of WHTN-TV in Huntington, saw me coming and sat their equipment on the field to give me a mock salute.

Morehouse, a kind and gentle man, was simulating driving a car while Jones was waving his arms similar to a seagull in flight. They were kidding me about driving while they were flying. "We'll be home in a couple of hours," Jones said.

I had been aware of Morehouse since I was a kid growing up. He was the general manager and sports director of radio station WJLS and the "Voice of the Flying Eagles" of Woodrow Wilson High School in Beckley. While Morehouse did Woodrow Wilson games when one of the county schools played in the Beckley area, he often came to call our games at rural Marsh Fork when the city school was off. When Morehouse showed up at the small schools it was like ESPN's arrival today. For kids in the coal camp like me, Morehouse announcing one of your games meant your school had made the big time. He was very modest and never saw himself as a star, but I always did. Still do. Because, he was.

We all shared the laugh at their gesture, and parted, them to the bus for the 40-mile trip to the airfield in Kinston, North Carolina, and me to the press box to finish work. In two hours, Morehouse, Jones and every Marshall player and nearly every coach I'd watched, spoken to and was going to write about were dead.

In the press box a young kid leaned over my shoulder and said, "Mr. Brown, do you mind if I use your phone to call in my story. I'm in a hurry. I have a plane to catch."

The youngster was Jeff Nathan, sports editor of The Parthenon, Marshall's student newspaper, who was covering the game for The Charleston (West Virginia) Gazette. Nathan, too, perished. Jeff's words were the last I heard from anyone in the Marshall group, and they've stayed with me all these years.

I think often, too, about the athletes on that team. To this day, Shoebridge remains one of the two most impressive athletes physically I have ever seen. The other was Willie McCovey, former All-Star first baseman for the San Francisco Giants.

Marshall did not have that many players following the NCAA problems of the year before, but they had some great ones. There is no question in my mind that running backs Joe Hood and Art Harris, cornerback Larry Sanders, wide receivers Dennis Blevins and Jack Repasy, kicker Marcelo Lajterman, and Shoebridge would have had a great chance for NFL careers. And, you could put backup quarterback Bob Harris in that group, too.

There were two players from Cabell County, where Marshall is located, on the team. They were players I'd covered in high school. Tom Howard was an all-state guard at Milton and Mike Blake was an all-state linebacker at Huntington East. Their coaches, Lewis Ball at Milton and Bob Sang at East, were especially devastated. That was true for the other players, too, but I was closer to Ball and Sang, especially Sang, and years later they still talked about "their boy." It's heartbreaking to this day.

Druid High School in Tuscaloosa, Alabama, had sent four of its sons to Marshall

— tackle Robert Van Horn, tight end Freddy Wilson, Hood and Sanders. They were at Marshall because Southeastern Conference schools weren't yet recruiting black athletes. And, they were good enough to play in the SEC, but for their skin color.

Famed Moeller High School of Cincinnati sent the Herd guard Mark Andrews, Bob Harris and Repasy. In my eyes, Repasy was the best possession receiver I've seen at Marshall and that includes College Hall of Famer Mike Barber, who played a handful of years in the NFL.

Dr. Joseph Chambers and his wife, Margaret, who died in the crash, also were Marsh Fork graduates. They were classmates and friends of my uncle, Jim Brown, and his wife, Judy. We had another common tie. Dr. Chambers' father was a coal company doctor, who had delivered me and three of my brothers and sisters.

I left the newspaper business in 1979 after 15 years and Huntington in 1991, and while in the city found attending the annual fountain ceremony very emotional, but still disturbing. I would often think that the widow I saw across the way could have been Shirley, or those children whose parents perished in the crash could have been Eva Carol and Katie. How would their lives have been different? Who would have raised them? Would they have gone to college? There still are so many what-ifs for so many.

For me, there are far more certainties. Today, I live in Savannah, Georgia, with Shirley. Eva Carol and Katie have blessed us with seven grandchildren — Andrew, John Michael, Sarah, Emily and Tommy Czerkawski from Eva Carol, and Brandon and Ben Brooks from Katie. My most precious gift, I believe, is the opportunity to grow old with Shirley, who's been with me since 1965 with no indication she wants to do otherwise. Neither do I.

Mike Brown, 64, is a semi-retired insurance agent who lives in Savannah, Georgia, with his wife Shirley. He also works as a freelance sports writer for The Macon Telegraph, Savannah Morning News, Statesboro Herald and The Associated Press.

Table of contents

Foreword

When I was asked to write the foreword for this book, I was extremely honored, but also wondered why they would want me. There are a lot of great people associated with Marshall University who are more qualified to do this.

When most people outside of the Huntington community think of Marshall football they think about the recent success the program has enjoyed and the big-time players who have come from there. Now with the "We Are Marshall" movie and with this book, people will be able to learn the rest of the story. It is a story that evokes all the emotions of life … tragedy, loss, sadness, mourning, but also triumph, victory, joy and celebration. It has all the ups and downs and in-betweens that every day can bring. Simply put, it is a story about LIFE told from the perspective of a football team and its fans.

My father, Frank Loria, was a 23-year-old assistant coach for the 1970 Marshall football team. He was a very special man. At Virginia Tech, he was a two-time All-American safety, an academic All-American in the classroom, and an all-around good guy. People tell me that they admired him not only for his success on the football field, but for how he carried himself off the field. He was a man of character who cared about other people.

Dad married my mom, Phyllis, while he was at Virginia Tech. My sister Vickie was born his senior year there. Even with all his success playing college ball, he was not drafted by the NFL. He tried out for the Denver Broncos, but was cut. When the call came from Marshall head coach Rick Tolley to join his staff, my father jumped at the opportunity. He wanted to be a head coach one day, and Marshall offered him his big chance. In the summer of 1969, he moved his wife and two little daughters (Julie had just been born) to the lovely community of Huntington, West Virginia. The first season was rough, but the 1970 team was really showing promise for the future.

I really wish I could go on with the story and tell you that my dad did really well as a coach, moved up in the ranks and today is a successful head coach. I wish I could say that he is surrounded by his family and friends and is living a great life. I really wish more than anything that I could just pick up the phone and talk to him right now. But that is not how things went. On November 13, 1970, he said goodbye to his pregnant wife and two daughters and left with the team for a game at East Carolina University. On November 14, 1970, he perished along with 74 other beautiful people in that terrible plane crash. I was born a month and a half later.

When people hear the story they usually respond with "I am sorry." While I appreciate that, I want people to know what happened; I want them to know of the tragedy. It gives us all an opportunity to reflect on our own lives today and realize that life can be difficult, but it is precious. It is easy to take things for granted, so it is important to reflect and give thanks for what we do have.

That 1970 team is an important part of college football history. It is good to remember, even celebrate, the lives of those we lost that day. The memories are precious. No, the sadness of that day will never go away but it helps to keep us grounded. It helps us to appreciate what we have today.

It also is important to remember that life went on. It is hard to believe, but here we are 36 years later. The story of my father continues with what happened after the tragedy, and that leads to my mother. My mom is a true hero. I cannot imagine what it was like for her on November 14, 1970. She was 22 years old, Vickie and Julie were ages 3 and 1 respectively, and Mom was 7.5 months pregnant with me. Her beloved husband was tragically killed and she was left to carry on. Life does not get any worse than that. I do not know how she did it.

I do know that she had the strength to pick up the pieces and to go on with life. She raised her children and provided us with a very good life. She did it with grace and honor and never once complained about what life had done to her. Today, she is happily married to a great man and they enjoy spending time with Vickie, Julie and me and our families. Mom has six beautiful grandchildren … and counting! Life continues to go on.

Over the past few years I have come to know some of the other family members who also lost loved ones in the plane crash, and I feel a connection to them. It is as though we are family — the Marshall family — composed of the university, the Huntington community, the football team and the fans. We have a unique bond and for the most part we feel an obligation to share our story with the world. Hopefully, our story can bring comfort to others who are going through adversity in their own lives as they can see how the Marshall family was faced with a devastating tragedy, and yet picked up the pieces and carried on.

I get chills when I hear the cheer, "WE ARE... MARSHALL." Those three words signify so much. There is a pause between the words "We Are" and "Marshall." In that short space of time is an opportunity to remember and honor that 1970 team and those we lost. Then, we are able to draw a deep breath from the very depths of our soul and really bellow out the word "MARSHALL" as a testament that we have overcome, we have persevered, we will not forget and we will continue to carry on.

Hopefully, with the release of the movie and book more folks will become Thundering Herd fans. We certainly will welcome them in and gladly have them join with us as we cheer, "WE ARE... MARSHALL."

Frank Loria Jr., 35, lives in New Jersey where he and his wife, Sarah, are the parents of Sophia, 4, and Frank Paul III, 2. Loria graduated from West Point, class of 1993, and currently works as a medical sales representative for Medtronic.

Acknowledgments

The authors and publisher are gratefully indebted to all the players, coaches and athletic department personnel who were associated with Marshall University football from 1967 to today. Without them the story of these four decades of the program could not be told.

Special thanks to Ernie Salvatore, retired columnist at The Herald-Dispatch newspaper in Huntington, West Virginia. Salvatore has followed Marshall football since his days as a student at the University in the mid-1940s. The authors greatly appreciate his contributions of insight and knowledge.

Thanks also is extended to the following people for a wide range of contributions and encouragement in the writing, editing and production of this book: Lars Anderson, Rick Baumgartner, Mike Brown, George Chaump, William "Red" Dawson, Mark Deal, Terry Echols, Carl Fodor, Thomas Forrest, Mark Gale, Charlotte Garnes, Ed Grisamore, Bos Johnson, Pat Jones, Ed Hamrick, Floyd Harlow, Rick Haye, Roger Hillis, Bill Hynus, Basil Iwanyk, Julia Keller, Menis Ketchum, Dr. Stephen J. Kopp, Carl Lee, Jack Lengyel, Jamie Linden, Frank Loria Jr., Mike McGee, Jerry Moore, Keith and Debbie Morehouse, Reggie Oliver, Stan Parrish, Chad Pennington, Joseph Person, Bob Plymale, Bobby Pruett, Sonny Randle, the late Nate Ruffin, the late Rev. R.F. Smith, Keith Spears, Rex and Debby Stoler, Mary Viola, David Walsh and Jason Wellman.

Thanks as well to The Charlotte Observer, The Chicago Tribune, The Greenville Reflector, The Herald-Dispatch, The Macon Telegraph, Marshall University sports information.

Chapter one

'This is going to kill us'

Marshall was getting in trouble with the Mid-American Conference because it didn't have any facilities. It couldn't host the spring championships. They could be held anywhere in the league but Huntington. The MAC was out of patience with Marshall. Marshall found itself in an impossible situation – no facilities, no money, no support. And the front office had no political clout whatsoever in the state capital.

The administration was very, very cosmetic. You couldn't get Dr. Smith to do anything. That eventually led to his being retired. All these inner workings began to take place. I wouldn't say that football or athletics was the only thing responsible for it. The whole school was in bad shape. You couldn't get new buildings, the campus was falling apart. You had all these new students coming into town to enroll at this school and there was no place to house them, no place to teach them. So, as for Smith's leadership, I think he was a prisoner of the situation itself. It was almost like an institutional change was beginning to take place, not just in athletics but in academics as well. The university status helped some, but, despite all the excitement and all the celebration, nothing much happened on the campus for the next 10 years.

Nevertheless, because of Charlie Snyder, a sound, fundamental coach, who believed in well-conditioned ball clubs, Marshall maintained a level of respectability in the mid-'60s and appeared ready to move up another level in the conference, except that two-platoon football killed him. The MAC voted not only to go along with the two-platoon system, but also voted to expand the number of sports it was going to sanction.

I remember riding back with Whitey Wilson from Columbus where the MAC had the meeting and he said: "This is going to kill us; you know that, don't you? This is going to kill us. How in the hell are we going to keep up with these guys when we can't do it now? This is going

Immediately after reassigning head football coach Perry Moss to other duties in the athletic department, Marshall President Roland H. Nelson Jr. glumly met the media to answer questions about the move during a news conference. Nelson said he considered the situation a "setback, but not a disastrous one."

to murder us unless we have a miracle happen." Now you have the seeds sown for the scandal. How is Marshall going to catch up? What is it going to do? So, out of that came this beautiful idea to go underground and do it illegally.

After all the months in the shadows, 144 alleged recruiting violations were brought up at a meeting of the MAC Council of Presidents. I mean guys were getting paid, guys were on the payroll, guys were getting spending money, guys were getting car expenses. Every damned rule in the book was being broken. If you're going to cheat, you've got to know how to cheat. So, they threw Marshall out of the league indefinitely. And then, of course, the NCAA was brought in. This was all a result of the crash program and upgrading Marshall athletics and bringing it into the 20th century – that was the big term – and the school wound up in disgrace.

– Ernie Salvatore

In the classic manner of most illicit love affairs, the Marshall University football recruiting scandal began innocently enough. The motives of the enamored – a small band of well-heeled alumni boosters – were well-intended. They were a decent bunch, proud of Marshall, devoted to it, protective of it, but also wearied by:

- The school's shameful lack of facilities, especially the deteriorating condition of off-campus Fairfield Stadium that Marshall shared with two high schools in Huntington.
- The subtle neglect of athletics by President Stewart H. Smith, and his administration, and his lack of influence in the West Virginia Legislature, which controlled Marshall University's financial destiny.
- A winless streak, starting in 1966, that had begun to draw embarrassing national attention.

The boosters simply wanted to correct these inequities by helping to rebuild the entire Thundering Herd athletic program. They also wanted to get the job done as quickly as possible. Success, they knew, would reap its own rewards. Football would be their centerpiece in the upward thrust since it faced the steepest climb. Immediate upgrading, they believed, was the only way Marshall could achieve parity in the Mid-American Conference without getting booted from it.

But a hitch developed. The group, which embraced a diverse collection of professional and business people, had reacted too late. Before it could commit a single fund-raising plan to paper, the MAC voted to abandon its middle-of-the-road image and go big time. This meant an expanded all-sports program that would require new, updated or enlarged football stadiums and basketball arenas, and new members.

Everybody else was doing it, the MAC's brain trust reasoned. In college athletics, TV money was becoming a prime revenue source as it began to surpass live gate receipts. So, as Commissioner Bob James warned his Council of Presidents and athletic directors, the MAC either had to keep pace or die. The MAC, of course, opted to live. And that nearly killed Marshall. The MAC's poor relative from West Virginia, with the scruffy image that the conference affluent deplored, now would have to upgrade its pitiful athletic program at an even faster pace just to keep up.

It was late summer 1966. The MAC's other members – Miami of Ohio, Ohio University, Kent State, Toledo, Bowling Green and Western Michigan, already were moving toward new horizons. Ball State, Central Michigan and Eastern Michigan were being mentioned as prospective new members. Northern Illinois, Louisville and Cincinnati were being courted outright. So, the small but influential group of Marshall helpmates decided to undertake a high-risk "crash" program of calculated "short cuts."

Perry Moss leaves the Old Main office of President Roland H. Nelson Jr. on August 23, 1969, after being stripped of his coaching duties. Nelson's action was taken following a decision by the Mid-American Conference on July 23 to suspend Marshall from the conference indefinitely. Shortly after his meeting with Nelson, Moss told reporters, "This thing has been so confusing. They've chopped my head off, but what the hell. I'm going to put it back on and go again." In March 1970, Moss left Marshall to assume a position as quarterbacks coach with the Chicago Bears. Moss coached just one season at Marshall, posting a 0-9-1 record in 1968. (Photo by Lee Bernard)

It seemed to be the only way to accelerate Marshall's so-called "catch-up phase" to keep pace with the MAC's expansion. The worst-case risk, of course, was exposure. But the plotters theorized that any National Collegiate Athletic Association punishment in the one- to three-year range would be a worthwhile "incubation period" for securing Marshall's place in the conference. The underground operations would coincide with the overt fundraising of the Big Green Club and without, of course, the knowledge of certain "key" school officials. The identities of the plotters were never made public. Their names were excised from all official findings filed with the NCAA and the MAC, including a 142-page report prepared by Marshall. Likewise, the names of those who knew about, aided or abetted the deception.

At this point, the flirtation had become a conspiracy. Before it ended in disgrace, three coaches would lose their jobs as a direct result of their involvement, dozens of student-athletes would leave school and many prominent private citizens would worry that one day they would be named by the media. The Marshall community's shock later would turn to anger when the MAC Council of Presidents voted to suspend Marshall indefinitely until it could prove it had cleansed itself of its sins. The transgressions that Marshall admitted to the conference included:

- Special loans for student athletes arranged by the athletic department staff.
- Money given to student athletes on a regular and irregular basis.
- Junior college fees for prospective student athletes paid by the athletic department staff.
- Special loans used to entice prospective student athletes to come to Marshall.
- Prospective student athletes contacted by the athletic department staff before being contacted by the Marshall admissions department, a violation of MAC regulations.

In ordering the suspension, the Council of Presidents instructed James to assist Marshall in rehabilitating its athletic program. It was a hollow commitment and one the Council of Presidents probably knew it wouldn't have to keep. Marshall officials stated at the time that the school was "trying to maintain an athletic program equal to those of schools with budgets four to five times the size of ours." It was a question of Marshall being the poor stepchild, who got the hand-me-downs, while its more affluent sibling, West Virginia University, received top-drawer treatment. And it was Marshall that now found itself on the scaffold with the noose tightening.

The MAC's official version was that Marshall was not being banished completely from the conference. To re-establish itself as a viable MAC member, however, would take resources that Marshall could only dream of harnessing. Before arriving at that unhappy state, the university would name three different committees to examine the athletic program and conduct investigations at various stages of the unfolding skullduggery.

The reshaping of Marshall's image began in earnest in 1966 when Smith was convinced by the boosters that firing Athletics Director Neal B. "Whitey" Wilson was a necessity. No one outside the small, clandestine clique knew the real reasons. That was the cabal's secret. But the clique's mouthpieces first convinced Smith that Wilson wasn't giving Marshall the dynamic leadership the "new Marshall" would need. Then the cabal's members accused Wilson of personal misconduct. Without giving Wilson a hearing or presenting him with a bill of particulars, Smith took the bait and Wilson took the fall. By mid-1967 it was goodbye, Whitey.

It was a shocking move. Wilson, a lawyer and a World War II combat officer who served in Europe in the 3rd Army under Gen. George S. Patton Jr., was from an old Huntington family. He often used his own money, or signed personal notes, to bail Marshall out of cash crunches. Wilson, however, had a glaring weakness, one he shared with his bosses: he had no clout in the state Legislature, which historically has been dominated by West Virginia University alumni. The clique's strategy was to penetrate the Legislature via Morgantown. They hoped to accomplish their goals by first making Wilson a sacrificial lamb, then hiring, on June 15, 1967, as his replacement Edgar O. Barrett Jr., West Virginia University's sports information director.

On its face, the theory that Barrett's West Virginia University background would influence the Legislature to look with favor on Marshall's sports needs was clever. But, in practice,

Neal B. "Whitey" Wilson was a highly popular athletic director for Marshall until his firing in 1967 by President Stewart H. Smith. The move was in response to mounting pressure from boosters who were putting together the ill-fated plan to restore Marshall's competitive balance within the Mid-American Conference. Wilson, an attorney who was an officer in World War II, often bailed Marshall out of cash crunches by using his own money or signing personal loan notes.

it was pitifully disingenuous. The problem: Barrett had almost no experience in sports administration. Also, his connections in the Legislature were equally modest. But, despite the clique's appalling naiveté, the first "hit" had been scored. Barrett was as innocent as Wilson had been. The new athletic director would himself become a victim of the duplicity.

The next execution came on November 14, 1967, when Barrett announced Smith's decision to reassign football coach Charlie Snyder to other duties within the university. Ironically, Snyder later became an assistant athletic director at Toledo. Snyder's dismissal, as unpopular as Wilson's had been, was particularly cruel because it came five days before the end of the football season. Snyder was a Marshall alumnus, a standout tackle and captain on the Herd's 1947 Tangerine Bowl team, and a disciple of legendary Marshall coach Cam Henderson. Snyder, however, was easier to fire than Wilson. Snyder's weaknesses were simpler to catalog; they were inscribed on his coaching resume. His record showed only two winning teams in nine years. Worse, Snyder's 1967 team went 0-10.

Snyder's failure paved the way for the hiring of Perry Moss two months later. Moss, a coach with the Orlando Panthers and Charleston Rockets of the Continental Football League, actually was Marshall's second choice. Burnie Miller, a backfield coach at Purdue, had been the first selection, but he backed off four days after he had been introduced as Marshall's new coach during a December 14 press conference in Old Main, the school's stately administrative building.

Miller's reason for changing his mind was as vague as was that for Wilson's firing. Miller apparently wanted no part of the "secret" mandate to get Marshall a winner. For the record, he blamed the lack of contract guarantees for more than a year for his staff. It became obvious when the NCAA completed its investigation two years later that the mandate called for taking various recruiting risks to turn Marshall into a quick winner. If the unthinkable – getting caught – occurred, all involved simply would accept the consequences.

Moss signed a $15,000 per year contract on January 16, 1968, in Smith's Old Main office, making the 41-year-old Oklahoma native the 17th football coach in Marshall's history.

"Everything tied together here," he said later that day during a news conference. "Everything was satisfactory, the salary and the recruiting expenses."

Barrett introduced Moss at the news conference, saying: "This is no job for the faint-hearted. We're trying to change the image of Marshall. We want to become competitive in the Mid-American Conference. We're not expecting a championship. We want to get competitive first."

That was not to happen. Not for a long time.

Moss' first and only team began the 1968 season with a 7-7 tie against Morehead State at Fairfield Stadium. The Thundering Herd went on to drop its next nine games. The dismal season included losses by substantial margins to Ohio University, Toledo, Miami of Ohio, Western Michigan, Bowling Green, Kent State and East Carolina, which appeared on Marshall's schedule for the first time.

But surely better times were just ahead. During the summer of 1968, Moss and his staff had assembled a group of freshman who were among the most talented football players in the country. While the varsity suffered through its season, the freshmen were beating the likes of Kentucky and Ohio. They finished their season 5-0.

A young defensive back from Quincy, Florida, was a member of the freshman team. Nate Ruffin, who was to suffer years of personal anguish as a result of his decision to attend Marshall, recalled the expectations for him and his teammates.

"That was one of the greatest things I remember," Ruffin recalled nearly 20 years after the scandal began. "When we came here in 1968, the word potential was what we heard all the time. We had the potential to be one of the most high-powered teams in this particular region because Perry Moss came out and recruited so many great athletes. I had met the guy in Florida when I was a junior in high school. Everybody knew him and he was big time. He was at all the big games in Florida. This guy recruited us and had us all in one week. They sold us on the idea of 'You guys can be the catalyst of something dynamite.'"

The talent of the freshmen didn't go unnoticed by their varsity teammates, who had earned the enmity of Moss during the pathetic 1968 season.

"We played the varsity every Monday in what they called

Marshall was coming off only the third winless season in the program's history — the others were in 1898 and 1920 — when new coach Perry Moss recruited Florida native Nate Ruffin to play defensive back in 1968. "They sold us on the idea of 'You guys can be the catalyst of a beginning of something dynamite.'" Ruffin, and many of his fellow recruits however, soon came to question the veracity of the promises Moss and his coaching staff made. Moss had the school's fourth winless campaign in '68, going 0-9-1, in his only season as coach. (Photo courtesy of The Herald-Dispatch)

the 'Toilet Bowl' out back of Twin Towers (dormitory). We would beat the varsity by about 45-0. We wouldn't even let them score. Our big thing was not to let the varsity score. They'd go out on Saturday and get beat up by everybody else and then our coach would say, 'All right, boys. Every Monday you're going to get the hell beat out of you again because I'm going to bring these freshmen back in and they're going to beat you again.' And we would. We'd beat them something bad."

But the freshmen had problems of their own. Some were beginning to question the veracity of promises made to them in exchange for their commitment to attend Marshall.

"A lot of students, a lot of good friends of mine, were in that group," Ruffin said. "They were told that once they got here they would be put on scholarships. They were fresh out of high school and they were trustworthy. About 125 of us came in here competing for probably 35 positions."

The competition late in the summer of 1968 that Ruffin described would better be defined as tryouts, a violation of NCAA rules.

"It was in August and numbers of guys were saying to themselves, 'We have to fight for a position.' The coach was saying, 'Hey, you don't have a starting position. But if you do real good, you might be able to knock this guy out of his scholarship and you can get it.' I saw the toughest practices that I've probably ever seen. It was like a massacre out there."

Questions also arose about assistance the players were receiving.

"When we signed a four-year renewable scholarship – that's what they called it – it was really a one-year scholarship," Ruffin said. "That was just the tip of the iceberg."

After some of the practices, said Ruffin, who already had been assured of financial aid, some of the recruits who had won positions would excitedly discuss how they had just signed their scholarships.

"Some of us had a little bit of sense reading and we'd say, 'Man, you just signed a loan, a student loan.' They didn't realize the difference between a student loan and a student grant. A student grant is given to you."

"Some of them got student grants … but they came in here under the premise of playing football. You couldn't get those grants under that basis unless there was a particular need established before you came. So (the recruiters) ended up not having enough money for all the people. Then they reverted to giving them loans. A couple of banks here probably lost their rear ends because they signed lots and lots of loans away to these students."

But the supporters, flush with the knowledge that they had landed some of the nation's best football talent, didn't seem to mind. It was a time to celebrate bringing Marshall out of its decline and into prominence. It was a time to show the recruits how much they were appreciated.

"We were the scandal," Ruffin said. "Several of the players in 1968 were given money. It was part of the deal. People were saying, 'OK, we have some superstars coming in this weekend. Let's show them a great time.' There were several of us who went to restaurants and had fancy meals. And when you picked up your plate, there would be an envelope under there for certain people. Only certain people got invited to the lunch. After practice on a day once a month, you'd go and receive certain things. You also had certain sponsors to look after you. They'd not just give you a meal, but if you needed certain things, they'd look out of you."

Ruffin recalled that Marshall's recruiting practices came to light when one of the play-for-pay members of the team decided to stop going to practice. The player missed several practices and was told by Marshall athletic department officials his payments were going to stop. The player shared his dilemma with a relative, who had ties to another school in the MAC. The relative shared his information with the conference, which acted on it early in 1969.

"The scandal broke loose and they kicked us out of the conference when the '69 season was coming up," Ruffin said.

Several of the players sought releases to attend other schools because of the sanctions laid down by the MAC and NCAA. Ruffin said he, defensive back Larry Sanders and quarterback Ted Shoebridge flew to Los Angeles to discuss attending UCLA.

"UCLA was going to take us," Ruffin said.

With the Marshall athletic department in shambles, no one could be found to sign the releases, leaving Ruffin, Sanders and Shoebridge stranded in California.

"UCLA coach Tommy Prothro said UCLA would only wait five more days. They waited five days and put us back on the plane."

Had the releases been signed, the futures of the three football players would have been altered dramatically.

Gone by now was Smith, who had retired in July 1968. Smith was given a new Pontiac by the university in appreciation for his years of service and he promptly drove off in it to the Olympic Games in Mexico City. In his place was Dr. Roland H. Nelson Jr. Faced now with investigations of his athletic department by the MAC and NCAA, he appointed several committees to deal with the embarrassing problems. The first of these panels became known as the "Blue Ribbon Committee" of faculty, administration, students, alumni and leading citizens. Made up of about two dozen members, it was formed by Nelson at the request of the University Council "to develop a positive plan for Marshall Athletics."

The request was submitted to Nelson on February 19, 1969. By then, the council, which had close ties to all facets on campus, had developed some strong reservations about the athletic department's operations, particularly in the areas of fund raising and the football program. The report of the Blue Ribbon Committee would confirm these fears with disastrous consequences. A brief chronology of events that followed the submission of the report to Nelson on May 5, according to the Marshall University Faculty Bulletin of August 14, 1969, shows:

- After receiving the Blue Ribbon Committee report on May 23, 1969, James, the MAC commissioner, acting on behalf of the Council of Presidents, notified Marshall by letter and telephone of alleged irregularities in financial aid, recruitment practices and federally insured loans.
- The MAC notified Nelson on June 11 that, based on complaints received by the NCAA, it would investigate Marshall. Nelson then appointed a "Three-Man Committee" to answer the questions posed by the MAC Council of Presidents.
- The MAC Council of Presidents on July 23 reviewed the answers and voted to suspend Marshall indefinitely. Nelson then asked the University Council and the Athletic Committee to review the report of the Three-Man Committee and make recommendations.
- The joint committee met on July 27, invited the three parties to present their views on July 29-30 and the draft recommendations to Nelson on July 31.
- Nelson discussed the recommendations with the three parties. Informed of their rights of appeal, they asked Nelson to form a faculty review committee to examine the recommendations. The review committee met August 11 and 13.

The three parties involved were Moss; Peter Kondos, freshman football coach and director of recruiting; and, surprisingly, Ellis Johnson, head basketball coach. The faculty review committee, in the 142-page report, recommended that Moss be reassigned to noncoaching duties for the duration of his contract, due to expire on June 30, 1970; that Kondos not be retained; and that Johnson be reassigned indefinitely to non-basketball coaching duties. Nelson complied on August 23, 1969, during an emotional news conference. He named Moss his special assistant to develop a plan for on-campus athletic facilities. Moss did not stay on long as Nelson's aide. By the following March, Moss had found a job with the Chicago Bears as an assistant offensive coach for quarterbacks. Kondos said he would resign, but not until June 30, 1970, an offer Nelson declined. Johnson, a highly popular and visible figure with fans, was accused by Nelson of running his program in an "incompetent and insubordinate manner" and was reassigned to the physical education department, where he served for several years before retiring.

Five days before Nelson's news conference, Barrett made the unusual move of resigning at his home on Sunday, August 17, saying that current conditions make it "highly unlikely that I will be able to carry out the type of program I want to direct." Barrett, with his wife and five children in the next room, emphasized that he was not quitting under duress.

"I've been under pressure for the whole two years," he said. "This has possibly been coming on day by day as the situation developed. I don't want to imply that the job can't be done here; it just can't be done by me under the circumstances. … I made a commitment to our financial supporters and they shelled out a lot of money. I don't feel I can continue to make that commitment."

Barrett stayed on long enough to help interim Athletic Director Charlie Kautz through the transition. In November 1969, Barrett announced that he would become an executive for a Huntington soft drink bottling company.

Meanwhile, the NCAA, showing rare compassion, placed Marshall on one-year probation – a mere slap on the wrist compared to the MAC's unprecedented overkill. Then, as if to ease the pain of the wrist slap, the NCAA adopted a resolution that commended Marshall for its forthright cooperation.

Many of the details of the scandal did not become public until Kondos filed a $465,000 libel suit against Nelson. The case went to trial in U.S. District Court in Huntington in August 1971. Kondos, who by then was driving a taxi cab in Massachusetts, contended that Nelson's accusation in a dismissal letter that Kondos was "incompetent" had prevented him from finding football-related work. Dr. Hunter Hardman, chairman of the Athletic

Committee that made its recommendations to Nelson, testified at the trial that during Kondos' appearance before the panel in the summer of 1969, the former coach admitted that he obtained money from Moss to pay fees at Beckley (W.Va.) Junior College for athletes trying to gain eligibility to enroll at Marshall. Kondos told the committee that he obtained the money from Moss without the head coach's knowledge of what it would be spent for.

Kondos testified that he came to Marshall in February 1968 with no previous experience in college coaching and that he was unfamiliar with NCAA rules. He said he depended on Moss to interpret the regulations for him and admitted that he transported two students to Beckley along with another Marshall assistant coach, Jim "Shorty" Moss (no relation to the head coach), who was transporting four other students. The trip was made "at the direction of my immediate supervisor, Perry Moss," Kondos told the jury in Judge Sidney L. Christie's courtroom. Kondos' statements appeared at odds with his case against Nelson, a point that was not lost on Christie, who seemed to be leaning toward a directed verdict of acquittal for Nelson.

"Much can be said for your argument and, in a different case, perhaps …" the judge told Nelson's attorney, Robert G. Perry, after he requested the directed verdict during the second day of the three-day trial. "But in this case, which has involved tremendous publicity and where the reputation of both parties is involved, I think it would be in the best interest of the two parties, justice and the public for the jury to decide."

It didn't take the jury long to determine that Kondos' claims had little merit. After deliberating about three hours and 45 minutes, a verdict was returned in favor of Nelson. But before the trial came to an end, Nelson was asked by Kondos' attorney, Thomas E. Medeiros, what had happened to the 142-page report prepared by Marshall in the summer of 1969 that outlined the university's MAC and NCAA violations. Nelson said he submitted copies of the report, with all names excised, to the MAC, which later returned them.

"Only one copy had any names in it and that one was kept in my office and not allowed to circulate," said Nelson, who resigned as Marshall's president in the summer of 1970 to take a teaching job at the University of North Carolina.

Nelson said he did not make the report public because "it reflected on many people in Huntington, who, through their own good intentions, gave illegal assistance to the athletic department and we did not want to embarrass them." Nelson added that many of the people named in the report were living and many were dead.

Medeiros told Nelson that he had been seeking the president's copy of the report to prepare for trial, but had no success. Nelson said the last time he saw the report was the day he left Marshall and placed it in the president's confidential file. John G. Barker, who had replaced Nelson as Marshall president, testified earlier in the trial that he had searched the files and could not find the report. The disappearance of the report and the names it contained probably saved the architects of the scandal from being identified during the trial.

This, then, was the framework of an ill-advised venture that remains one of the darkest chapters in the history of Marshall athletics. But as impossible as it would seem, Marshall soon would be plunged into another tailspin that was eminently more tragic.

Chapter two

A promise unfulfilled

I've often wondered how far Rick Tolley would've taken Marshall's disgraced football program had he lived. None of us will ever know. What was obvious, however, at least to me, was that they couldn't have made a better choice to restore order and sanity to the football program when they – meaning President Roland H. Nelson Jr., really – named Rick interim football coach. He turned out to be a perfect pick. Rick was only 29, but looked and acted like someone 10 years older. There was a strong sense of command about him … of leadership. He had broad shoulders; he had a thick neck and a handsome, finely chiseled face, the kind that inspires confidence. He was deadly serious about the task that had been handed him. More important, he considered himself the head coach. And, as far as he was concerned, if Perry Moss ever tried to get it back, he'd go head-to-head with him before any selection committee to keep it. Rick got the job two days before the start of preseason practice on August 27. What he'd inherited was a disaster, so he ran his program like a Marine boot camp. And before the 1969 season was over, many dramatic things would occur. Then, just when things were getting back to normal and the pain and the embarrassment of the scandal were wearing off, the plane crashed coming back from the East Carolina game and Rick Tolley and 74 other people were dead. What a horrible epilogue that turned out to be.

– Ernie Salvatore

Head coach Rick Tolley coached Marshall in 1969 and 1970, posting a combined record of 6-13. He faced a monumental task when he stepped in as acting head coach two days after Perry Moss was relieved of his duties in August 1969. That summer's events in the Marshall athletic department had rocked the football program to its foundation and team morale needed a dramatic overhaul less than a month before the season kickoff. But within the next year, Tolley and his assistants had reason to be excited about the Herd's fortunes, as shown in this photo of Tolley viewing game film on July 22, 1970. A little more than four months later, Tolley died along with most of his coaches and players in a plane crash. (Photo by Havern Summers)

H.B. "Deke" Brackett brought the expertise of a 40-year college coaching career to Marshall when he came to work for Perry Moss in 1968. He stayed with the program when the reins were assumed by Rick Tolley after Moss was reassigned shortly before the 1969 season. Brackett, who played quarterback at Tennessee in 1931-33, asked graduate assistant coach Gale Parker if he could have Parker's seat on the charter flight from East Carolina instead of returning to Huntington by car with fellow assistant Red Dawson, who he'd been on a recruiting trip with in the days before the game in Greenville, N.C.

Marshall University's administration moved quickly to hire a replacement for Perry Moss. It had no choice. There was no time to conduct a long search for a coach to try to rebuild the football program, someone to lend it a degree of credibility after the embarrassing scandal that forced Marshall President Roland H. Nelson Jr. to reassign Moss. The timetable dictated moving with dispatch: Moss was removed as coach on August 23, the start of the 1969 football season was only 28 days off, the team was to report for fall practice on August 27, and there were rumblings that at least two of the Thundering Herd's most promising players were considering asking for releases to attend the University of Tampa.

Marshall's unenviable situation was compounded further by a non-winning streak that had reached 21 games at the conclusion of the 1968 season. The Thundering Herd, which had admitted to the NCAA that it had cheated concerning recruiting practices and had been placed on indefinite suspension by the MAC for its sins, now was a cruel misnomer. Marshall and the Thundering Herd were becoming synonymous with frustration and failure. It was truly a no-win proposition for anyone stepping into the Marshall coaching job. In the preceding 17 seasons, there had been just three winning teams and 51 wins in 164 tries.

It took Nelson two days after reassigning Moss to settle on one of the former coach's assistants for the job of putting the football program back in order. Rick Tolley, a 29-year-old interior line coach, who had joined the Thundering Herd staff seven months earlier, accepted the position as interim head football coach. It was a busy day for the Marshall president, who also named Charlie Kautz as acting athletics director and Stewart Way as interim basketball coach. Kautz replaced Edgar O. Barrett Jr., who resigned a week earlier in the wake of the scandal; Way succeeded Ellis Johnson, who was accused by Nelson of running

Marshall head coach Rick Tolley, with rolled paper in his hand, talks with his players during Press Day at Fairfield Stadium on August 28, 1969. Assistant coaches William "Red" Dawson, to Tolley's left, and Frank Loria listen along with the players, including guard Jeff Angle (62), tackle Danny Gordon, guard-center Richard Dardinger (50) and split end Dennis "The Menace" Blevins (80). (Photo by Lee Bernard)

the basketball program in an "insubordinate manner" and reassigned to teaching duties.

Two days after Tolley's appointment, the former Wake Forest and Ferrum Junior College assistant and 1961 Virginia Tech graduate told sports columnist George Rorrer of The Herald-Dispatch newspaper in Huntington that he was not taking the Marshall job in a caretaker capacity. He also was not concerned that Moss might be waiting in the wings for reinstatement.

"I'll tell Perry or anybody else if at the end of this year I feel I've done the job, I'll be trying to keep it," Tolley said in Rorrer's column.

He made it clear that suggestions he was too young for a top college job would go unheeded.

"I feel I'm ready for a head coaching job," Tolley continued.

The first, and most pressing, task facing Tolley was reversing the tide of player

Halfback Joe Hood (33) runs for a portion of his 77 yards in Marshall's 17-7 opening-game victory against rival Morehead State University on September 19, 1970. Hood carried 18 times in the game, which was the Thundering Herd's first on artificial turf at Fairfield Stadium. Quarterback Ted Shoebridge scored two touchdowns and kicker Marcelo Lajterman kicked a field goal and both extra points. Marshall's defense held the Eagles to 153 total yards, intercepted three passes and recovered two fumbles. The game ball was given to West Virginia Gov. Arch Moore. (Photo by Lee Bernard)

defections after the fallout during the summer over the recruiting scandal. Two players upon whom Tolley counted most to help end the non-winning streak – quarterback Ted Shoebridge and offensive tackle Ron Mikolajczyk – were at home in Lyndhurst, New Jersey, when the Thundering Herd reported for practice on August 27. They were considering transferring to Tampa, but Shoebridge said there was a chance that they might return to Marshall for their sophomore season. Two days later, Shoebridge, who led the freshman team to an undefeated season in 1968, and Mikolajczyk, the Thundering Herd's best line recruit in several years, told Tolley they would report for fall practice. It was good news for the coach, who welcomed only 41 players back on the first day of drills. In addition to Shoebridge and Mikolajczyk, tackle Dan McCoy, halfback Rob Giardino and center Bob Olson – all starters in the spring – were out of camp. Also missing was reserve tackle John Zukowsky. McCoy was getting married, Giardino and Olson were considering going to Tampa and Zukowsky was dropping out of school.

"We're thinner than we thought we'd be, but we're still going to be able to play football," Tolley told the media on the opening day of practice, despite having barely enough players to scrimmage.

Shoebridge, a versatile athlete who had worked out during the summer of 1969 with the Philadelphia Phillies, and Mikolajcyzk, described by Rorrer as "Hercules unchained," were regarded as the nucleus of the sophomore-laden team. Few thought the Thundering Herd would win many games in 1969, but the margins of defeat were expected to be much slimmer. The only reduction, however, came in the number of names on the Marshall roster. The Thundering Herd had 83 players in spring drills, but six seniors, seven juniors and 29 sophomores did not return in the fall. Twenty-six of them simply quit, Rorrer wrote, including the six seniors who had never played in a winning game during their Marshall careers; two were academic casualties; 12 were at Marshall on government-guaranteed loans and failed to earn scholarships as they had hoped; one was sidelined by injury; and another – sophomore quarterback Gary Kaluger – was killed in a car wreck during the summer. Shoebridge and Mikolajcyzk returned; the quarterback for the season and the tackle for two days. Hercules changed his mind and decided to labor for Tampa. Others followed. At least four players quit, saying they had lost their desire to play for Marshall.

"I'm getting a little tired of hearing people tell me that," Tolley told Rorrer after the fourth player left the team.

Mike McGee

Mike McGee watched thousands of hours of game film in his nearly 25 years as a college football coach. There remains an hour or so from one game that McGee has never been able to lay eyes on. It is the November 14, 1970, game between Marshall University and East Carolina University, where McGee was head coach.

"I've never gone back and watched it," said McGee, now 67 and living in Colorado after his retirement in 2005 as Athletics Director at South Carolina.

The film chronicles East Carolina's lone victory that season, a 17-14 decision against the Thundering Herd. It also details the last hours of life for the 37 Marshall players who suited up for the game that day at Ficklin Field in Greenville, North Carolina, as well as other athletic personnel, fans and most of their coaches. A couple of hours after the film's final frame, they all died in a plane crash while returning to Huntington, West Virginia.

"There's some things that have never been the same since," McGee recalled. "It's just one of those great shocks."

McGee was in his first and only season as head coach at ECU in 1970.

It was his first head coaching job after seven years as an assistant at Duke, Wisconsin and Minnesota respectively. He had been a standout lineman at Duke, where he won the Outland Trophy in 1959 before being taken in the second round of the NFL Draft by the St. Louis Cardinals in 1960.

The coach was celebrating the victory with members of his coaching staff and their families at the restaurant at the local Holiday Inn when he received the news about the crash from his school's sports information director.

"He said it had just come across the TV that the Marshall plane had crashed," McGee remembered. "There was no other information about possible survivors."

McGee and his brother Jerry, who was an assistant on his staff, and another coach then went to the Daily Reflector, the newspaper in Greenville, in hopes of finding out more details from wire reports. "It rather quickly became apparent that it was a catastrophic accident," the head coach said.

Shortly after the group sat down for dinner, the manager of the hotel had informed them that there were still at least three families of the Marshall players who were spending that night at the hotel. Upon returning to the hotel, McGee called his team physician and the team's chaplain with the thought they could help the families once the news was out.

"I called (families) and asked them if I could come by," McGee recalled. "I went up there with the team doctor and when they

Tolley's reputation for toughness was well-earned and played a role in some of the players' decisions to leave the team or not report at all.

"You were talking about a guy who wasn't messing around when they brought old Ricardo in here," Nate Ruffin, a defensive back on the 1969 team, recalled of Tolley. "He came in and said, 'Boys, I don't play no favorites.' "

Tolley often found himself less than satisfied with the team's pre-season conditioning. His practices consisted of tough workouts and countless wind sprints during the sweltering days of late August and early September.

"They need a lot of running," Tolley told Rorrer after the second day of practice. "They're out of shape. Linemen are always the hardest ones to get in shape. A few more days in this hot weather and they'll come around."

Tolley also had little tolerance for minor injuries, Ruffin said.

"We went through those drills where you had to pound the other guy's helmet with your arm and everybody had to participate," Ruffin said. "I had big calcium deposits inside my arm where I had bruised it real bad and we never did take care of it. We'd come back to practice day after day and (Tolley) would say, 'Nobody's hurt today, right?' And we'd say, 'No, sir!'

"We went through so much. We liked playing the games so much because you could get a break. There was no such thing as a Sunday or a Monday break. During the whole season from August until the last day, there wouldn't be any breaks. We found ourselves literally being beat to death on the practice field."

Ruffin said he and his teammates soon coined a nickname for their coach.

"We called Tolley the 'Dog Man.' We said the man was fair; he treated everybody like dogs. You know how some people let up on the quarterback in practice? If you let up on the quarterback, you knew you'd get killed. None of the players ever got mad at each other because we knew the coach was the man who ran the show. He was definitely the man in charge. Everybody respected him for that, but we really hated his practices. I worked for the railroad out on a road gang from 6 a.m. to 6 p.m., but I never worked harder than those three or four hours out there on the practice field."

Short on numbers but long on conditioning, Marshall opened the 1969 season on the road at Morehead State. Shoebridge, showing great poise and potential, ran up 257 yards in total offense. His statistics included 12 of 27 passes for 193 yards and nine rushes for 64 yards. He scored a touchdown and completed a 60-yard pass to John Hurst for another. But Eagles quarterback Bill Marston out-dueled Shoebridge, throwing four touchdown passes in the 27-14 Morehead win. It was a question, Tolley said, of the Thundering Herd's youth and inexperience in the secondary. Marston riddled sophomores Larry Sanders, Craig Greenlee and Ruffin for 19 completions on 27 attempts for 243 yards. Dennis Crowley, a former Marine who won a Purple Heart decoration during a tour of duty two years earlier in Vietnam, caught two of Marston's touchdown passes. Marshall also was hurt by 180 yards in penalties, a school record that still stands. Predictably, losses followed to Toledo, Northern Illinois, Miami of Ohio, Louisville and Western Michigan. The streak stood at 27 and was expected to climb to 28 against Bowling Green in the seventh week of the season. One more loss or tie and Marshall would equal the record then held by Kansas State and Virginia.

After the 48-14 loss to Western Michigan, Marshall's worst of the season, preparation for Homecoming and the visit by the Falcons became known as "Stop the Streak Week." Stickers exhorting the Herd to "Stop the Streak" cropped up across Huntington and the campus. Stickers even showed up

opened the door, they were watching TV, but the details had not come across, but there was enough of an indication that they were in a state of shock and the beginning of the realization of what had happened and the beginning of the grief.

"We just kind of stayed with them for a period of time. I asked them if they would like to have a chaplain."

McGee then turned to his team. He found his captains and he and the staff were able to meet with the team on campus.

"It was 11 o'clock, maybe midnight," he said. "It wasn't only the team, but also some students. We had an impromtu prayer service. It was one of these moments where everyone frankly was in shock and disbelief and grief."

McGee flew to Huntington with the governor of North Carolina the next day to attend the memorial service that Marshall held after the crash at the Memorial Field House. He was seated among family members of those who perished in the crash. He remembered that nearby were the six surviving children of Dr. Ray Hagley and his wife Shirley.

"It was one of those terribly unfortunate accidents," said McGee, who left coaching in 1978 to begin a career in athletic administration that took him to directorships at Cincinnati and Southern California before his 12 years at South Carolina. "Since then, Marshall has always been one of those teams I root for. They obviously came back in great fashion, but it took a long time." (Joseph Person, contributor)

on the players' helmets during practice. No one – coaches, players and fans – wanted to see Marshall's name appended to the ignominious streak list. But in spite of the gimmicks and encouragement, it seemed that loss No. 28 was imminent. Bowling Green, 4-2, had history and the numbers on its side: The Falcons were a 27-point favorite coming in against Marshall; they had beaten the Herd 14 straight times, the most recent a 52-28 thrashing in 1968; and they were jockeying for a postseason bid to the Tangerine Bowl.

After the Homecoming Parade made its way through downtown Huntington in a cold, intermittent rain, about 7,000 Marshall fans filed through the turnstiles at Fairfield Stadium, hoping that this would be the Saturday that Marshall could shed the embarrassing distinction of holding the country's longest string of non-winning games. A little more than two minutes into the game, the dream looked as if it would become just one more nightmare in the three-year-long losing slumber. Bowling Green quickly drove 64 yards in seven plays for the first score of the game, a touchdown blemished only by the failure of kicker Art Curtis, whose field goal had beaten Miami of Ohio 3-0 the previous week, to convert the point after. After Marshall failed to move the ball on its first possession, the Herd punted and Bowling Green started another drive. But Herd linebacker Jerry Stainback, one of several transfers from Ferrum Junior College's 1968 national championship team, recovered a fumble by BG's Isaac Wright at the Marshall 38-yard line. A Bowling Green offside penalty then set up a first-and-5 from the MU 43. On the next play, Shoebridge sprinted to his right and found tailback Dickie Carter open over the middle. Aided by blocks from tight end Larry Carter and fullback Hurst, Dickie Carter took the ball in for a 57-yard score. Hurst's extra-point put Marshall in front 7-6.

Both defenses stiffened until late in the first half when Bowling Green moved from its own 34 to the Marshall 15 behind the sharp passing of Vern Wireman, the MAC's leading quarterback. But with second-and-7 at that point, the BG quarterback dropped back to throw and the wet football slipped from his hands and into the grasp of the Herd defensive tackle Mike Bankston at the Herd 29. Three plays later, Shoebridge rolled around left end for a 21-yard gain to the Bowling Green 39. With 50 seconds left in the half, Shoebridge hit receiver Jack Repasy, who had beaten two defenders deep in the end zone, for a 39-yard touchdown. Hurst again hit the PAT for a 14-6 Marshall lead at halftime. A miracle in the mud was developing, but 30 minutes of football still remained.

As the second half opened, Marshall's defense stopped two drives, the first when

Ruffin intercepted Wireman at the Herd 5 and the second when a Wireman sneak was stopped on fourth-and-1 at the MU 15. Late in the third quarter, after defensive end Mark Andrews recovered another Wireman fumble at the Marshall 34, Hurst cut around right end and eluded the Bowling Green secondary for a 46-yard pickup, leaving the Herd 20 yards from increasing its lead. But Shoebridge misfired on a pass to Larry Carter and then was sacked at the BG 34. The Herd quarterback regrouped to find Larry Carter for a 9-yard gain and then hit Repasy for a gain to the BG 3. Four plays later on fourth-and-goal from the 1, reserve tailback Kevin Gilmore plunged over for the score. Hurst's extra point put the Herd in front by 15 points with 12:23 left in the game.

The Falcons came back on their next possession, driving 67 yards in eight plays. The touchdown came on a 4-yard pass from Wireman to Fred Mathews, who set a then BGSU school record with 13 catches for 138 yards in the game. Bowling Green closed the difference to 21-14 on a two-point conversion pass from Wireman to Mathews. The Falcons got the ball back with 8:52 left, but Wireman fumbled again to Bankston with first-and-10 on the BG 48. After Hurst missed a field goal, the Herd turned away another BG drive when Sanders intercepted a frustrated Wireman at the MU 5. Faced with poor field position, Herd punter Skip Williams knelt in the end zone for a safety that gave BG two points and Marshall a free kick with 36 seconds left. Bowling Green ran three ineffective plays to end the game and the streak. Marshall 21, Bowling Green 16.

Tolley was ecstatic.

"This is the greatest thing that has ever happened to me," he said to reporters after the game. "I think it is to the kids, too. We felt and the kids felt all along that we were going to do it (break the streak). We knew we could come through if we'd stop making big mistakes. Today, all the kids gave a great effort. This really ought to help them. We've got some good football players. It was a matter of getting over this hump. Now that the pressure is off, these kids could go on and become a good football team."

The credit for winning the game belonged to the Herd defenders. Although they gave up 415 total yards, 299 coming on passes by Wireman, they made the big plays at critical junctures. Interceptions by Ruffin and Sanders stopped BG drives deep in Herd territory and Marshall forced the Falcons into five fumbles, four by Wireman. Bankston, who would be named runner-up national lineman of the week for his defensive efforts, recovered three fumbles, forced another and had 15 tackles. Shoebridge, inching closer to single-season

Marshall posed for its team picture during media day in mid-August 1970, amid Fairfield Stadium renovations that included increased capacity 6,492 seats to 17,200, a new Astroturf playing surface, and locker room facility. Only a handful of those photographed that day missed the November 14 plane crash that killed 75 players, coaches, athletic officials, fans and crew members. (Photo courtesy of The Herald-Dispatch)

records for passing and total offense, led the Herd with eight completions on 16 attempts for 202 yards.

Falcons' coach Don Nehlen, meeting the next week with the Bowling Green booster club, reassessed his first impressions about the Herd win. "I thought we'd played terribly until I saw the game films on Monday," he told the group. "Actually, we didn't play that badly against Marshall."

The Herd took Tolley's words to heart the next week. Traveling to Kent State with only 32 healthy players, the Herd embarrassed 75 Golden Flashes 31-20 before their Homecoming crowd. Shoebridge, playing in only his eighth varsity game, set the Marshall single-season total offense record with 16 of 39 passes for 238 yards and two touchdowns and 42 yards rushing. His total of 1,309 total yards broke Bob Hamlin's 1962 mark of 1,170. The Herd was 2-6 with two games left. Games that Tolley and his players believed they could win.

East Carolina, in the second of a three-game package that would see Marshall travel to Greenville, North Carolina, in 1970 to complete the deal, came to Fairfield Stadium and left three hours later, a 38-7 victim of a stampeding Herd. More milestones and records fell in the Marshall win. It was the Herd's largest margin of victory since a 46-7 win over Morris Harvey in 1955 and the most points scored since Marshall defeated Findlay 40-22 in 1962. Shoebridge passed for 156 yards and two touchdowns, breaking John Oertel's 1969 single-season passing record of 1,251 yards by 57. Shoebridge's 10 touchdown passes for the season broke Ogden Thomas' record of nine set in 1951. The 1969 finale was against Ohio University, but during the week of preparations for the Bobcats, Tolley was concerned that members of his team had more than football on their minds. Early in the week, Hurst, Shoebridge and 26 players petitioned Gov. Arch Moore to reinstate Moss to his head coaching job. They argued that they had been recruited by Moss and, therefore, were his players. If Moore did not comply with their request, they then would seek releases from their Marshall scholarships. It was a situation that was less than conducive to getting a team ready for its season finale.

"I don't know whether they'll be mentally ready for Ohio or not," Tolley said after the petition was given to Moore, who helped convince Shoebridge and other players to return in September. "I guess we'll find out by halftime."

Hurst was confident the Herd was more concerned about Ohio than the petition.

"I don't think it will bother us," he said. "This is the last one and we want it badly."

Shoebridge completely discounted the effect of the entreaty to the governor.

"Our minds are definitely on the game. We'll worry about that other stuff later. I think morale is higher on the team than it has been all season."

The Herd's state of mind, however, was not enough to stop the Bobcats. With the assistance of questionable penalties against Marshall, Ohio University drove 63 yards in the closing seconds of the game to come from behind and defeat the Herd 38-35. The last penalty of the drive was a pass interference call against Ruffin in the end zone that put the ball on the Marshall 1-yard line. Ohio's Paul Kapostasy scored from there with five seconds left to seal the victory. The partisan crowd was enraged and a group of fans leaped from the stands and assaulted two of the officials, Robert M. Walker of Canfield, Ohio, and Ollie Freese of Cincinnati, before police and Marshall officials restored order. With Marshall still on suspension from the MAC, the incident did little to enhance the Herd's chances for reinstatement by the league's Council of Presidents.

MAC Commissioner Bob James called the crowd's actions "mob violence in its lowest form." He went on to say that the league's athletic directors would have to determine the "desirability of sending their athletic teams into such an unsportsmanlike atmosphere for future athletic competition." He had already stated that no MAC officials would be permitted to call future games in Huntington. Two months later, on February 19, 1970, the Mid-American's Council of Presidents denied Marshall's application for reinstatement to the conference. The Council would not, it said, review its decision until 1973. Its reason: Marshall's admitted violations of NCAA rules governing recruiting practices and its woeful lack of facilities. The MAC had, for all intents and purposes, finally cut all ties to its poor, barefoot cousin from West Virginia. Nelson was bitter. He believed his efforts at a thorough housecleaning months earlier in the wake of the admission of wrongdoing would convince the MAC to retain the Herd after 15 years as a member in good standing.

"It comes through to me loud and clear that the Mid-American Conference does not want Marshall as a member. … I see no future for Marshall in the Mid-American Conference," Nelson said.

The Herd remained an independent until gaining membership in the Southern Conference on May 14, 1976.

Kautz, who had been given the job of athletics director permanently during the football season, ended the soap opera that had developed over the coaching situation by giving the job to Tolley on December 1, 1969. True to his word, Tolley said he would apply for the position if he believed he had turned the Marshall program around. Tolley won out over Moss, who also had applied. Tolley met immediately with Shoebridge, whose father, Ted Shoebridge Sr., had said he would advise his son not to return to Marshall for his junior year if Moss were not reinstated. The quarterback, who in his first season held Marshall records for single-season yards passing (1,620), total offense (1,756), passes attempted (226), passes completed (104) and touchdown passes thrown (13), assured Tolley he would be back to lead the Herd in 1970.

Tolley, now solidly in charge of the football program, approached his second season optimistically.

"We were as good as any team at our level of competition during the last four games of 1969," Tolley said in the Herd's preseason prospectus. "And if our kids could pick themselves off the floor to make the comeback they did last year, we could have a pretty fair football team in 1970 with everything back to normal. We'll have a good attitude and we're going in with confidence. We should be better in every department."

Positive pronouncements notwithstanding, Tolley was displeased when the Herd donned pads for the first time in preseason practice on September 1. His team got through its morning session in good shape, but Tolley said the players "loafed" in the afternoon heat. He immediately ordered an evening session with pads to insure that there would be no lapse in his team's performance the next day.

With Shoebridge easily in reach of nearly all Marshall career passing records and the total offense mark, it looked, indeed, as if the Herd would field a "pretty fair football team" in 1970 and improve on the 3-7 ledger of the 1969 season. The "Jersey Jet," as Huntington sports writers had started to refer to Shoebridge, was joined in the offensive backfield by running back Carter, a senior who quit later in the season, and sophomore Art Harris Jr., a transfer from the University of Massachusetts. Joe Hood of Tuscaloosa, Alabama, a sophomore running back, and Bob Harris, a Cincinnati junior who was Shoebridge's backup and also played at flanker, were two other key backfield components. Harris completed 20 of 33 passing attempts during the spring varsity-alumni game while Shoebridge played for the Marshall baseball team.

"Bob is an outstanding quarterback and between he and Shoebridge we have as good a 1-2 quarterback corps as there is in the country," Tolley said.

Marshall opened the 1970 season in Fairfield Stadium, but the old field had a new face. Improvements were the result of a special $1 million appropriation from the West Virginia Board of Regents that was designed to help rehabilitate the Herd's inadequate facilities, one of the MAC's original complaints about Marshall. The stadium featured a new Astroturf playing surface. Renovations also were under way that, by season's end, would increase Fairfield's seating capacity by 6,492 to 17,200. The new surroundings agreed with the Herd as it defeated Morehead State, 17-7. It was Marshall's first win in an opener since beating the Golden Eagles, 27-20, in 1966. Marshall's defense was splendid, putting on one of its finest exhibitions in years. The Herd held Morehead to 153 total yards and intercepted three passes — two by Felix Jordan and one by Sanders. The Eagles did not pick up a first down until their first possession in the third quarter. They did not score until the fourth quarter when Marshall was up 17-0. Shoebridge completed only 6 of 15 passes for 105 yards, but scored two touchdowns rushing. Marcelo Lajterman added a 29-yard field goal.

Marshall quarterback Bob Harris (12) rolls to his right behind the blocking of center Richard Dardinger (50) and guard Tom Howard (60) in the Thundering Herd's 17-14 loss at East Carolina University on November 14, 1970. The defeat was a major disappointment for Marshall, which had whipped the Pirates 38-7 in Huntington a year before. "East Carolina wanted it more than we did," Marshall coach Rick Tolley told reporters shortly before boarding a Southern Airways plane for the flight back to Huntington. Less than two hours later, Tolley and every Marshall player would be dead. (Photo by Thomas Forrest)

The next Saturday was a disaster. Toledo pounded the Herd 52-3 in the Glass Bowl. The first half was a series of three Herd downs and a Lajterman punt with the Rockets scoring to break the monotony. Shoebridge suffered a horrid game, completing but nine passes in 43 attempts for 137 yards. He was relieved by Harris, who was equally ineffective, passing six times and completing one. Marshall managed only eight first downs, one via a penalty. Toledo out-gained the Herd 513-170 in total offense. The only glimmer of success for Marshall was a 27-yard field goal by Lajterman. The Herd rebounded in its next game at Xavier. Led by Shoebridge's two touchdowns and Sanders' 52-yard return of an interception for a score, Marshall out-dueled the Musketeers 31-14. Lajterman also kicked a 38-yard field goal, giving him one in each of the Herd's first three games.

Marshall's preparations for Xavier gave it little time to take notice of the news that on the day before the Herd's meeting with the Musketeers a plane had crashed in Silver Plume, Colorado, in the Rocky Mountains. The aircraft was one of two planes carrying the Wichita State football team to Logan, Utah, for a game with Utah State. Twenty-nine people were killed, including 13 players. The other plane, with the rest of the Shockers aboard, continued to Logan without incident.

Marshall, its record at 2-1 and off to its best start since the Herd opened at 4-0 in 1965, now faced perennial bully Miami of Ohio, which led the Herd in the series 18-3-1. In a steady rain, the Herd showed the Redskins that it was not going to be pushed around on its Fairfield Stadium playground. It took a 47-yard runback of a punt by Miami's Dick Adams late in the game to clinch the 19-12 win. The game featured 15 fumbles – Miami had nine and lost five; Marshall bobbled six and gave up four. The Herd's next opponent was Louisville and the game left Marshall's home crowd of 6,500 holding its collective breath until the last seconds. With the Cardinals leading 16-14, Lajterman attempted a 57-yard field goal that fell about a foot short of the crossbar. The last of three straight visitors to Fairfield, Western Michigan's Broncos ran roughshod over the Herd, 34-3, to drop its record to 2-4. Western picked up 505 yards in total offense, 409 of it coming on the ground. Lajterman proved again that the Herd kicking game was going to great lengths to reach consistency, booting a then school record 47-yard field goal for Marshall's only score. The trip to Bowling Green brought more heartache for Marshall fans. Stu Shestina, the Falcons' kicker, made a 38-yard field goal with 1:04 left to give Bowling Green a come-from-behind 26-24 win. In its eighth game of the season, it was finally Marshall's turn to win a close contest. After trailing Kent State 17-13 going into the fourth period, Hood capped a 10-play, 69-yard drive with a 2-yard touchdown run to give the Herd the go-ahead points. Lajterman's

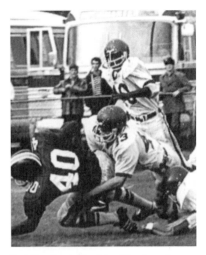

East Carolina tailback Les Strayhorn is brought down by Marshall defensive back Stu Cottrell (43) and defensive end Scotty Reese (on the turf). In the background is Herd defensive back Larry Sanders (40). (Photo by Thomas Forrest)

Marshall team captain Dave Griffith (81) wraps up ECU fullback Billy Wallace near midfield. Coming up to assist on the tackle is defensive lineman Tom Brown (65). Pirates quarterback John Casazza (11) watches the play. (Photo by Thomas Forrest)

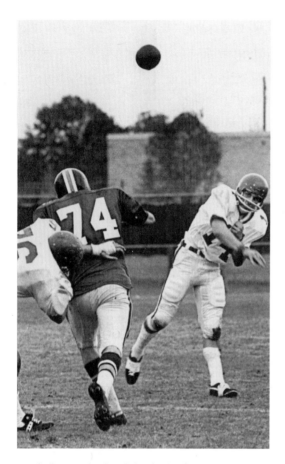

Marshall quarterback Ted Shoebridge fires a pass over East Carolina tackle Chuck Zadnik (74), who gets past the block attempt of Marshall's Dave DeBord (76). The play, which resulted in an interception, came with nine minutes left in the game. Playing in the second half, Shoebridge completed 14 of 32 passes for 188 yards and one touchdown. (Photo by Thomas Forrest)

PAT set the final score at 20-17.

The Herd was 3-5 with two games to go; a .500 season, a ridiculous notion only two years before, was within the grasp of Tolley and his players. No longer could the Herd be regarded as a "breather" on an opponent's schedule. Tolley and the Herd had extended six of the eight teams it had played and beaten three of them. Granted, a 5-5 year still would be a tough goal to accomplish; ahead were two road games, the first at East Carolina and the second at Ohio University.

The Herd flew by charter to its game in Greenville, North Carolina, at Ficklin Field on November 14. There was a crowd of 8,711 on hand. It included former Marshall football great John "The Sheik" Zontini, who had been inducted earlier that year into the West Virginia Sports Writers Hall of Fame. It was the first time Zontini had seen the Herd play since he graduated in 1935. There was another man present at Ficklin that Saturday who also would become intimate with Marshall football. On the staff of Pirates coach Mike McGee was a 34-year-old former All-Pro receiver with the National Football League's St. Louis Cardinals. Although he could not know it at the time, Sonny Randle, who was in his first year of college coaching, would figure prominently in the Herd's future.

The game, won by East Carolina, concluded with a controversial play and ended Marshall's chances for its break-even season. With ECU leading 17-14, Marshall started its final drive on its own 12-yard line with about 90 seconds left on the clock. Sixty seconds later, Shoebridge had moved the Herd to the East Carolina 25, well within field goal range for Lajterman. From there, Shoebridge missed on pass attempts to Blevins and Bob Harris.

Linebacker Jerry Stainback (56) and defensive back Bobby Joe Hill (41) chase East Carolina fullback Billy Wallace. Stainback was the game's leading tackler with nine tackles and 13 assists. (Photo by Thomas Forrest)

On third-and-10, Shoebridge dropped back again, but this time was collared by defensive end Jim Gudger at the Pirates' 44. Shoebridge got the pass off before being downed, but was called for intentional grounding even though running back Art Harris had fielded the ball after only one bounce. The ball was spotted on the East Carolina 49 and Shoebridge's pass on fourth down for Hood fell incomplete, insuring another losing campaign.

"We had a number of opportunities to win it, but we couldn't capitalize," Tolley said in his post-game press conference. "Our offensive execution was not as good as it has been and defensively we just gave up too many yards on the ground."

The Herd left Ficklin Field about 6 p.m. for the 40-mile trip to Kinston Airport where it boarded a DC-9 for the 45-minute flight home. A light rain was falling when the charter made its approach to Tri-State Airport. It was about 7:45 p.m. Weather conditions and visibility were poor. As the jetliner started its descent toward Runway 11 at Tri-State, Hugh M. Artis, an employee of the Ashland Oil refinery located just west of the airport, noticed that the plane seemed to be coming in low as it glided in from west to east.

"I don't think I've ever seen a plane come in that low," he remembered telling a co-worker. "Then I heard the intensity of jet engines increase as it dropped out of view over the hill."

Moments later, he saw a flash on the other side of the hillside that separates the refinery and the airport. The light from the flash lasted for 15 to 20 seconds before diminishing to a dull glow.

"I told my assistant, 'I believe that jet has crashed,' even though I didn't want to believe it," Artis said.

Immediately after the plane disappeared from Artis' view, it struck treetops on a

On November 15, 1970, the morning after the crash, members of the Kenova and Ceredo volunteer fire departments sift through the shredded wreckage of the Southern Airways jet in thick woods just west of Tri-State Airport. A light snow dusted the ground as recovery of the bodies continued. (Photo by Jack Burnett)

ridge just west of the airport. Seconds after its impact with the trees, the plane slammed into the hillside at a speed of 160 miles per hour and burst into flames. An investigation by the National Transportation Safety Board later would determine that the 95-seat plane clipped the first tree 66 feet above the ground on a ridge just west of West Virginia 75, tumbled while cutting a 95-foot swath across that hillside and crashed on the east side of the highway. Killed instantly were 37 Thundering Herd players, eight coaches and administrative personnel, 25 fans and the jetliner's crew of five. There were no survivors among the 75 people on board. It was Southern's first fatal crash in 21 years of operation. It was, and remains, the worst sports disaster in the history of the United States.

Heat from the fires that burned across the hillside, the darkness of the cold night and the rain that turned the scene into a muddy bog hampered the efforts of emergency personnel. Searchers combed the area by the eerie, reddish light of flares. Recovery of the bodies was delayed until the next day and completed as a light snow dusted the twisted

Eugene Payne of the Charlotte (N.C.) Observer illustrated Marshall's tragic loss from the plane crash by showing an empty stadium and bench in this line drawing that appeared in the newspaper following the crash. The Thundering Herd's final scheduled game of the 1970 season against Ohio University was canceled after the crash.

The Rev. Robert Scott of Marshall's Campus Christian Center led prayers during a Memorial Service at Fairfield Stadium on November 21, 1970 — one week after the plane crash. Scott also was the Thundering Herd team chaplain. He prayed for "eternal peace and rest" for the crash victims. Similar tributes took place before the start of college football games throughout the country that day. (Photo by Lee Bernard)

Right: Marshall equipment manager John Hagan stands among the equipment of Thundering Herd players in the team's Gullickson Hall locker room six days after 37 members of the team perished in the plane crash on the return flight from the game at East Carolina. Hagan didn't accompany the team on the ill-fated flight, rather deciding to drive a truck to and from the game. "Something just told me not to go on this trip," he later said.

remains of the charred wreckage. With the exception of the plane's engine pods and part of its fuselage, there was little left that could be easily identified as part of an aircraft. The Marshall and Huntington communities were numbed and shocked by the tragedy. It seemed that nearly everyone knew someone who was on the plane — a family doctor, a friend or a familiar face from television.

Kautz, Tolley, assistant coaches Deke Brackett, Frank Loria, Jim "Shorty" Moss and Al Carelli Jr., Marshall sports information director and radio announcer Gene Morehouse, Herd trainer Jim Schroer, MU director of admissions Brian O'Connor, and Jeff Nathan, sports editor of Marshall's student newspaper The Parthenon, were killed.

Also among the dead were prominent Huntington residents Dr. Ray Hagley and his wife, Shirley; Dr. H.D. Proctor and his wife, Courtney; Dr. G.H. Preston and his wife, Phyllis; Dr. Joseph Chambers and his wife, Margaret; Ken Jones, WHTN-TV sports director; Huntington City Councilman Murrill Ralsten and his wife, Helen; business executive Michael Prestera, who had been elected to the West Virginia Legislature just 11 days earlier; automobile dealer Parker Ward; Norm Weichmann, Chemetron Corp. plant manager and a volunteer who had filmed Marshall football games for several years; Donald Booth, an employee of H.K. Porter Co., another volunteer photographer; business executive E.O. Heath and his wife, Elaine; and insurance executive Charles Arnold and his wife, Rachel. In one of the sadder ironies of the crash, Art Harris Sr., the father of Herd player Art Harris Jr., was killed along with his son.

It was the team's only air trip of the year and Kautz told former Herald-Dispatch sports writer Mike Brown on the Wednesday before the flight that he chartered Southern Airways because he wanted the Herd to fly with a larger airline rather than on the smaller, older planes the team had used for trips in the past.

"He said because it was the only trip of the year he wanted it to be first class," recalled Brown, now a retired insurance executive in Savannah, Georgia, and a former member of the school's Big Green Scholarship Foundation.

Some people missed the plane because events intervened. Gale Parker, a graduate assistant coach, flew with the team from Huntington to Greenville, but Brackett, who had been on a recruiting trip by car with assistant coach William "Red" Dawson, asked Parker if he would mind giving up his seat on the plane to a "tired old man," Brown recalled. Parker complied and drove back to Huntington with Dawson, who was put in charge of the program immediately after the crash.

"Gale and I were driving through Greensboro (North Carolina) and heard on the radio that the plane carrying the Marshall football team had crashed," Dawson said. "I thought that because it had crashed while landing it might not be too bad. I found out later that it was."

Equipment manager John Hagan noted that the plane was leaving Huntington on Friday the 13th and chose to drive to the game. Jordan had been hurt, but the coaching staff had a difficult time deciding on whether to risk another injury to the sophomore defensive back against the run-oriented Pirates or hold him out for Ohio University and its passing attack. Jordan's equipment made the trip, but the player was removed from the traveling party at the last minute. Defensive back Richard Taglang simply was late for the departure of the team bus for Tri-State Airport.

Strangely, a death and a dream kept lineman Ed Carter from making the trip. His father had died a week earlier and Carter had gone to Wichita Falls, Texas, to attend services. On the day he was to leave to meet the team in Greenville, his mother told him that she had dreamed the night before that he would be killed on the flight back from East Carolina. She convinced him to stay at home. Assistant coaches Carl Kokor and Mickey Jackson were in University Park, Pennsylvania, scouting Ohio U. against Penn State on the weekend of the crash. Injuries to Frank James, Greg Finn, Pete Naputano and Ruffin prevented them from going to East Carolina.

The task of identifying the bodies was painfully slow. Over a period of several days, obituaries slipped into The Huntington Advertiser and The Herald-Dispatch as positive identification occurred. On the Friday after the crash, identification could be made on only four of the last 10 bodies that remained in a temporary morgue at Tri-State Airport. Those were the bodies of defensive end Al Saylor, Tolley, Schroer and O'Connor. Marshall officials announced that a joint burial service would be conducted the following Tuesday in Huntington's Spring Hill Cemetery for the final six victims whose bodies could not be identified — players Kevin Gilmore, Allen Skeens, Barry Nash, Tom Zborill, Dave Griffith and Tom Brown. The six were buried in adjacent graves. A monument noting their sacrifice and that of their teammates watches over their graves. Ruffin, who died of cancer in 2001, was buried adjacent to his former teammates.

Seventeen months and three days after the tragedy, the NTSB released its conclusions on the crash. The board stated that on its approach the plane had dropped below the "minimum descent altitude" in bad weather without visual contact with the runway. The probable causes for this, it said, were "improper use of cockpit instrumentation data" or "altimetry systems error." Earlier in the investigation, testimony had established that water that had seeped into the plane's altimeter could have given the pilots, who had never before flown into Tri-State Airport, a false reading, indicating that the plane was higher than it actually was.

But regardless of how the crash occurred, its pervasive damage was done. Seventy-five people, most of them important to the future of Marshall football, were dead. And a football program that had succeeded in turning the corner in its effort to erase its image as a loser and put behind it the recruiting scandal and banishment from the Mid-American Conference now faced the bleakest moment in its history.

Chapter three

Picking up the pieces

When I think of the post-crash era, I'll always think of Jack Lengyel in the context that he represented exactly what Marshall needed at that time. And he was actually the third choice. Jack Lengyel had an excellent reputation in the profession. He was working his way up at the time, granted, but he had a good reputation and a good background and people liked him. So, when they saw an honorable guy like Jack Lengyel in here trying to do an impossible job, it really enhanced Marshall's reputation. He changed it from one of pity to one of respect. You've heard about the Young Thundering Herd, but what he had was a makeshift ballclub. Hell, he wasn't hired until after St. Patrick's Day of 1971, and the crash had happened the preceding November. Jack Lengyel was the guy who set the foundation for what has happened today. Jack Lengyel worked a coaching miracle.

– Ernie Salvatore

Jack Lengyel entered an impossible situation believing there was nothing that could not be achieved. It was the only attitude a man in his position could have after accepting the job of rebuilding the Marshall University football program. Lengyel knew his job would be difficult. Just how tough is something he never imagined.

"It would have been easy to say, 'Let's give up,'" Lengyel said. "No one would have criticized Marshall. In a time when people were criticizing athletics and students

---

Quarterback Reggie Oliver (12) rolls left behind the blocking of Terry Gardner (26) during Marshall's 35-21 home loss to Ohio University on November 24, 1973. Oliver and Gardner had hooked up for the game-winning touchdown two years before in the Young Thundering Herd's shocking 15-13 victory over Xavier. (Photo by Tim Grobe)

Marshall Coach Jack Lengyel poses with his three seniors from the 1971 Young Thundering Herd team. From left are defensive back Felix "Flip" Jordan, guard Ed Carter and defensive back Nate Ruffin. Because Jordan and Ruffin were injured and Carter was attending his father's funeral in Texas, they were not aboard the flight that crashed near Tri-State Airport the previous November. (Photo courtesy of The Herald-Dispatch)

were rebelling against discipline and administrations were concerned with the financial crisis that faced their institutions, it would've been easy to give in. And I doubt very seriously if anyone would've criticized them."

The decision to continue the program wasn't a foregone conclusion. The school's administration was under the direction of Donald N. Dedmon, who was named acting president in July 1970 upon the resignation of Roland H. Nelson Jr., whose departure ended 22 troubled months at the school for him. Student protests and riots over the Vietnam War and drug busts on and around campus, along with the athletic misdeeds that led to Marshall's NCAA probation and expulsion from the Mid-American Conference, were among the problems he faced.

Dedmon was executive vice president at Marshall before succeeding Nelson on an

THE WHITE HOUSE

WASHINGTON

September 7, 1971

Dear Coach Lengyel:

There will be a deep sense of sadness as Marshall University football begins again this season, but it will be mixed with warm pride that last year's freshmen have responded so positively to the great tragedy that struck your campus.

The 1970 Varsity players could have little greater tribute paid to their memory than the determination to field a team this year. Friends across the land will be rooting for you, but whatever the season brings, you have already won your greatest victory by putting the 1971 Varsity squad on the field. Congratulations to you and to every member of your team.

Sincerely,

Richard Nixon

Mr. Jack Lengyel
Head Football Coach
Department of Athletics
Marshall University
Post Office Box 1360
Huntington, West Virginia 25715

President Richard Nixon sent a letter to Marshall coach Jack Lengyel on September 7, 1971, congratulating Marshall for its decision to field a team after the plane crash of 1970. Marshall played its first game on September 18, losing to Morehead State University, 29-6.

interim basis. Dedmon remained at Marshall as vice president for academic affairs after John G. Barker took office in March 1971 and left Marshall in 1972 to become president of Radford College, guiding the school to university status in 1979 before retiring in June 1994. He died February 13, 1998, in Naples, Fla., at age 66.

"Dedmon demonstrated deep compassion as well as extraordinary leadership ability that elicited genuine admiration in the days, weeks and months that followed the crash," wrote former Marshall history professor Charles Moffat in his book "An Institution Comes of Age." At the heart of that compassion was the decision to continue the football program in the wake of the tragedy.

Dedmon and his colleagues went back and forth on the subject in the days and weeks after the crash. Those in favor of dropping the program cited its lack of success, its increasing costs, and the fact that money could be better spent on a basketball program that always had held more favor with fans and now was an emerging national power. Those who wanted to keep football, however, had the strength of emotion on their side. Their most effective argument: That it would be a disservice to those who died not to field a team again. They won out with the help of impassioned pleas to the administration from the players who had missed the game at East Carolina and those who were freshman recruits in 1970.

"There were really no raging debates about the issue," recalled Mike Brown, who covered the football program for The Herald-Dispatch newspaper in Huntington. "The call for dropping football mainly came from the faculty and their voices weren't very strong. It was their view that, financially, the sport was a drain and now would be the perfect time to get rid of it."

The decision to play was cemented with the hiring of Joe McMullen as athletics director on February 7, 1971. McMullen had been an assistant football coach under the legendary Rip Engle at Penn State, and had been head coach at Akron and San Jose State before entering athletic administration.

"In the end, everyone realized what football meant to Marshall no matter what state it was going to be in for a while," Brown said. "When Joe Mac (McMullen) was hired as athletic director all of that talk of dropping football promptly went out the window. Joe Mac was a football man and they were going to play football at Marshall."

With the decision to play ball, McMullen set out to find a coach, but Lengyel, then coach at Wooster (Ohio) College, wasn't the first choice. That was Penn State University assistant coach Bob Phillips, who applied for the job, but turned down Marshall's offer.

Marshall athletics director Joe McMullen, right, and assistant AD Ed Starling, on McMullen's right, joined others on November 14, 1974, in placing a wreath at the site of the memorial in Huntington's Spring Hill Cemetery where the six crash victims who could not be positively identified were buried. At the far left, is Thundering Herd coach Jack Lengyel. (Photo by Howard Cazad)

The second choice was Georgia Tech freshman coach Dick Bestwick, who accepted the job February 24, 1971, but resigned a week later, citing family reasons. Bestwick said he did not want to be separated from his family for three months, nor did he want to relocate them to Huntington.

Enter the miracle worker. Lengyel, then 35, began spring practice in April 1971 determined that he could help lift the Thundering Herd from the ashes of the plane crash just five months before and make it a respectable team. In fact, he said prior to the season, his goal was for the team to go 10-0. Despite this optimism, he knew privately there was no way that could happen.

"That was the attitude I felt was necessary for us to sustain a major college schedule under the most trying set of circumstances that ever faced any university at any time," said Lengyel, who had played for McMullen at Akron.

But Marshall had lost too much in the crash. Lengyel discovered just how frustrating that picking up the pieces would be from the first day of practice.

"It was more difficult than I thought it would be," he said. "It was one of the toughest things I ever had to go through. It's something I hope no one has to go through ever again. All the equipment was gone. We used what little gear we had until we could get new equipment. But it was a tragedy far deeper than a football tragedy. Marshall lost great boosters, leaders and administrators. It lost radio and television people and an athletic director along with the team and coaches. It wasn't just a football team lost. The crash cut a wide swath across the whole town."

Lengyel immediately hired three assistants and then set out to recruit players — another extremely tough task. Two surviving assistants who were on Tolley's staff — William "Red" Dawson and Mickey Jackson — had continued recruiting players during the search for a head coach.

One of those players was Roger Hillis, a two-way tackle from Hazel Green, Alabama. Hillis knew nothing about Marshall other than it had just lost most of its football team in a plane crash a month or so earlier when Kenneth McKinney, his coach at the rural high school, said some coaches from the school were interested in talking with the player about a scholarship. The lure of a college education was as much a reason for Hillis to listen to Dawson and Jackson as continuing to play football.

"I was from a family of laborers in an area full of cotton farmers," recalled Hillis, now a career counselor at Sparkman High School in Hazel Green. "I was really excited more about going to college than about football. It was a really big thing for my family. I had a great family with a great life, but college wasn't something I thought about. Now, all of a sudden, it was attainable."

Hillis agreed to make a recruiting visit to campus not knowing for certain where he was headed. When he started checking on Marshall, he heard rumors that Sam Huff was being considered as a candidate to become coach.

"I knew about Sam Huff," Hillis said. "I thought it would be something to play for a guy like that."

Huff's candidacy was nothing more, of course, than talk circulating around the home state of the former West Virginia University All-American linebacker and future NFL Hall of Famer. Huff or no, Hillis headed to Huntington where a snowstorm turned a weekend visit into a stay of nearly a week. The hospitality he enjoyed while in town was more than enough to secure his signature when the coaches later offered the scholarship. Hillis' recruitment, however, wasn't typical for first Dawson and Jackson and then three colleagues and Lengyel after the head coach's hiring.

"We couldn't offer the recruits the possibility of a championship team or a bowl bid," Lengyel said. "We weren't even a conference team and we were on probation. In effect, all we could offer, as Winston Churchill once said, was 'blood, sweat and tears.' And those who did come would have to come to play."

The NCAA amended its rules and permitted freshmen to play at Marshall. Lengyel assembled 13 freshmen, 17 sophomores, five juniors and three seniors for his initial season. The team was dubbed the "Young Thundering Herd."

"We felt that we needed a name to identify these men who would accept such a challenge," Lengyel said. "We were to return to the 'Thundering Herd' after four years when we had our first graduating class."

The Young Herd that first stepped on the field with Lengyel was supplemented with a collection of players other schools on Marshall's schedule would most likely spurn. Among them were walk-ons who weren't good enough high school players to earn college football scholarships, a former basketball player from the Virgin Islands' Pan Am Games team and three transfers from the University of Buffalo, which had dropped football. There were students from campus who had never played organized football, freshman Dan Norrell, whose brother, Pat, was killed in the crash, and a soccer player named Blake Smith, who later played a key role in likely the greatest upset in the history of college football.

"They had a walk-on day near the end of two-a-days (practices)," Hillis recalled. "There must've been 150 guys show up. Most of them ran a little and were gone, but every now and then some guy would do something. I remember one guy ran a pass pattern, caught the ball and sprinted off. The coaches didn't need to see anything else. He was over with us."

Filling out the roster with players who survived the walk-on session sometimes meant a revolving door in the locker room. It was common to be on the field with a player one day and never see him again in uniform — or on campus, for that matter — because of the tedious task of tracking eligibility.

"There was this one guy, a fullback, who was just killing people in practice," Hillis said. "I mean he was running all over the place on everybody. I went back to South Hall (dormitory) after one practice and there's this guy sitting over in the corner with his head down, almost in tears. I went over and it was the guy who'd been running over everybody. I asked him what was wrong and he said the coaches had found out he'd played pro ball in Canada."

Although there were those who had discouraged Marshall from trying to rebuild its football program, others admired the Young Thundering Herd. One of those was President Richard M. Nixon, who sent a letter to Lengyel congratulating Marshall for its decision to field a team in 1971. The University of Toledo, a member of the Mid-American Conference — the league that placed Marshall on indefinite suspension in 1969 — sent a sculpture and plaque in remembrance of those who died in the crash.

Nate Ruffin, a senior defensive back who had missed the flight to East Carolina with an arm injury, was selected team captain. He was joined by Gary Morgan, Pete Neputano, Felix Jordan and Ed Carter as the only veterans from the 1970 team to play in 1971.

"We were almost a freshman team with a few sophomores and three seniors," Ruffin said. "Reggie Oliver and all those young guys were on that team. I felt like an old guy around a lot of young kids. I'd be at a party and people would tell me that all those kids were going to get me killed. I had similar thoughts, but then realized a lot of responsibility was falling on me."

Ruffin said he became an adjunct member of the coaching staff, often attending meetings with coaches long after the rest of the team had finished practice. The pressure on him was enormous.

"A player might have had a little drug problem or something and the coach would suspect it, but couldn't prove it," Ruffin said. "So the coach would tell me to find out about the guy and help him deal with it. But maybe I was doing the same thing as some of the other players – out there smoking a little grass on the side – and here I was trying to herd them in. I felt so out of place in the captain's position and I think it pushed me more than I was ever pushed before because I was the captain of the team and we had to keep it together."

Forging a team from scratch and convincing the players they could win was Lengyel's biggest challenge. He told them they could be a good team if they played together. Lengyel set goals for each part of the team. The kicking game was to score six points in each outing, the defense was to hold the opponent to two touchdowns and the Marshall offense was to score two touchdowns. Although he didn't want the players to know it, Lengyel knew the goals were unrealistic. He resorted to gimmicks to make up for the team's lack of skill.

"It was difficult because we didn't have the talent," Lengyel said. "But we were long on commitment and desire. We always changed fronts and disguised the defense. We were gamblers. We had to be to cover up our weaknesses. We couldn't play a straight-up defense. For a while, sometimes, we had the equalizer of surprise. But we couldn't fool them too long."

Hillis, who played on the offensive line, said he and his teammates knew nothing of their deficiencies. They were football players and approached every game with the mindset that they had a chance to win, regardless of what others said.

"I don't think we knew any better," he said. "The coaches did a good job preparing us mentally. I've never been in a game where I didn't think I had a chance of winning and that includes every one I played at Marshall. Kenneth McKinney taught me that, and the coaches at Marshall reinforced it."

Lengyel's offense was based on positioning two receivers in extremely wide formation. One reason was that Oliver was a good passer and could get them the ball, but the principal strategy behind the move drew two defensive backs away from the center of the field. Lengyel said he believed that his team had a better chance playing nine-on-nine in the middle of the field than it did playing 11-on-11.

On April 12, 1971, the Marshall coaching staff visited West Virginia University, which was led by Bobby Bowden, now a legend at Florida State where he has become the winningest coach in major college football history. The Herd staff was taught the Houston veer. The option-oriented offense became Marshall's modus operandi. The Young Herd unveiled the veer in its spring game against a group of alumni players and won 26-0.

"It was a game I felt we needed to win in order to make the first step on the right foot," Lengyel said. "I can assure you, there wasn't a dry eye in the stadium."

The players quickly recognized that their presence was therapeutic for the community and they embraced the connection, even the youngest like Hillis. Normally,

Assistant coach Red Dawson called the bootleg screen that enabled quarterback Reggie Oliver to throw a 13-yard touchdown pass to Terry Gardner for the winning touchdown in Marshall's 15-13 victory against Xavier on Sept. 25, 1971. Oliver took the snap from center just before time expired. (Photo courtesy of The Herald-Dispatch)

Right: Jubilant Terry Gardner crosses the goal line for Marshall's winning touchdown in the Young Thundering Herd's dramatic victory against Xavier. With one second remaining on the clock, quarterback Reggie Oliver rolled to his right, then threw a bootleg screen pass back to his left to Gardner, who sprinted 13 yards for the touchdown. The victory is regarded as one of the most stunning upsets in college football history. (Photo by Chris Spencer)

Marshall fans mob victorious Young Thundering Herd players on the Fairfield Stadium turf after MU's miracle victory over Xavier. The celebration took place just seconds after Terry Gardner scored the winning touchdown in Marshall's first victory after the crash. Ironically, on the same date, Wichita State defeated Trinity College, 12-8, for its first win since 13 members of the team died on October 2, 1970, in a plane crash in Silver Plume, Colo. (Photo by Chris Spencer)

visits to schools and other organizations were handled by upperclassmen. Since Marshall had precious few, everyone had his share of trips into the community as a team representative. They quickly realized this bond was something they had never before experienced.

"It wasn't a mournful kind of thing, but more like a parenting situation," Hillis recalled. "It was healing for them to have us with them again. I know we could not have been treated better."

Marshall's first regular-season game was September 18 at Morehead State and about 4,000 Marshall fans made the 90-minute trip from Huntington to see the game. The Golden Eagles dominated the statistics, out-rushing Marshall 304-57 and out-passing the Young Herd 149-84, but the score was a respectable 29-6. Marshall trailed just 16-6 with 9:21 left in the third quarter after a 10-yard screen pass from Oliver to tight end Tom Smyth. The scoring strike was the first of only two touchdown passes Oliver would throw all season. His second, and most important, would come a week later.

"We lost the game," Lengyel said. "But we won a great victory in our rebuilding program."

No victory, however, was more gratifying than the one that came the next Saturday, a cool — for September — afternoon at Fairfield Stadium. In an incredible finish, Marshall upset Xavier 15-13 when Terry Gardner scored on a 13-yard screen pass from Oliver on the game's final play before a then-stadium record crowd of 13,000, including Gov. Arch Moore.

Marshall took a 3-0 lead when Smith kicked a 31-yard field goal on the last play of the first quarter and that margin held up until halftime. The Musketeers, who were favored by three touchdowns, came back to go ahead 6-3 on a 1-yard run by Ivy Williams with 6:47 left in the third quarter. The Herd regained the lead on a 2-yard quarterback sneak by Oliver with 11:58 left in the game. Then with 5:18 left to play, Marshall faced a third-and-1 at its 19-yard line.

"I told our quarterback to get two first downs and then punt the ball away, if necessary, to run the clock down," Lengyel said.

But Marshall could not convert; sophomore fullback John Johnstonbaugh was stopped an inch short. Bob Eshbaugh punted the ball away and Xavier's John Gompers returned it 47 yards for a touchdown for a 13-9 Xavier lead.

The Young Herd's next drive stalled at its own 45 and Eshbaugh punted. The Marshall defense, though, stiffened and stopped Xavier on three downs, forcing a punt that gave the Herd the ball at the Musketeers' 48 with 1:18 to play. Three straight incomplete passes darkened Marshall's hopes for victory. Hillis recalled thinking that he and his teammates were reduced to divine intervention with only one play remaining to get a game-extending first down.

"It had been cloudy, but then the clouds over the stadium were gone," Hillis said. "We pretty much knew we needed a miracle. Maybe that was a sign."

Hillis might have been right. Oliver hit wide receiver Jerry Arrasmith with an 11-yard pass for the first down to extend the drive. The quarterback followed with an 11-yard completion to wide-out Kelly Sherwood. Then, facing a fourth-and-5 at the Xavier 18, Oliver threw five yards to Arrasmith for the first down to set up the game's final play – a 513 bootleg screen.

"We were yelling on the sidelines to snap the ball," Lengyel said. "It was snapped with one second left. We had a bootleg screen pass to Terry Gardner called. Red Dawson called the play from the press box."

Most of the defense followed Oliver as he rolled right. The sophomore from Tuscaloosa, Alabama, then whirled and threw back to Gardner on the left side of the field. One Musketeers defender stayed back, but was leveled by tackle Jack Crabtree and Gardner sprinted into the end zone, completing the 13-yard pass play to give Marshall its first post-crash victory.

"We ran that play earlier in the game and it didn't come off quite right," Oliver recalled. "I don't know what gave the coaches the confidence to call it again, but, because they did, we won the game and went from being the Young Thundering Herd to the Thundering Herd."

Oliver, who did not learn he would start the game until about five minutes before the team took the field, said he was certain that Marshall could score on the final play.

"I'd completed 19 passes before that one," Oliver said. "I knew we had good receivers and enough time to get that play off. It was all or nothing. They put on a heavy rush and a lot of them chased me on the bootleg fake. Then Jack made that incredible block and the rest was history."

Added Hillis: "I don't think my feet touched the ground the rest of the day. I remember coach Lengyel saying we didn't know how big a game we'd just won. I don't think we did."

The significance wasn't in any way diminished for those who witnessed the outcome. An hour after the game, as Marshall players drifted from the locker room, they found more than 4,000 people remaining in parts of stadium. Some in disbelief, some in revelry, some in tears, but all in celebration.

"There were all those people still there," Lengyel said. "People were hugging and crying and holding onto each other, not believing what had happened. The newspapers called it a miracle. It was a miracle."

Marshall went from miracle to massacre in seven days. In the Young Herd's next game, national power Miami of Ohio crushed Marshall 66-6 in Oxford, Ohio. It was the most lopsided loss in Marshall's modern history and the worst since an 81-0 loss in 1923 to West Virginia.

Oliver didn't play because of a separated shoulder and was replaced by his roommate, fellow sophomore Dave Walsh. The statistics were as one-sided as the score. The

Redskins led 31-0 at halftime. Miami had 11 first downs; Marshall had none. Miami amassed 186 total yards; Marshall had minus 22. The Redskins led 52-0 before Jordan blocked a punt and returned it 36 yards for a touchdown to give the Young Herd its only score. Marshall's leading rushers were Johnstonbaugh and Gardner, each with two yards, which also wound up being The Young Herd's total offense for the day. Miami, on the other hand, had five runners gain more than 30 yards. The Redskins had 24 first downs to Marshall's two. Miami gained 359 yards rushing and held Marshall to minus 21.

Oliver said his most vivid memory of the game was the Miami mascot, which was a student dressed as an Indian.

"Every time they scored that Indian would run out on the field and dance around," Oliver said. "We never got on that end of the field anyway, and they kept scoring, so after a while the Indian just stayed out there on their end of the field and waved his tomahawk around when they scored. That was the worst whipping I've ever been associated with. It was men against boys. Miami was one of the powers of college football and they showed it."

Lengyel said Marshall made far too many mistakes to stay on the field with the powerful Redskins. "We compounded our problems by losing our poise and we suffered a humiliating defeat."

The overmatched Herd was powerless to stop the potent Miami offense and the performance embarrassed Lengyel. Miami was a superior team, but wasn't 60 points better than his club. The Redskins scored their final touchdown by running the quarterback up the middle on 11 straight plays. Lengyel used the opportunity to drive home the point that Marshall could be better than it showed — that it must be better if the football program was to continue.

"We collected the team at the 50-yard line after that game," Lengyel said. "We had them look back at the scoreboard so they would remember what it was like to suffer such a humiliating defeat. And we wanted them to remember that Miami wasn't 60 points better than us. We didn't keep our poise. We contributed greatly to the loss. We had the heavy part of our season ahead and we certainly didn't want to have another game like the Miami massacre."

The next week, while Marshall practiced at Fairfield Stadium, Lengyel had the scoreboard turned on, with the score 66-6 posted as a reminder of what had happened against Miami. The action brought about its intended reaction.

"The coaches wanted to teach us a lesson after we beat Xavier and they did," Hillis said. "They felt (Miami) kind of run (the score) up on us, and they probably did. But that never ever left our memory. It was an embarrassment. You never mind getting physically beat by someone who's better, but you never want to be embarrassed no matter how good they were. We were beaten after that, but never embarrassed."

Marshall's next game was at Northern Illinois and marked the first time the team was to fly since the crash. Lengyel told the players that anyone who did not want to fly would not have to. He recalled that only one player declined to make the trip. Still, there was an uneasy feeling among those who boarded the plane. Lengyel held a team meeting and explained to the players every detail about the plane and the flight. He also reassured the players that no portion of the flight would be at night, as was the return trip from East Carolina.

"Although many people joked as they put quarters in the insurance machine, there was apprehension on everyone's part regarding our first flight," said Lengyel, who took his wife, Sandy, on the trip. "It was a terrible prop plane. As Father Robert Scott, who was our team chaplain, said, the players had to reconcile this matter within themselves and remember that they couldn't live with fear."

The flight to DeKalb, Illinois, and back to Huntington was smooth and without incident. Marshall lost to the Huskies 37-18, but Oliver passed for 247 yards in the second half, leaving Lengyel optimistic.

"It was a tough game," he said. "Although we lost, we put on a tremendous display of a passing attack. That gave us great confidence going into the next game."

That was at home against the Dayton Flyers and the optimism Marshall enjoyed concerning its offense disappeared in a dismal 13-0 defeat. The Herd passed for only 47 yards and had only 134 in total offense. It penetrated as far as the Dayton 23 late in the game before an interception stopped the threat. The Marshall defense, though, was outstanding, holding Dayton All-American running back Gary Kosins to 88 yards on 29 carries.

"The defense did an outstanding job against Kosins," Lengyel said. "He was an outstanding back. We gambled and set our defense to stop him, but we failed to develop any offense to establish a scoring punch for ourselves."

Marshall's defense continued to bear the burden the next week on a windy day at Western Michigan; the Young Herd trailed only 6-0 at halftime. The larger, stronger Broncos, however, wore down Marshall in the fourth period and posted a 37-0 victory.

"This was a very strong and very big football team," said Lengyel about Western

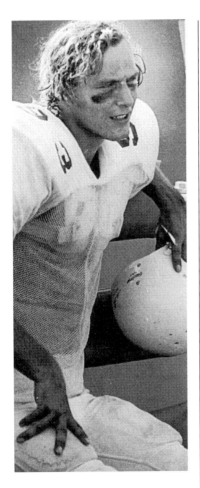

Wide receiver Bill James was better known to Marshall fans as a basketball player, but he was one of several Herd athletes from other sports to use their fifth year of eligibility to help rebuild the football team. James, a cat-quick, 6-foot-4 high-jumping wing player on the highly successful basketball team, was regarded by many Marshall observers as the school's best all-around athlete during his years with the Herd.

Michigan. "People were wondering why they weren't pushing us all over the field. We did an outstanding job on defense, but again we couldn't generate any offense. Although we lost the game, we gained a great deal of respect."

Marshall established even more credibility a week later by pulling off one of the greatest upsets in the school's history.

The Young Herd entered its homecoming as a heavy underdog to MAC power Bowling Green. The Falcons were 5-1, had the fifth-ranked offense in the nation and were expected to win their final five games and go to the Peach Bowl. They had running back Paul Miles, who averaged more than 100 yards rushing per game, and they had beaten Miami. Before the game, Nehlen said he didn't believe Marshall could run on his team. Uncharacteristically, he was wrong. The Young Herd not only out-rushed the Falcons 193-127, but beat them by a score of 12-10.

"They had a back that averaged 100 yards," Lengyel said. "We were lucky to have 100 yards as a team. They had a team that by all standards would annihilate Marshall."

Almost everyone thought Bowling Green would do to Marshall what Miami had done to the Herd – everyone except Lengyel.

"Whitey Wilson (former Marshall athletic director) asked me at an alumni party before the Bowling Green game what I thought," Lengyel said. "I said to him that I thought we'd win it. He said, 'You can't be serious.' I got mad about that. I told him that if I didn't think we could win the game we wouldn't play it. After we won, he was the first to come up to me and apologize."

Bowling Green was at a disadvantage from the outset. The Falcons' coaching staff did not realize Marshall had installed Astroturf at Fairfield. The Falcons played in cleats made for running on grass and struggled all day. They also wore heavy, wool jerseys on a day when the temperature climbed well into the 80s.

"It was tremendously hot," said Oliver, who would later serve as an assistant coach at Bowling Green. "They were dumping ice and water on their players all day, trying to keep them cool. Coach Lengyel had us a giant cooler on the sideline. It was air conditioned and had a plastic front. We sat in it and watched their players drop like flies."

Marshall led 6-0 at halftime, scoring when Johnstonbaugh took a handoff from Oliver and ran four yards up the middle for a touchdown with 9:52 left in the first half. Incredibly, Marshall outrushed stunned Bowling Green 113-58.

Marshall was stopped on its first possession of the third quarter, but Eshbaugh pinned the Falcons deep in their own territory with a 62-yard punt. Eshbaugh was a key in keeping the Falcons bottled up, punting six times for an average of 42.2 yards. Bowling Green, though, ran 11 plays, driving from its own 36 to the Marshall 10, where it had a first down. Jerry Fields was stopped on a run up the middle for a gain of a yard. Miles took a pitch left, but was stopped for no gain and Reid Lamport followed with an incomplete pass intended for Roger Wallace, forcing Bill Witte to kick a 27-yard field goal with 6:27 left in the period.

Marshall held the 6-3 lead through the end of the third quarter and extended the margin to 12-3 early in the fourth quarter, driving 80 yards in 15 plays with Walsh scoring from two yards on a quarterback sneak. The key play of the drive was a screen pass on third-and-10 at the Marshall 20 from Oliver to fullback Ned Burks that picked up 35 yards.

The Young Herd's elation, however, quickly was erased as seconds later Tony Bell fielded the ensuing kickoff at the Bowling Green seven and returned it to the Marshall 20. On the next play, Lamport hit Rick Newman with a touchdown pass and Witte added the extra point to make it 12-10.

Marshall's defense took over to stop two excellent Bowling Green scoring opportunities. The Falcons recovered a Walsh fumble at their own 49 just seven plays after scoring. Bowling Green then ran two plays, gaining 9 yards, setting up a third-and-1 at the Marshall 41. But the Young Herd defense held as Lamport threw an incomplete pass and Miles was stopped on fourth down for no gain. The Falcons had one final chance to win the game, driving from their own 26 to the Marshall 20 before Witte attempted a 37-yard field goal. The kick, though, was no good and Marshall called four plays to run out the clock, completing one of the most stunning upsets in college football history. Marshall finished with 330 yards in total offense, the most any team compiled on Bowling Green that season. The Young Herd defense held Miles to 92 yards, breaking a streak of 33 straight 100-yard games. Johnstonbaugh finished with 98 yards.

"From the opening whistle to the final gun we controlled the game," Lengyel said.

Oliver said Marshall's defense was the key in the victory. Of particular significance was freshman linebacker Charlie Henry, who was only 17 when he enrolled at Marshall. Oliver said the play of the 5-foot-11, 180-pounder, inspired every Marshall player during the Bowling Green game and for the entire season. Against Bowling Green, Henry totaled 20 tackles, including eight solos, and deflected a pass.

"Charlie got hurt in the third quarter," Oliver said. "They had to carry him off the field and he had an air cast on his leg, indicating his leg was broken. But I remember looking up and there he was back out there. He went back out and played. He was a tough little guy and he was such an inspiration to all of us."

Henry also was a favorite of Lengyel.

"One player who exemplified what football is all about and what we were trying to do was Charlie Henry," Lengyel said. "He started all four years for us. He was wiry and quiet, but exemplified everything you could want in a football player. I was very proud of Charlie. He played as hard as he could play and he was a good one. He's one of the glues that held us together."

The next week, Marshall saw an opportunity for another win slip away when it lost 21-0 at Kent State. The Young Herd was inside the Golden Flashes' 10-yard line eight times, but failed to score and the defeat was one of the most frustrating for Lengyel in his four seasons at Marshall.

"We needed two in a row," Lengyel said. "We particularly needed one on the road, because a successful team must win on the road. Kent State was a team I thought we could beat. We had three opportunities inside the 20-yard line in the first six minutes and couldn't score. I felt the first team to score would win the ball game. It was a very disappointing loss."

Henry again played well despite Kent State's offensive domination of Marshall. Henry again had 20 tackles, including five solos, and a fumble recovery.

Marshall's next game was November 13, the eve of the one-year anniversary of the plane crash. The players held a memorial service before the game in the stadium and at the gravesites of the players who had been killed. The Young Herd played host to Toledo and the Rockets owned the nation's longest winning streak — 32 games. They extended the streak to 33 with a 43-0 victory, running a then school record 104 plays in front of the largest crowd – 14,750 – ever at Fairfield. But the Young Herd played well for three quarters and trailed only 21-0 entering the fourth period. Marshall had three players – Chuck Wright, Odell Graves and Dave Homa — finish with more than 20 tackles each.

"It was a game mixed with many emotions and was certainly one of the toughest to play," Lengyel said. "Because of the weekend it was on, it was difficult for both teams."

Marshall ended the season at home against Ohio University, a team that earlier that year had defeated Kentucky and Tulane. The Young Herd offense was unable to sustain any major drives that day and the Bobcats rolled to a 30-0 victory. Marshall's first post-crash season had concluded. Despite the Young Herd's won-loss record, Lengyel assessed the year as a success.

"We had two victories on the scoreboard when many said we wouldn't win a game," Lengyel said. "There were many more victories in the hearts and minds of the players and the staff and the people who supported the team. One thing we lacked was experience. You could fault our team for mistakes born out of inexperience, but you could never fault them for their determination and effort on every given weekend. Each Monday they came back with the attitude of 'Who do we play this week and how do we beat them?' "

Oliver, who later would play in the World Football League, was a skilled quarterback and could have left Marshall for another school after the crash. Several schools contacted him, but leaving was something he could not do. He believed he was obligated to finish what his late teammates had started.

"I was so close to everybody in the crash," Oliver said. "I had four high school teammates on that team (Joe Hood, Larry Sanders, Robert Van Horn and Freddy Wilson). If Marshall was good enough for them to give their life for, then it was good enough for me. I wouldn't trade the experience. We had our ups and downs and we lost a lot, but Jack held us together pretty well. Because the powers that be decided to build the program from the grass roots, a lot of guys got to play who wouldn't have played anywhere else."

Most of the 1971 team returned in 1972 – a season that once again saw Marshall win only two games. Both victories, though, were against local rivals Morehead State and Ohio University to open and close the year, respectively.

Marshall opened at home against Morehead in a game that saw the lead swing from one team to the other. The Young Herd scored a winning touchdown with just 2:52 to play when sophomore tailback Bob Crawford went seven yards up the middle for a touchdown and Larry McCoy kicked the extra point to make it 27-24. The victory gave Lengyel and the Marshall fans hope that the Herd could near the .500 mark. It was not to be.

That reality was driven home the next week when Marshall was beaten 39-0 by Dayton. That defeat was followed by a 24-7 loss to Northern Illinois, a respectable 22-7 defeat against Miami, a 14-0 loss at Xavier and a 34-0 homecoming loss to Western Michigan. Bowling Green gained revenge for the 1971 upset with a 46-7 pounding of the Young Herd. Marshall lost another game, 16-14 to Kent State, that it hoped it could win. The Young Herd led the Golden Flashes until the 1:09 mark when Herb Page kicked a 29-yard field goal. Next was a 21-0 loss to Toledo, setting up the finale at Ohio University.

Not only did Marshall beat the Bobcats, it did it soundly, 31-14. The victory broke a streak of 11 straight road losses and marked the first time Marshall had won in Athens since 1965.

Despite the 2-8 record, Lengyel said the 1972 season was one of the most important in Marshall football history. It was a year when Lengyel began to make real progress in rebuilding the program. Recruiting, while still difficult, was somewhat easier and scholarship players were replacing walk-ons in the lineup. That, however, was a mixed blessing and eventually was greatly responsible for Lengyel's resignation two years later.

"We were getting stabilization of material," Lengyel said of 1972. "We were a semblance of a college football team coming back together. We were getting some players, but not what we needed to sustain a competitive program. The university was struggling, too, and we couldn't do a lot of things we wanted to, but you could still see progress."

That progress was even more evident in 1973 when Marshall finished 4-7 and with a few breaks could have gone 6-5. The Herd opened with a 24-17 victory over Morehead and later beat Northern Illinois 39-36, Toledo 17-14 and Dayton 37-14. Marshall lost two other close games, 30-28 to Xavier and 24-21 to Bowling Green. Both of those losses were games Lengyel believed his team should have won.

Marshall entered the 1974 season with the most talented team and its highest expectations since 1970. But it also faced possibly the toughest schedule in the school's history, with games against Akron, Miami, Temple, Western Michigan, Bowling Green, Kent State, Toledo and Ohio. The schedule proved to be too much for Marshall – still a very young team – to handle. The Young Herd finished 1-10, beating only Akron. The Herd lost four other games, though, by a total of nine points.

The 1974 season took its toll on Lengyel and, on December 12, he resigned. The reason was only in part that Marshall was 9-33 in his four years. A greater factor was that those players who were recruited and walked on to the team as freshmen in 1971 were being beaten out by players Lengyel recruited two and three years after the crash. It was a strain on Lengyel to tell those who helped lay the foundation in 1971 that they were being benched in favor of the recruits. That, more than anything, led to Lengyel's decision to resign.

"Those who lettered for us on the '71 team were being beaten out by freshmen we were bringing in," Lengyel said. "They gave us a commitment the two years when we didn't have anybody. The psychological aspect of telling that letterman that a freshman was beating him out was a great strain, especially after all the things they did the first two years. We were trying to convince them that that was a part of football and they needed to accept their roles. Some couldn't accept it."

Lengyel himself was not convinced that benching his veterans was a part of the game and he had trouble accepting it. The situation tore Lengyel apart throughout the 1973 and 1974 seasons and he finally decided that resigning was the best way to handle the problem, despite the urging of Marshall President Robert Hayes that Lengyel stay one more season.

"It was a very difficult situation, putting the class structure back together," Lengyel said. "It was very frustrating for the student-athletes and for me. But I had an obligation to make sure of the competitiveness of the team."

With a team composed overwhelmingly of freshmen in 1971, only six earned the distinction of becoming the first four-year lettermen in NCAA history. In addition to Hillis, the others were offensive lineman Allen Meadows, Burks, Eshbaugh and Henry.

"That's a statement to what Marshall faced in rebuilding," Hillis said. "Looking back, there were so many guys who just weren't physically ready and couldn't stay healthy to play four years against the teams we played. (Six who lettered) were lucky, I guess. All the adversity we survived, we're kind of like brothers."

After he resigned, Lengyel moved to Louisville where he worked in the furniture business. He later became the athletic director at Fresno State University. From there, he moved on to become the athletic director at the University of Missouri. He resigned that post to become the athletic director at the U.S. Naval Academy in Annapolis, Maryland, serving 13 years before his retirement in 2001. Since his retirement, Lengyel has served as interim director of athletics at Temple University, Eastern Kentucky University, and most recently, the University of Colorado. He now resides in the Phoenix, Arizona, suburb of Surprise.

Chapter four

Running on a treadmill

This was a nondescript period. Like a nothing interlude. Probably the two things I remember most about the Ellwood years were that they broke the long losing streak against Miami of Ohio and Fuzzy Filliez was in there catching passes those first couple of years. But aside from that, it was just like treading water. There wasn't anything being done. They weren't raising a whole lot of money; they weren't in a conference until the last two years. There just wasn't that much excitement.

– Ernie Salvatore

There were more than 100 applicants for the Marshall coaching vacancy created with Jack Lengyel's sudden resignation in 1974, but Frank Ellwood – the man who got the job – wasn't among them. After reviewing the applications at hand, President Robert B. Hayes and Athletics Director Joe McMullen began a search of their own and ended it by naming Ellwood as the Thundering Herd's coach two days before the New Year of 1975 dawned. Hayes and McMullen selected Ellwood from the staff of Ohio University coach Bill Hess where Ellwood served as defensive coordinator.

"We went after him," Hayes said, explaining the circumstances surrounding Ellwood's choice. "He showed great insight in our talks together. To my questions, he gave straight answers, right on target. After 10 weary years (the length of time since Marshall's last winning season), it's time to turn this program around. We have a person

A weekly dose of frustration like that felt by Marshall linebacker Ed McTaggart became all too familiar during Frank Ellwood's tenure as the coach of the Thundering Herd. This installment for McTaggart and his teammates came in a 44-16 drubbing at the hands of visiting Southern Illinois in the final game of the 1976 season.

Frank Ellwood had high hopes when he took over the Marshall football program as head coach in 1975. However, his teams won only nine games in four seasons, including a 1-10 record in 1978 — his final season coaching the Herd. (Photo courtesy of The Herald-Dispatch)

from a winning program and I believe winning is contagious."

Ellwood was among a group of six prime candidates for the position. He was interviewed in the middle of the group and was so impressive that Hayes canceled the others and decided Ellwood was his man.

"I figured, why wait?" Hayes said after introducing his new coach. "The credentials these others had were no stronger than Ellwood's."

In Ellwood, Marshall had a 39-year-old coach who had been in the big wars as a quarterback at Ohio State and a highly successful assistant at the Air Force Academy, Ohio State and for 10 seasons at Ohio University. As a Buckeyes' player for Woody Hayes, the native of Dover, Ohio, played in the same backfield as 1955 Heisman Trophy winner Howard "Hopalong" Cassady when the Buckeyes won the Rose Bowl. Ellwood was an academic All-Big Ten and All-American selection at Ohio State where he earned two degrees in education. Among his recommendations were those of Air Force coach Ben Martin, Michigan's Bo Schembechler, Hess and Hayes. All extolled Ellwood's expertise with a football team both on and off the field. He even had his former players at OU singing his praises.

"He's the one guy who can turn it around for Marshall," OU linebacker Mike Nugent – a Bobcats' co-captain – said after Ellwood was named Herd coach. "He's an organizer and dedicated to the cause. He's so organized I haven't found a weak spot in him."

But for all the winning Ellwood had done at his other stops, he couldn't do the same at Marshall, which moved from an independent to a member of the Southern Conference during his tenure. He won only nine games – 10 if a forfeit over Morehead in 1976 is counted – during his four years. None of the victories came in the nine games against SC opponents during his final two seasons in 1977 and 1978. But Ellwood and his teams provided

Marshall and its fans with memories that rank among the tops in school history.

At the top of the list was one of Marshall's biggest victories ever. In the second game of Ellwood's second season, Marshall ended 37 years of frustration against Miami of Ohio by dealing the nationally ranked Redskins a 21-16 loss at Fairfield Stadium. It was Marshall's first win over Miami since 1939. Ellwood's teams also were memorable in defeat, especially on four Saturdays during his final season when the Herd lost four games despite leading with four minutes left in each.

There also were record-setting individuals during Ellwood's years. John "Fuzzy" Filliez parlayed precision pass routes and excellent hands to catch at least one pass in a then-NCAA record 42 consecutive games from 1973 to 1976. Filliez was the Marshall career receiving leader until Stan Parrish and George Chaump brought pass-oriented offenses to Marshall in the mid-1980s. Ellwood also brought Marshall its first 1,000-yard rusher in C.W. Geiger, who originally signed with Michigan State out of East Bank (W.Va.) High School only to transfer to Marshall after two years. The "Geiger Counter" rolled up 1,039 yards on 247 carries in 1977, before seeing his career come to an unceremonious end with a suspension the next year in a dispute with Ellwood over playing time for him and three fellow seniors.

And it was Ellwood who shocked Southern Conference writers at the league's annual preseason gathering by predicting that the Herd, in its first year in the league, would win the championship.

Marshall was 0-3 in 1975 before Ellwood broke into the win column with a 36-3 triumph at home against Illinois State. Marshall's only other victory of the season came in a 21-19 decision over Western Michigan on Homecoming. The Herd finished the year 2-9.

Marshall opened 1976 just as inauspiciously as the season

C.W. Geiger became the first 1,000-yard runner in Marshall history when he ran 247 times for 1,039 yards. Known as the "Geiger Counter" during a consensus high school All-American career in East Bank, W.Va., Geiger signed with Michigan State out of high school, but transferred to Marshall in 1976.

before, losing 31-14 at Morehead State. The game went into the record book with an asterisk beside the score when Morehead discovered it had used ineligible players against the Herd and forfeited the victory. The Herd limped home from Morehead to prepare for Miami, which despite a 14-10 loss to North Carolina in its opener would come to Huntington as the 20th-ranked team in the country. Miami owned a host of weapons, chief among them tailback Rob Carpenter, a 6-foot-1, 215-pound senior, who had finished sixth in the nation in rushing the previous season with 1,022 yards on 235 carries.

"They're not unbeatable," Ellwood said the day before the game. "But we'll have to play a good game and take advantage of any breaks we get or make."

Miami looked as though it wouldn't have much trouble covering the 30-point spread by which it had been favored when Marshall fumbled on its first two possessions to help the Redskins to a 9-0 lead after a quarter. Marshall quarterback Bud Nelson teamed with receiver Ray Crisp for touchdown passes of 23 and 4 yards, however, to give Marshall a 14-9 lead at halftime. Tailback Mike Bailey crashed in from two yards on a fourth-down play midway through the third period for a 21-9 lead and, as it turned out, all the points Marshall was to need for the upset. Miami, which lost four fumbles, got its last score by returning a Marshall fumble on the game's final play.

The outcome was such a shock, not only in West Virginia and the Midwest, but around the country, that The Associated Press ran the score three times in succession on its national wire so its clients would be certain of its authenticity. Carpenter's post-game comment best summed up the magnitude of the victory for Marshall, which hadn't scored 21 points on the Redskins since the win in 1939.

"I never thought I'd see us get beat by Marshall," said Carpenter, who went on to a Pro Bowl career in the NFL with the Houston Oilers and New York Giants. Carpenter was not on the field for the end. He was ejected for arguing with an official with a little more than seven minutes left in the contest.

Spurred by the victory, Marshall went on to gain an even split after eight games which put that elusive winning season in sight with two of the remaining three games at home. There were, however, no more wins to come as the Herd lost to Villanova 23-10, Toledo 39-8 and Southern Illinois 44-16 to close out Ellwood's best season.

The coach was optimistic before the 1977 season, Marshall's first as a challenger for the Southern Conference championship. So confident was Ellwood about his team's capabilities that he started his address to the media at the SC's annual preseason Football

Above: Fuzzy Filliez tries to elude a Miami (Ohio) tackler after one of his five receptions in Marshall's 21-16 upset of the 20th-ranked Redskins. Marshall was a five-touchdown underdog against Miami, which hadn't lost to the Herd since 1939. Filliez was one of the greatest receivers in Marshall history and is tied with Randy Moss for seventh place in career receptions with 168. (Photo by Tim Grobe)

Left: Reserve quarterback Larry Berkery (10) and safety Harold Wetzel embrace near the end of Marshall's stunning victory over Miami (Ohio). (Photo by Lee Bernard)

Rouser in Pinehurst, North Carolina, with the statement: "I'll open by saying that we'll probably be the conference champion." His bold prediction sent those in attendance scrambling for their pens and tape recorders to catch any other off-the-wall remarks that might follow and created a legendary tidbit of cocktail-hour conversation for all future Rousers.

And as with so many other predictions, this one would fail to meet reality. After losing its opener to Ohio University, Marshall defeated Morehead State and Toledo, but then dropped its final eight games to finish 2-9. The closest the Herd came to winning a game against SC opposition was in a 28-20 loss to Appalachian State. That game served as Marshall's debut as a member of the league and started a streak of frustration against conference teams that would continue into the 1981 season.

The disappointment of 1977, however, could not match that of 1978, a season in which it appeared Marshall was simply not meant to find any success, regardless of its efforts. The Herd even had problems with the coin flip; it lost nine of 11 calls, including its first eight.

"That whole season, from start to finish, it seemed like it just wasn't meant for us to have any success," recalled Ed Hamrick, a senior kicker on Ellwood's final squad. "And the shame of it all was that there were players good enough to win with."

But from the start of pre-season practice until the end came in mid-November, the team and coaches operated with the pressure of knowing that this was the make-or-break season.

"A sense of urgency probably is the best way to describe everything surrounding how that final season was approached," Hamrick said. "Everything was intensified. We had some intense contact in the middle of the week – even in midseason. You'd think by that time everything should've been established and there was no need for that, but there was the added pressure that seemed to just keep mounting every week."

Marshall opened 1978 on the road with a 17-0 victory over Toledo only to see its mark level at 1-1 with a 28-7 loss at home to Appalachian. Then came what seemed to be a weekly dose of heartbreak.

Tennessee-Chattanooga came to Huntington with its usually potent offense and rugged defense and appeared as though it would leave with another victory after taking a 20-7 lead early in the third period. The Herd, however, struck back with a pair of touchdowns – the second on a 58-yard interception return by linebacker Greg Kendziorski – and a 28-yard field goal by Hamrick for a 23-20 lead at the quarter's end.

Marshall's defense protected that cushion with one solid stand after another until the Moccasins were left with one last chance at their own 21-yard line after a Herd punt. On came back-up quarterback Dennis Berkery in relief of an ineffective Tony Merendino, who had failed to complete a pass the entire second half. Berkery, the younger brother of former MU quarterback and baseball pitcher, Larry Berkery, was not new to this relief role. He had bailed out the Mocs with a 21-yard touchdown pass the season before against Jacksonville State. Berkery misfired on his first pass after Mike Smith managed just two yards on a draw play, and was incomplete on another throw. With less than two minutes remaining and the Marshall fans believing their frustration against SC opponents was near its end, the Mocs called a timeout to discuss the fourth-and-8 play.

The subject of punting never came up between Berkery and coach Joe Morrison, only finding a play that would gain the necessary yardage for a first down. They selected a hook to wide receiver Joe Burke. The sophomore flanker broke off the line and moved in behind the Herd's dropping linebackers and in front of the secondary over the middle. Berkery was on target with the pass, and when Burke hit the ground after his leaping grab, he was met by two Herd defenders. Amazingly, the Marshall pair collided. Free from the bonds of the defenders, Burke regained his balance and raced for the end zone to complete a miraculous 77-yard play with 1:40 remaining.

"I just ran a hook into the middle," Burke said. "I was just trying for the first down – we just wanted to keep the drive going. About three of them hit me and I just bounced."

Until that play, Ellwood was confident victory was a minute or so away.

"The script was written," Ellwood said afterward. "We'd put them in a position where it would take a freak play to win and that's what they got."

Marshall got its second dose of heartbreak in Cullowhee, North Carolina, where Western Carolina's Gerald Harp hauled in a 22-yard pass from quarterback Mike Pusey with 56 seconds remaining to give the Catamounts a 21-14 victory. Marshall had taken a 14-13 lead on Bud Nelson's 11-yard run earlier in the final period.

If the devastation at Western wasn't enough to send the Herd reeling, the losses that followed at home to Miami and on the road to The Citadel certainly were. Four of the team's top players – Geiger, Nelson, Bailey and Crisp – were suspended indefinitely after missing practices following the Miami loss. That came on the heels of the suspension of punter John Huth for violation of a team rule.

Ellwood said the situation would benefit the team the rest of the season, and it appeared for a while he was right as the Herd took a 17-14 lead into the final period against Kent State. Marshall held the advantage until Kent quarterback Tom Delaney hit running back J.C. Stafford off a scramble with a 14-yard TD pass on fourth down with just 4:03 left in the game. The Herd had two possessions after the Golden Flashes' score, but had passes intercepted both times.

The Herd then dropped home games to Furman and Western Michigan. That left games at Southern Illinois and East Carolina. By now, speculation about Ellwood's future with the program was circulating. Some stories had him being fired, others had him resigning, while others had him returning, but only if he would replace certain members of his coaching staff.

"Frank was a class individual and I believe he was a very intelligent, disciplined and capable head coach who was dedicated to his team and staff," said Hamrick, whose younger brother, Mike, was a teammate. "But that dedication, especially to his staff, was in all likelihood what led to his downfall. He could've made some moves that maybe would've saved his job that year, but there was that loyalty. He waited too long to do anything. By the last year, it was too late."

Despite the mounting pressure, the team still displayed a gutsy drive on the field in an effort to regain some measure of respect. Marshall took that resolve to Carbondale, Illinois, to meet the Salukis where, despite a fumble and four pass interceptions, it clung to a 14-12 lead late into the fourth quarter. But as had almost become the norm, the Herd made one mistake too many. This time it was a blocked punt – the first in Huth's 53 kicks – that led to a 22-yard field goal by Paul Molla with 4:26 remaining in the game.

"As we lost each week, you could feel the pressure building," Hamrick said. "It was transmitted from the coaches to the players. It manifested itself in practice and off the field. Each one of those close defeats played a role in the next one. There was the drop in morale with each one and every one was harder to take than the one before. None of those games was easy to deal with from an emotional standpoint. You'd worked so hard and had victory in your grasp, but then in the final seconds it was taken away. Maybe we could've come back from one or two, but to have that happen four times, it's still pretty unbelievable."

Two days after the Southern Illinois defeat, there were no more rumors concerning

Ellwood's future. An announcement by McMullen that the contracts of the coach and his assistants would not be renewed took care of any speculation that still lingered. McMullen's statement came after Ellwood refused an offer to resign. The decision to dismiss the staff, McMullen said later, had been made three days after the loss to Western Michigan. With the season finale at East Carolina still remaining, the timing of the firing prompted far more criticism in the community than the action itself.

"I was told to set up a timetable in which to inform the coach," McMullen said. "I had to decide whether to do it Friday, Sunday morning or Sunday afternoon. I chose Sunday afternoon."

McMullen said he chose not to wait until after the final game so the search for a successor could begin immediately.

"I would be hypocritical not to say the decision was based on the bottom line," McMullen said. "It would've been a tough decision if this was a 4-7 or 5-6 year."

The handling of Ellwood's dismissal is still a sore point with Hamrick, who also served as president of Marshall's student body for a year.

"As far as the program went for that year, yes, everything was pretty much gone," said Hamrick, a former director of West Virginia's Division of Natural Resources. "Still, it was senseless for the university to fire a coach with just one week remaining. That little time made no difference in finding another coach. In view of the conduct Ellwood had shown in his four years, I think he was owed that. I think they owed it to him not to dismiss him in a way that would embarrass him or his players. There were far too many things to look at in Frank Ellwood than the wins and losses."

Ellwood had no apologies for his four years worth of effort.

"I'm not running out of Huntington with my tail between my legs," the coach said. "I know how hard we've worked and I have no apologies. The bottom line is winning and losing. … I had a great coaching staff and a great bunch of kids. They all worked like dogs and for a while there we were up the side of the mountain, but we just couldn't get to the top."

Ellwood's tenure closed with a 45-0 loss at East Carolina.

Now, two coaches had been given the task of bringing Marshall a winner. Although both came close, neither was able to attain the goal. Marshall had traveled two different roads in search of those coaches. Lengyel had been a small college head coach, Ellwood a major college assistant. The school decided to try a third path – one that would take it on a search for a coach with major college head coaching experience.

Chapter five

Setting the table

All of a sudden, Marshall had a name and this time it looked like football was for real. Sonny Randle comes in and it starts looking like Marshall is going to make a move. But the problem was that Sonny came in here under two handicaps. One was the Ellwood years themselves – there was nothing here as far as talent. And there were Sonny's own problems at Virginia where he'd been fired and his reputation followed him here – to his detriment as far as the faculty was concerned. But, as far as the public and the student body were concerned, it was one of the most popular appointments in Marshall's history. There weren't very many victories, but this was an extremely popular guy. He later had the handicap of a switch in athletic directors when Joe McMullen was fired and Lynn Snyder was hired. Snyder wasn't an inspiring person to begin with and Sonny was stuck with the guy.

He came in here under a five-year plan. He took a look at what he had and knew he couldn't do it in four and he didn't want to be a victim of the four-year cycle. But his timetable was a year off. He thought he could do it in four and win in the fifth. But it was the fifth year he had that set the table for Stan Parrish.

I'll always remember Sonny as a colorful guy who worked hard and talked the language of the people here. They liked him. He was a country boy. Sonny was popular even when he was losing. There never was an anti-Sonny movement, even when they fired him. And when they fired him, it was an unpopular firing.

– Ernie Salvatore

Athletics Director Joe McMullen made it clear from the beginning that Marshall

Colorful Sonny Randle brought a new intensity to Marshall's football program when he took over from Frank Ellwood after the 1978 season. That intensity, though, did not translate into many victories. Randle coached the Thundering Herd for five years, posting an overall record of 12-42-1. (Photo courtesy of The Herald-Dispatch)

would spare no expense or effort in finding a coach to right its football program. He wanted someone who had been in the "big wars." No longer would Marshall tap the resources of programs for young coaches looking for a move up to the top position. That strategy had failed with Lengyel and Ellwood. Marshall was looking for not only a man with experience in the trenches, but one who might bring a higher level of recognition to the program.

It found both on November 28, 1978, when Ulmo Shannon "Sonny" Randle succeeded Ellwood. Randle had been head coach at East Carolina and Virginia, his alma mater. At East Carolina, the former National Football League All-Pro receiver won two Southern Conference championships and compiled a 22-10 record in three years, including 9-2 marks in each of the final two years. His two-year stint at Virginia was less enviable, however. His first team in 1974 went 4-7, but he was fired before the final game of a 1-10 season the following year. Virginia's strict academic requirements and his efforts to bring the Cavaliers a winner were incompatible, Randle said in explaining his firing. Football for players at Virginia became a full-time job with Randle's hiring. Not only were there hours of practice on the field but nearly as many spent in meetings, leaving little time for the stringent scholastic standards of the university. Almost from the day he returned to the Charlottesville campus, this put him at odds with those whose support he needed to succeed. His conduct off the field also clashed with the image the school strived to project.

He drove his players nearly as hard as he drove himself, but had trouble coping when their level of desire didn't match his. His practices were, to put it mildly, severe and often elicited stories of undue physical and verbal abuse. These were spawned by numerous players who had quit under Randle's strict regimen. He had an equally volatile relationship with officials and some members of the media. It was in only the second game of his tenure at Marshall that Randle boiled over in a post-game interview when a local TV sports director pursued a point about the game a bit too far in the coach's view.

Despite working until near midnight, then rising at 4:30 a.m., there never seemed to be enough time for Randle and his football. He walked quickly, talked rapidly and drove even faster. He was a master at driving and eating, often wheeling his car well above the speed limit with a sandwich in one hand, a bag of French fries in the other and a soft drink resting between his thighs. His ability to eat and drive was second only to the litany of remarks he could direct at any driver impeding his progress on the road.

Because Randle was divorced he was viewed as a playboy, which led to a mistaken image of him as a heavy drinker. Actually, he never touched alcohol. He attended church regularly and was never without a chaplain for his teams. His lone visible vice was betting on the horses, which he did quite well. Randle, who grew up around race tracks before spending much of his youth in military school, owned an interest in a horse named "Quick Post" with former St. Louis Cardinals quarterback Charley Johnson and often had a bet on a race every day. While Randle was on the field conducting practice at Marshall, it wasn't uncommon for a manager to keep an ear on the radio, listening for race results. The only thing that brought more attention to Virginia than his image was his dismissal, which came with the program in turmoil and drew embarrassing media attention nationwide. Randle, however, was in public view long before his coaching career began. He spent 11 years in the NFL as a wide receiver, earning All-Pro honors four times. He was best remembered as Johnson's favorite receiver at St. Louis in the early 1960s.

Very few of the labels he acquired concerning his conduct on and off the field while at Virginia were lost when he came

The late Joe McMullen, who hired Sonny Randle at Marshall, used a dictatorial approach in running the university's athletics from 1971 to 1979. (Photo courtesy of The Herald-Dispatch)

to Marshall. His straightforward image was evident to others on the first meeting. He pulled no punches and left little room for gray areas. One night, early in his career, he was questioned by a person on his radio call-in show about why his team wasn't playing better. His answer: "You can't make chicken salad without the chicken," a telling comment that demonstrated Randle's wit. Later in a post-season question-and-answer interview, Randle shocked a writer by saying that if it weren't for football he'd probably be in prison. And he meant it. But for all the faults most saw in Randle, nobody could question his loyalty to his players or those who came to know him well.

"He was simply an intimidating personality and that made him misunderstood by most people," said Terry Echols, who started at linebacker for Randle from 1981 to '83. "But he had a lot of compassion for people when they got to know him. Regardless of all that was said about his practices, he cared for his players. He really treated his players well, from the scholarship guy he saw as a team leader to the walk-on who was on the scout team."

Billy Hynus, a wide receiver who played for the Herd in Randle's final three years, felt much the same way. Hynus married and became a father while playing for Randle and the coach showed the compassion of which Echols spoke.

"Coach Randle was a lot more than what he showed on the field," Hynus said. "He was great with his players. I know when I got married and had the baby on the way he helped me find an apartment and checked on how the change would affect my scholarship. He wanted to see that my family was taken care of and I was still able to go to school and play ball."

From the time Randle's interest in the head coaching position became known to Marshall, he was the school's leading candidate. He was the only man interviewed in person and he made it widely known that he coveted the post. The position he had held the past two years as athletics director and football coach at Massanutten Military Academy in Woodstock, Virginia, was beginning to bore him. He saw his time there as ample penance for his sins at Virginia. Now was the time to move back to the college ranks and he saw Marshall as his chance.

"I realized when I left (Virginia) I had to go somewhere and pay my dues for a while," he said. "I knew one day there'd be an opportunity to be a head coach, but it had to be the right one."

Marshall, Randle believed, was right for him.

"The job I was looking for had to have everything a program needs in order to make it work," he said upon his hiring. "Marshall is right for Sonny Randle and I'm right for Marshall University. The chemistry is excellent."

Marshall and Randle seemed right in step.

"We wanted someone to come in and shake up the program," Hayes said.

"They got the right guy," Randle countered. "When you're given what it takes to do the job, there will be no excuses for losing. They won't have to fire me. I assure you of that."

But as right as Randle seemed to be on his choice of Marshall, he was just as wrong about how his employment as Thundering Herd coach would conclude. He repeated it often during a five-year tenure that began in a storm created by remnants of the controversy at Virginia and ended in calm just short of its goal. He would be fired in November 1983, a day after one of his biggest victories, just the 12th in his 55 games as the Herd's coach. His firing, however, didn't come at the hands of the men who had hired him. A different power structure was in place when the end came for Randle and that played a role in his demise.

Sam Clagg, a former player and coach for the lengendary Cam Henderson, was the interim president, replacing Hayes, a staunch Randle backer. Hayes had been deposed by the West Virginia Board of Regents in 1983. Lynn Snyder was now athletics director, taking over for McMullen, whose contract wasn't renewed by Hayes after the summer of 1979. McMullen and Randle quickly were at odds, with the administrator eventually losing out to the coach's core of supporters. Clagg, acting as little more than a caretaker for the school, left Randle's fate to Snyder, who came on board from an assistant's position at Illinois just before Randle made his fall debut. Snyder, like McMullen, saw his relationship with the coach deteriorate to one bordering the adversarial and chose not to renew Randle's contract after the 1983 season.

When Randle started his five-year run as Marshall coach in 1979, he began much in the manner of his predecessors; he wasted little time in trying to inject life into the program. He promised the fans an exciting game plan that accentuated the pass on offense and a multiple look on defense.

"We'll be throwing the ball when we step off the bus," Randle said. "I've never been adverse to throwing on first down or fourth down. We'll be wide open and aggressive."

His talk of wide-open football even spawned a record titled "Let's Make Thunder" that received local airplay. To the players who would have to execute the attack, Randle promised a clean slate for the start of his first spring practice.

"We gave the players a new lease on life. Each and every player on our team is starting from scratch," he said.

Randle quickly discovered, however, regardless of the posture he took trying to live up to the second promise he didn't have the personnel to execute the first, at least not in the early stages. To carry out the plan, Randle advocated a team built on speed and quickness. He knew that to have any chance of competing with the rest of the Southern Conference, he needed those two elements before anything else.

Unfortunately, what Randle found in his bag of Ellwood leftovers was only size, which was fine for the power game that his predecessor had played, but only third on his list of priorities. And what speed he did find was on the bottom end of his rating scale. Regardless of the physical attributes a player possessed, it quickly became evident that it would take one with a special emotional makeup to play for Randle.

His practices were, in the words of former players, "torture," "brutal," "murder," "insane," "ridiculous" and, simply, "a bitch." In the beginning, they served a two-fold purpose. The first was to define the players who had the toughness Randle was seeking and the second was to get them in the physical condition he was convinced they would need to succeed.

"So much of the problem came because guys had been pampered in high school," said Echols, who as a free agent played a year with the Pittsburgh Steelers. "The practices challenged more than anything your mental toughness. Don't get me wrong, they were tough physically for sure, but Sonny used them to play on the mind more than anything. Were you strong enough to endure it? A lot of guys weren't. And some of them were really good athletes – I mean some of the best at their position I've ever played with. The guys who were like me, we looked at it like, 'He's not going to break me,' no matter how tough it got.

"That first year or two, he made it tough because he wanted to weed out the guys who didn't meet his standards. Except for the last few games, practices were just as tough when I started as they were when I finished. But because he had his guys in there, you didn't have guys quitting or complaining and who didn't get the press that the ones did when he started. There was only one thing I found tough and that was Sonny was from the old school about water. We got one break in the middle of practice and one at the end.

Luckily, nothing happened. He did ease up on some things off the field the last couple of years. He let us wear high whites (socks) and have some music in the locker room. Again, it was because he had his players."

Although some players hung on, a few just so they could retain a free trip through school, many departed in the face of the extreme workouts. Players left the squad almost daily during the first pre-season practices. Of the 23 players Randle announced in his first class of scholarship recruits, a handful left without playing a game, and only four were around for their senior seasons. Some members of the class, including prize receiver Chris Adkins, didn't last a week. One who did last the duration was defensive back Carl Lee, who went on to earn All-Southern Conference honors twice before being a seventh-round draft choice by the NFL's Minnesota Vikings in the spring of 1983.

"I never had a practice in Minnesota as hard as I had at Marshall," said Lee, who was a three-time Pro Bowl selection during a 12-year NFL career — 11 with the Vikings and one with the New Orleans Saints. "Honestly, training camp was easy compared to what coach Randle put us through in preseason. I couldn't have been better prepared when I was a rookie. Even when Bud (Grant) retired and Les (Steckel) took over, I didn't have a practice as hard as college and all everybody kept talking about was how tough Les' practices were. Guys would bitch and bitch and bitch about how tough we had it under him. I told them they should've been with me at Marshall if they wanted tough."

Echols found an equally easy atmosphere in the Steelers camp.

"I never had a practice as tough as college when I was with the Steelers. You get geared up for the pros, like 'Oh, this has to be tough.' Then you go through one and say, 'This is it?' "

It wasn't only the work on the practice field that drove some players away; the time they spent in meetings left precious few moments for those who took their studies seriously. Eric Janssen, a pre-med major from Columbus, Georgia, was a good example.

"He felt my academics were in the way of football," said Janssen in a July 1981 interview with The Columbus Enquirer. Janssen, a two-year starter at wide receiver, decided to return to Marshall as a senior but not to football. "It was like a 40-hour-a-week job and working overtime," he said of playing for Randle.

Randle's penchant for grabbing a player's facemask and lacing his practices with abusive language was something that Echols said was blown out of proportion. Echols didn't deny, however, that it was extensive.

Coach Sonny Randle tries to make a point with some of his offensive players along the sidelines in the 1980 season opener against Morehead State. Marshall started the season impressively, routing Morehead 35-8 on the Eagles' home field, then beating Kent State 17-7 at home. From there the Herd managed only a 13-13 tie with Western Carolina and eight defeats to finish the season with a 2-8-1 record. (Photo by Frank Altizer)

"You should've seen the stuff I had done to me in high school," said Echols, a key recruit out of Mullens (W.Va.) High School in Randle's 1980 class. "Sonny was just as likely to grab your mask and pat you on the head for something good as he was to grab it and scream at you. It was his way of getting your attention. Coaches did it all over the country and still do. It just got blown up in the press because of what happened at Virginia and the fact all those guys quit that first year. It never bothered me and, believe me, I got my share of grabs."

The coach was equally tough on his players about their off-field conduct. It was often the norm rather than the exception that Randle would have a player or two join him for his 4:30 a.m. jog on "the path." Many times that wasn't all. The violation also often meant a run

A tug of one of his player's facemask by coach Sonny Randle did not always mean the coach was upset. Here, Randle is congratulating defensive back Kevin Smith for making a good play against Toledo in 1979. (Photo by Tim Grobe)

of the steps at the stadium after practice or a few laps around the field with a couple of tires on the shoulders.

"The first thing was that Sonny was a disciplinarian, then a coach," Echols said. "He thought you had to have the discipline before you could play. He had guys running with him all the time. I can't count all the times I was with him. I think a lot of times he did that to some of us just because he knew we could take it and it would set an example for the other guys. There the last couple of years, it was an exception when I wasn't running with him or on those steps. I know one thing … I was in the best shape of my life then."

Despite all the controversy surrounding his practices, Randle couldn't have asked for more – either from his team or its fans – when it came time for his first game.

"They certainly were gassed for that one," Randle recalled.

With a then record crowd of 17,240 in Fairfield Stadium, favored Toledo – a preseason pick to win the Mid-American Conference – raced to a 14-0 lead and the fans feared they were in for a rerun of past seasons, but with a different director. As it would turn out, they were, but only after having at least one victory to savor. Undaunted by the deficit, Randle's charges roared back with 31 straight points to shock the Rockets, 31-14. Freshman walk-on Ron Lear and junior quarterback Danny Wright spearheaded the attack. Lear, who would become the brightest spot of an otherwise dull year, debuted with 126 yards on 27 carries to lead a rushing game that ripped Toledo's defense for 267 yards. Wright added 104 yards total offense and ran for two touchdowns. The defense held the Rockets to just 203 yards and recovered three fumbles. Nobody knew it at the time, but the victory was a far greater upset than it appeared that night. The Rockets would lose just two more games that year and finish second in the MAC, prompting Randle to say later, "I guess they didn't know how bad we really were."

Powerful Western Carolina promptly took the luster off the opening victory by dominating a sluggish Herd, 24-0 at Fairfield. The outcome left Randle livid about the effort of his team. In what would become a trademark line during his tenure when his team played with no emotion, Randle said, "Put this one on me. They weren't ready to play and when that happens, it's nobody's fault but mine." The shutout was the first of five the Herd would suffer in its next six games with the last coming in a 48-0 loss at powerful Mississippi State.

Marshall's lone chance for victory after the opener came at home against The Citadel, the SC leader, in the ninth game of the year. The Herd again rode the running of Lear and Wright and a big-play defense to take a 16-10 lead deep into the third period before the Bulldogs rallied with a touchdown and extra point. Marshall appeared to have ended its run of futility at eight games in league play when John Huth lined up for a 28-yard field goal with just 2:08 left in the game. The sophomore kicker powered the ball toward the goalposts and when he looked up from the tee, he saw the ball sailing over the left upright. He leaped in the air triumphantly with arms held high. The kick was good, Huth thought. He was wrong. Referee Tom Giles signaled wide left, viewing the ball had hooked left before it went over the crossbar.

"It was slicing through. I couldn't believe it when I saw (the official's) hands signaling no good." Randle said simply, "I guess it wasn't meant to be."

The Bulldogs ran out the clock to preserve the 17-16 win.

Losses to VMI and Appalachian State followed as the Herd closed the season 1-10. The disappointment of the record was soothed somewhat by the knowledge that the bulk of the players who had key roles for the Herd would return, including Lear. The diminutive Lear ran himself into the NCAA record books as the first Division I walk-on in history to rush for more than 1,000 yards in a season. "Jet," as Randle called him, turned down walk-on offers from Kentucky and Austin Peay to join the Herd. He earned a scholarship by running for 1,162 yards, at the time, the fifth-best NCAA total by a freshman.

Hopes were high in 1980 after the Herd dispatched Morehead State on the road and Kent State at home in its first two games. Before 18,051 fans at Fairfield Stadium, Randle, ever the showman, sent the Herd out in new gold pants and green jerseys, replacing the plain white pants the team traditionally wore. The wardrobe change seemed to have the right effect; the Herd drubbed Kent State 17-7. There would, however, be only one other bright spot the remainder of the year. That would come on a chilly October afternoon in Cullowhee, North Carolina, against Western Carolina. Freshman Barry Childers would turn Marshall's losing streak in the Southern Conference into a winless string when he kicked a then NCAA-record 59-yard field goal with one second left in the game to lift the Herd into a 13-13 tie with the Catamounts. The kick, which tied the mark for a freshman held by Texas A&M's Tony Franklin, not only surprised Western, but Marshall as well.

"I went over and sat on the bench," Echols said. "He wasn't going to make that field goal. It was cold and there was a cross wind. He had a great leg, but how do you figure he's going to make that? We'd lost. That's what I thought. Then I heard him hit the ball. You knew when he hit one because it sounded like a shotgun. I got up and the ball was headed for the post and I said, 'That's got a chance.' "

Randle was elated that his team could come away with a tie.

"We haven't won, but at least the streak is over. This should give our kids a lot of confidence."

Not enough, however, to avoid losing its remaining four games.

The off-season was punctuated by the loss of Lear, who despite a variety of injuries that limited his play, led the Herd in rushing in '80 with 617 yards. The 5-foot-8, 180-pounder was sent to the sidelines for good when a follow-up test after a routine examination uncovered a spinal condition that threatened paralysis if he continued to absorb further blows to the neck and back. He finished his career with 1,779 yards, at the time, fifth-best on

Tailback Ron Lear was Marshall's chief offensive weapon in 1979 and '80. Lear ran into the NCAA record book as a freshman when he became the first walk-on to rush for more than 1,000 yards in a season when he set a school-record with 1,162. The Lexington, Ky., native added 617 yards in an injury plagued sophomore season, but "Jet," as coach Sonny Randle called him, had his career end in spring practice 1981 when it was discovered the spinal cord injury he'd suffered the season before could lead to paralysis if he continued to play.

the Herd's career rushing list. It was a devastating loss to Randle, who held a special place for Lear because of his determination to play despite his walk-on status. With quarterback problems continuing to plague the Herd, it also was a severe blow to the team.

"For two years, Ron Lear has been a super asset to the Marshall program," Randle said announcing Lear's department. "It's sad that such a dedicated young man won't be able to play a game he loves so much."

A crowd of 18,212 saw the Herd win its third straight opener for Randle, 20-17 against Morehead State, in 1981. That victory would represent half of the Herd's win total for the season, but the other half proved to be one of the biggest wins for Randle and the program. It came in Boone, North Carolina, against Appalachian State and ended Marshall's frustration against SC opponents at 26 games. Ironically, the streak had started in Boone under Ellwood four years earlier. The win also ended a long drought against a conference foe. The Herd's last win in a league game had been in 1966 against MAC member Kent State. Sophomore Larry Fourqurean keyed the 17-10 victory over Appalachian by running for a then school record 245 yards on 32 carries. He scored what proved to be the winning touchdown on a 5-yard run with 8:03 left in the game. Echols sealed the victory when he recovered an Appalachian fumble in Marshall territory with 1:53 remaining.

"There wasn't anything special about that game," Echols recalled. "It was one time that the offense and defense seemed to put it together long enough. It was a great feeling, knowing we could beat somebody other than a Morehead or a Kent State; somebody that could mean something for us."

A few hundred people greeted the Marshall team bus when it arrived at the Hodges Hall dormitory after midnight to celebrate the win.

In 1982, the Herd opened with a victory for the fourth straight year, this time 30-17 against Kent. But just as during the three previous seasons, the excitement was short-lived. Although the defense remained solid, the offense continued to struggle in the face of inconsistent play at quarterback. Ted Carpenter, who had gained the starting role as a freshman walk-on in '81, retained the job in '82, but was pressed by freshman Carl Fodor and junior college transfer Dan Patterson. Fodor finally took over against Western Carolina and had an inauspicious debut. The Weirton, West Virginia, native hit on just 9 of 25 passes for 65 yards and suffered four interceptions. Fodor rebounded to guide the Herd to a 12-10 win over Akron the next week and two weeks later would help it to a 22-20 win at VMI. A rocky start against East Tennessee in the final game of the season prompted Randle to give Patterson a shot and set up a controversy that would leave its imprint on the next season.

Long before the first crack of a pad in the 1983 season, Randle knew there must be major improvement in the program or he wouldn't see 1984 as the Herd's coach. In his mind, the school was so desperate for a winner that downgrading the program to Division II or even discontinuing it were possibilities if he and his staff didn't deliver a winning year.

Carl Lee was the prize player in Sonny Randle's first recruiting class and the defensive back from South Charleston, West Virginia, lived up to the coach's expectations. Lee started all four years of his career and was first-team all-Southern Conference as a junior and senior while leading Marshall in tackles in three of his four seasons. He was selected in the seventh round of the 1983 NFL draft by the Minnesota Vikings where he went on to earn Pro Bowl and All-Pro honors as a cornerback.

He said as much on the drive to the Southern Conference Rouser in Boone a week before pre-season practice opened.

"I honestly think, if we don't get it done, they'll drop it down or maybe even just end it all," he said to his companion. "I sincerely mean that. I think they know we'll have done everything in our power to bring them a winner and that they won't find anybody anywhere that'll work any harder or do any more to get it done than we have. If we don't do it, maybe they'll give somebody else a shot. And they might get it done. But I guarantee you they won't work any harder than we did."

The next day, Randle told the media assembled at the Rouser that it was time for him to "Get it done or get gone."

Unhappy with the team's offensive performance in spring practice, Randle made a last-ditch effort to prop up his chances for bringing Marshall a winner by scouring the country for a junior college quarterback. Although he still had Fodor, who showed promise in his brief stint as a freshman, as well as Carpenter and Patterson, Randle decided new blood was needed at the position. Shortly before the start of pre-season practice, he signed Tim Kendrick, a 6-3, 210-pound transfer from Gulf Coast Community College in Mississippi. Kendrick brought sparkling credentials to campus. He had passed for more than 1,200 yards and 15 touchdowns in nine games at Gulf Coast. His availability, however, at such a late date was the result of a broken leg suffered in the ninth game of the year. Despite the injury, Randle pronounced Kendrick fit and heaped praise on the transfer.

"He's got as fine an arm on him as I've seen," the coach said. "He's got all the tools you want in the guy who's pulling the trigger."

Although he insisted from the day Kendrick was signed that he was just another face in the quarterback picture and his inclusion was to create more competition, it was evident who had the inside track.

Although Kendrick got the bulk of the work with the first unit, Randle maintained the job was still open as late as the week before the opener at Eastern Michigan. He didn't name Kendrick the starter until a day before the game. But for all the work Kendrick received, he was anything but prepared. Kendrick threw only 14 passes in the opener and most of them were on out patterns. He threw the ball down the field only twice and one of those was intercepted. For all Kendrick's problems, though, Marshall was able to stay in the game on Fourqurean's running and Pat Velarde's punting.

The Herd marched 58 yards on its first possession of the game to take a 3-0 lead on Scott LaTulipe's 40-yard field goal. That drive displayed the only offensive consistency Marshall would show on the night. Fortunately for the Herd, the Hurons, in their first game under new coach Jim Harkema, were equally inconsistent. Thanks to Fourqurean, who gained 124 yards on 27 carries, the Herd was able to cover enough ground from its own territory to get Velarde, who averaged 43.9 yards on seven kicks, in position to pin Eastern deep in its end of the field. The game settled into that back-and-forth exchange and it probably would have ended that way with Marshall walking away a 3-0 winner had it not been for Fourqurean's fumble at midfield with 8:12 remaining in the game. Three plays later, Eastern had a touchdown and, for all intents and purposes, a 7-3 victory. With Kendrick seemingly awestruck in his debut, the Herd had no chance of coming back with the passing game. Eastern was able to contain the Herd's running game the rest of the way and claim its only win of the season.

The loss was a bitter one for Randle, who later would point to the defeat as probably the difference between Marshall having a winning season and a losing campaign. With the exception of Kendrick's inadequacies, the Herd was the better team in that game and Randle knew it. Marshall's defense limited Eastern to just 231 yards, but the Herd could manage only 196. Randle masked his view of Kendrick's effort in his post-game interview, but privately, he couldn't hide his disappointment.

"That one really hurt," Randle said. "It was right there for us and we didn't get it. And the guy pulling the trigger, well, he wasn't there at all. He went out on that field, his eyes got as big as saucers, his fanny slammed shut and we were done."

Hoping Kendrick was suffering from nothing more than first-game jitters, Randle sent the quarterback out again the next week in the home opener with Illinois State. The result was even more disastrous than the first week. The junior threw interceptions on

Marshall's first two possessions then fumbled the ball away on its third. But despite the problems, Marshall again was in the game, trailing 7-3 at the half. That quickly changed in the second half. Kendrick suffered his third interception on Marshall's second possession of the third period and the Redbirds turned it into a 10-3 lead. Randle gave Kendrick one more series. The Herd lost four yards on the possession and Illinois State countered with a 64-yard drive that ended in a touchdown for a 17-3 lead. Patterson came on for Kendrick and although he completed 8 of 13 passes for 119 yards, he couldn't get the Herd in the end zone as it suffered a 27-3 defeat.

Relief came the next week in a 35-0 romp against a poor Morehead State team. Patterson was in at quarterback, but to do little more than hand off to Fourqurean and back-up Robert Surratt, another junior college transfer. The duo ran their way into the school record book as the first two players in school history to gain more than 100 rushing yards in the same game. Fourqurean led the way with 158 yards on 16 carries, and Surratt added 110 on 15 tries. Both scored two touchdowns. To his credit, Patterson did contribute four pass completions, including a 44-yard touchdown, in eight attempts. Marshall simply dominated the Eagles, who many observers felt was the worst team Marshall had faced in years.

Earlier in the week, The Parthenon – Marshall's student newspaper – reminded Randle of his promise to resign if the Herd didn't have a winner. He took the opportunity in his post-game interview to deliver a verbal salvo to his critics.

"I guess this (victory) will keep the vultures away for a while," the coach said in his sternest southern drawl. "They'll have to stay up there circling for at least a week. You can tell them to put the rope away."

The win at Morehead did little more than to stop the Herd's bleeding. The losing gash was ripped open again the next two weeks with losses at Furman, 31-7, and back home against Western Carolina, 21-7. Marshall simply was outclassed by the Paladins, while the Catamounts took advantage of a "flat" Herd to post the victory. It was the effort before the Homecoming crowd that particularly bothered Randle, who time and again during his stay in Huntington had juiced up his team to play above its capabilities against a favored opponent.

"I was scared to death before the game in the locker room and I've never felt that way before in football. We weren't ready to play and I have no one to blame but myself," he said, the shame creasing his face. "When you're not enjoying much success, it's hard to work during the week like you need to in order to be successful. Saturday at the stadium is supposed to be a fun day for these guys, but lately it certainly hasn't been anything like that. There's got to be a reason and that's where I'm to blame."

For advice, Randle sought the help of Dr. R.F. Smith, then senior minister at Huntington's Fifth Avenue Baptist Church and the team's chaplain. Carrying a burden to Smith wasn't unusual for Randle. The coach had gone to his confidant for help with problems on and off the field since deciding he wanted Smith to be team chaplain. The decision was beneficial to both parties. Randle found a source of inspiration and Smith a means to fill the void in his life created by the death of his teenage son just a few months before Randle came to Marshall. Smith, however, didn't accept the role unconditionally.

"We went out to lunch and I told him up front that if he just wanted window dressing to look good in the religious community, I wasn't his man," Smith recalled. "I had to have a green ticket to minister to every ear – coaches and players. Sonny gave me a blank check. I had an open-door policy. I was included in executive sessions with coaches and the team. I felt free in their office and they felt free in mine. Now, Sonny and I had some head-to-head discussions, but regardless of disagreements we might have, he never reneged on his commitment to me from that first meeting."

There were times, particularly early in Randle's tenure when criticism of his coaching methods was prevalent, that Smith and Randle conversed almost daily, and not necessarily about football.

"There were a lot of one-on-ones in those early days," Smith said. "We spent many hours in my library at home, secluded, talking not just about football, but life in general. Sonny became as close to me as a brother."

Nothing, however, had the impact on Randle and his program as did the meetings Smith conducted with the coach, his staff and players in the days after the loss to Western Carolina. The players voiced their concerns on the season to date, their individual performances, the job their coaches were doing and their hopes for the rest of the season.

"I went in and jotted down on the back of an old program their list of concerns," Smith said of the team meeting. "I assured them I'd take the information to Sonny and the other coaches with no names attached, and so many of the problems were simply tied to communication and a misunderstanding of the motives."

Randle had listened before and at times acted. But this time he took the concerns to heart. With various adjustments in the work he demanded from his players both on and off the field, the coach depressurized the setting in which they had to perform. Practices, although still conducted under the same regimen but without much contact, were more spirited almost immediately.

"You could sense a world of difference in those first couple of days," Echols said. "It was like the Herd was a new team. It felt good to get ready to play, then great when Saturday finally came."

Hynus gave much of the credit to Smith.

"I don't know what Dr. Smith did, but it made a world of difference in coach Randle the last part of that season. He changed off the field, in practices and on the sidelines, and it really helped our team."

Smith insisted he performed no miracles. It was all a part of Randle's maturing process. It was a process that brought him more in touch with the changes football and society had undergone since he had entered coaching more than a decade before.

"We had a long conversation about philosophy and some theology, and really what the whole business of leading people was all about," said Smith, himself a former athlete. "There are two schools of thought in coaching – one group coaches football and another coaches young men. And there is a decided difference in the two. Sonny started out coaching football, but in his later days, he moved his thinking to, 'These are men I'm coaching,' and started to relate to them more in that light. One of the things that was key in the whole situation was that he was now dealing with a group of players who were products of a more permissive society.

"No longer was the military influence under which Sonny and I grew up in prevalent. It was, 'Yes, sir,' 'No, sir,' a salute and do the job. It was no longer a group of kids reared in the '50s and early '60s. The players now were questioning things. Slowly, Sonny grasped this and started implementing changes. To Sonny's credit, he moved 110 percent on those players' concerns."

The moves paid dividends against East Tennessee State. Marshall won 13-10 with its most impressive outing to date. Kendrick returned at quarterback and played his best game of the season while the defense snuffed the Buccaneers' final two scoring chances with interceptions. It was exactly the kind of effort Randle was looking for and it would go a long way toward changing the course of the rest of the year.

Tailback Larry Fourqurean led Marshall in rushing as a sophomore and senior en route to finishing his career as the school's leading rusher 2,232 yards. "Queen Bee" as Randle called Fourqurean, gained a then school record 245 yards in Marshall's 1981 victory against Appalachian State. (Photo by John Klein)

"Instead of doing things Sonny Randle's way, we let the kids do it their way," Randle said. "We played with a lot of emotion and when we do that we're good enough. This is a new start, a new Herd and a new beginning."

Marshall had an open week to savor the victory before traveling to Chattanooga. Although it would lose the game 23-16, Marshall gained much more than the won-loss column could detail. After scoring a safety early in the first period, Marshall saw the powerful Mocs roll up 23 straight points, threatening to turn the game into a laugher. UTC, however, couldn't settle for letting the scoreboard do the talking. Its players had to get in the taunts and words for which they'd become noted around the league. Mocs' linebacker Zack

One of the highlights of Sonny Randle's five seasons as coach of the Thundering Herd was his very last game. Marshall walloped VMI, 56-7, on November 19, 1983, for its most lopsided victory in 36 years. Randle was carried off the Fairfield Stadium turf by players Glenn Bates, left, and Stephon Blackwell after the game. (Photo by Chris Spencer)

Irvin delivered the verbal shot that sent the Herd back in retaliation.

As teammate Lawrence Green was returning an interception, Irvin began to taunt MU lineman Ray Lamb near midfield. Punches between the two quickly followed. The altercation moved to the sidelines, where Green's return ended, as other Mocs' players followed Irvin's lead with words. Instead of backing down, the Herd jumped in the fray with both feet. Its spirit would set the tone for the rest of the game.

Fodor, who had taken over for an ineffective Kendrick late in the opening period, and Brian Swisher served notice that Marshall had no intention of giving up by combining on a 70-yard touchdown pass on the first play of the second half. Fodor later hit Todd Evans with a 4-yard pass for a score with 6:04 left in the game. Marshall's defense, meanwhile, stuffed the Mocs. It took a circus-catch interception by UTC's Gary Woodburn in the game's final two minutes to end the Herd's upset hopes.

"There wasn't one head ducked in the locker room at halftime," Echols recalled. "We knew they weren't any better than we were. We didn't end up winning, but it told us all something. For the first time, we really felt like a team."

And at the center of the team now was Fodor, who many observers believed should have been given the opportunity to play long before the Chattanooga game. Privately, Fodor felt the same way, but after his first appearance, he was told by an assistant coach to say nothing of his previous inactivity.

"One of the coaches caught me in the shower room, told me I was going to get some press and to think before I said anything," Fodor recalled later. "He told me to say that the coaches said they were going to give me a chance, and I got it, and I'm happy. That hurt me because I could've done the same thing long before. Maybe if they wouldn't have waited until the seventh game, the season wouldn't have turned out for us like it did."

As he had shown as a freshman, and later would display in his junior and senior seasons, Fodor at the controls made Marshall a much better team. The next week he led the Herd to a 26-10 victory over The Citadel.

Marshall was doomed to its 19th straight losing season the next week at home in a 48-24 loss to William & Mary. As had become almost expected with the program, one play turned the game for Marshall. Trailing 17-14 at the Herd's 39-yard line with the clock ticking down in the first half, Indians' quarterback David Murphy lofted a Hail Mary pass in the corner of the end zone that receiver Stan Sutton hauled down among three Marshall defenders for the touchdown. The play stunned the Herd and the crowd of 8,808 and spurred the Indians to victory. Randle sidestepped questions about his future, saying only, "We can't have a winner, but we've got two more left in the conference so we can do some damage. Getting those are our goals now."

The Parthenon, though, didn't let Randle off the hook. The paper called for him to quit in an editorial headlined, "Sonny Randle Must Resign."

Team chaplain R.F. Smith was instrumental in Marshall's improved play late in the 1983 season. In describing Sonny Randle, Smith once said there were two Sonny Randles. "There was never a more noble gentleman socially and never more of a tiger on the field." (Photo by Lee Bernard)

Despite not being able to give Marshall a winner, Randle held out hope that wins in the final two games would be enough to earn him another year. Snyder was keeping silent on the subject. Randle's hope for two wins came to a chilling end the next Saturday in Boone as Appalachian State defeated Marshall 28-19. Although Snyder wouldn't make Randle's firing public until eight days later, it was after the loss to the Mountaineers that he made up his mind not to retain his coach.

Unknown to everyone but Snyder, the season finale at home with VMI would close Randle's tenure. In a style that was fitting for someone who had worked so hard to reach a goal but fell just short, Randle was given a send-off by his team that will long be remembered by the 6,311 in attendance. The final score of 56-7 – at the time Marshall's widest margin of victory since 1947 – was emphatically indicative of the Herd's dominance of the Keydets on that warm November afternoon. The defense limited the Keydets to 176 total yards while recovering two fumbles and intercepting a pass. Fourqurean capped a stellar career by running for 83 yards and three touchdowns to finish with 2,232 rushing yards for his career and the most in school history at the time. Randle was carried off the field on his team's shoulders and a group of fans brought down the goal post in the stadium's north end zone.

Although Randle had told his players to "play for themselves and nobody else," they clearly hoped a big finish might sway Snyder. While in the locker room the players discussed circulating petitions around town in an effort to save his job, Randle savored the victory and said he wouldn't resign.

"That day in Yankee Stadium a long time ago when I caught 17 passes was about as perfect as I've ever been associated with," he said. "But this afternoon, well, I think that beat it. Everything went exactly as you could hope for it to go. I've never had a team that's had a better win. … When you think about the way things were five years ago and look at them now, you can see just how far things have come. This is a good football team going in the right direction. … With nine starters returning on offense and eight on defense, I don't think there's a coach in America who wouldn't want to be a part of a situation like that. I think next year, you'll see (the team) as good as you'll ever want. … The table is set for these kids. The sky is the limit for them."

Randle and Snyder met the next morning. Snyder waited until that night to announce that he wouldn't rehire the coach. Randle was in Charlottesville visiting his children when the announcement was made. He never made comments on the record about his dismissal and declined the post-season question-and-answer interview with The Herald-Dispatch that he had conducted annually. His only response after the firing came in a letter to the newspaper a few weeks later. In it, Randle thanked the community for its support during his five years. He said he was a better person for the experience of trying to bring Marshall a winning program and had gained a new perspective on himself and football because of it. In the 1990s, Randle returned to the Marshall program as a television analyst and maintained the positive outlook on his tenure on broadcasts.

"There were two Sonny Randles," said Smith, who died in 2003 and served as counsel to other Marshall coaches and players until his retirement from Fifth Avenue Baptist in 1999. "There was never a more noble gentleman socially and never more of a tiger on the field. There was Sonny the football coach and Sonny your friend. Sonny the individual had to change before Sonny the coach. And it wasn't until the one off the field began to bleed over into the more intense one on the field, did the maturing process which proved so beneficial in his last days begin."

For Randle, it hadn't come soon enough. And, because of that, Marshall had to begin another search for a football coach to direct a program that at long last appeared on the verge of success.

Chapter six

Finding the quick fix

Stan Parrish was a guy who did exactly what he said. One of the first things he said he wanted to do was make football fun again and boy did he make it fun. He puts in this quick-fix offense by accentuating the pass with a perfect guy like Carl Fodor to play the role. Then, with all this "Air Parrish" business, he plays something resembling a defense and gets away with it. The schedule, however, was fixed up for him so it would work. He and Lynn Snyder got together and, if you look at the schedule, it was set up perfectly for a fast start. They played a lot of their games at home at the start of the season. That got big crowds to come out to see what was going on at Fairfield Stadium. The quick fix worked. It pumped up the players and the people in town. They won and football was fun again.

– Ernie Salvatore

Stan Parrish made a winning season the only priority when he was summoned by Athletics Director Lynn Snyder to replace Sonny Randle as the Thundering Herd's head coach.

"The word rebuilding is not part of my football vocabulary," said Parrish, who came from Purdue University where he was quarterback coach for a year, at his hiring. "We want a winner next year. Six (wins) is the goal – the first goal and foremost one in our minds."

He wasn't deterred by the fact that he would be trying to succeed where the past five coaches over the last 19 seasons had not.

"Even though a lot of people thought otherwise, when I looked at the job, the

Stan Parrish charged up the Marshall fan base with a passing offense that was a threat to score from anywhere on the field and a defense that gambled its way to big play after big play. The coach, who resembles "Wheel of Fortune" host Pat Sajak, gave Marshall its first winning season in two decades and put the program on the national stage with victories over some of the perennial contenders in NCAA Division I-AA. Of the top 10 crowds at Fairfield Stadium in Marshall history when Parrish left for Kansas State after the 1985 season, six came during his two-year tenure. (Photo by Tim Grobe)

positives far outweighed the negatives," he said.

Parrish, who resembles "Wheel of Fortune" host Pat Sajak, brought impressive credentials and the calm of a seaside breeze to the position. As head coach at Division III Wabash College in the five seasons prior to moving to Purdue, the Cleveland, Ohio, native posted a 42-3-1 record. One of his first tasks was to pump up the morale of the returning players, who, for the most part, wanted Randle to receive another year. He did that in part by offering them more off-field freedom, discontinuing team film sessions, nightly meetings and mandatory study hall. All the moves were in direct contrast to Randle, much like Parrish himself, was to his predecessor.

"The players will have the rules and I've got confidence they can handle the freedoms," he said. "I'll give them a lot of rope, but if I see they can't handle it, I'll pull some in."

The changes were well received by the players, especially to those such as wide receiver Billy Hynus, who was married and had a young daughter.

"Coach Randle's years, I had an 8 a.m. class, then practice, then dinner, then a meeting. A lot of times I wasn't getting home until 8:30 or 9 o'clock," Hynus said. "That made for a long day for anybody, but for me, with a family, it was especially tough. With coach Parrish, you were out at 6 o'clock and that was it. You didn't worry about dinner, a meeting or study hall. He was more business-like with the players in that respect. You were in college to get an education first then play football. That was your responsibility and it was yours to accept without him holding your hand."

The way Parrish handled his team was an extension of his personality. He took a matter-of-fact approach to the job, stressing organization and effective use of time. An avid golfer, Parrish and a companion once played 18 holes in two hours and 20 minutes (in a cart, of course). And although the coach would make time for visitors to his office, he gave few an opportunity to make themselves comfortable in the chair. As a husband and father of a young son and daughter, Parrish kept his football in perspective. His days started early and were filled with plenty of preparation for the upcoming opponent, but practice ended the work day on most nights. He respected the time of his players and his assistants.

"Coach Parrish was laid back, but he still kept things in a business perspective," Hynus said. "He had an objective and that was to win and he knew what he wanted to do and what he wanted us to do to reach that. He didn't need a lot of ranting and raving to get your attention. He expected you to understand what he said, have confidence in it and do it."

Recalled Parrish: "All those kids needed was just a little change in direction. A few pats on the back can go a long way. We gave them a new angle to the same purpose and a sense of confidence that they had the ability as a team to reach it."

The coach's other major change was to hand the reins of his controlled passing game to Fodor, the on-again, off-again quarterback under Randle, despite his obvious talent.

Quarterback Carl Fodor flourished in Parrish's innovative passing offense. The junior from Weirton, West Virginia, was an on-again, off-again starter in his first two years under Sonny Randle, but his talents came to the fore with Parrish's confidence. Fodor finished his Marshall career as the school and Southern Conference leader in nearly every passing and total offense category for single season and career, and began the school's string of standout performers at the position. (Photo by Tim Grobe)

"It was evident very early that Carl was going to be our quarterback," Parrish said. "We were committed to throwing the football and he was clearly the best guy to do it."

Parrish informed Fodor over the semester break that he would be his top quarterback in the spring.

"Coach Parrish's confidence in me brought everything out," said Fodor, who would go on to set a host of Marshall and Southern Conference passing marks during his two seasons under Parrish.

"That kind of offense made as much difference as anything else he changed," Hynus said of the Parrish system. "We had the players who were suited for it. It was geared for our team and we didn't have any problems catching on. We never did have a problem pass blocking. And in that new offense, we had a lot more options because we had more than two or three guys in patterns. All Carl had to do was read it right and we had a great chance of completing the pass. It caught a lot of people off guard and that really helped us win."

With 16 starters returning, a new philosophy that had been accepted by the players and a schedule that included four straight home games to open the season, Parrish had what most believed an excellent chance to pull off the winning season.

Marshall's memorable 1984 season started inauspiciously when Fodor fractured a bone in his foot just two days into pre-season practice. The break required surgery for insertion of a pin to insure proper healing. After some tense early moments, his rehabilitation time was placed at three to four weeks, meaning he was questionable at best for the opener September 1 against West Virginia Tech. Fodor, though, was off crutches and on the practice field within a week and running lightly shortly thereafter. He participated in workouts during game week, but was placed in the role of backup to Carpenter, who had received the bulk of the preseason work in Fodor's absence. The start for Carpenter, though, was nothing more than a token gesture by Parrish, who knew full well that Fodor would be the key to the offense.

After an ineffective first quarter by Carpenter, Parrish got Fodor off the bench and the strong-armed junior didn't disappoint his coach or anyone else in the late-arriving crowd of 16,623. After three misfires in the first series, Fodor steadied to complete 21 of his final 32 tosses for 254 yards and three touchdowns in a 33-10 win. It was the effort Parrish had hoped he would see from his quarterback and the beginning he so desperately needed to keep his team on a positive level.

Fodor continued his onslaught at home the next two Saturdays, first throwing for a then school record four touchdowns and running for another in a 40-6 romp of Morehead State. It was the first of three games in which Fodor would toss four scoring passes in the record-breaking season. He was equally brilliant in a 24-17 win against Mid-American Conference opponent Eastern Michigan, having a hand in all three of Marshall's touchdowns – two passing and another running. Tight end Tim Lewis was on the receiving end of 11 of Fodor's 29 completions for 156 of the quarterback's then school record 389 yards.

With this new passing attack, Marshall opened the season with three consecutive victories for the first time since 1965, the last team to post a non-losing season at 5-5. Parrish and his troops were halfway home to clinching that coveted winner. But the coach and his staff knew full well the remaining eight opponents would be nothing like the first three. So tough were the games that Parrish admitted privately that Marshall could lose them all. The first big test came against Furman in a fourth straight night game at home. The Southern Conference's perennial kingpin entered the game ranked No. 4 in Division I-AA and fresh from an upset win against Division I-A North Carolina State that ran the Paladins' record to 3-0. Despite its accomplishments and a No. 11 I-AA ranking, the Herd was rated at no better than an 18-point underdog to the Paladins.

Marshall served notice to the Paladins and the crowd of 18,065 it was ready to play by driving for a touchdown on its second possession of the game for a 7-0 lead. Fodor capped an 89-yard march with a 13-yard pass to Danny Abercrombie for the first of his four TD passes on the warm night. The Herd appeared headed for a 10-0 advantage on its next drive, Scott Latulipe's field goal was blocked. That changed the momentum and Furman raced to three straight touchdowns, the last with just 1:19 remaining in the half. Undaunted,

Marshall's offense lived up to its quick-strike billing as Fodor hit 6 of 8 passes in a 78-yard drive that took only 57 seconds. The last of the six completions covered 17 yards to Swisher, who hung on despite a vicious hit by a pair of Furman defenders.

The Paladins, though, put the Herd in full catch-up mode when Robbie Gardner raced 88 yards for a score on the first play of the second half before running mate John Drye added a 3-yard burst seven minutes later for a 35-14 lead. Fodor got one score back with a 4-yard pass to Lewis in the third period. After Kevan Esval tacked on three points for Furman with a field goal, Fodor hit Abercrombie with a 17-yarder with seven minutes left in the game. That was all Marshall could muster as it suffered a 38-28 loss.

Although a loss, the game proved Marshall had closed the gap with the top of the conference. Fodor had one of his finest days for the Herd completing 35 of 60 passes for a then school and SC record 436 yards. His total offense of 427 yards also broke school and SC records at the time. Abercrombie caught 11 passes for 141 yards. The Herd, however, was hampered by three interceptions and a lost fumble and the defense allowed 498 total yards, including 380 rushing.

"We gained a large measure of respect with that game," Parrish later recalled. "I think it gave the kids some credibility with other Southern Conference players that none of them had felt before. They were finally seeing themselves as equals."

Emotionally drained from the loss to Furman, Marshall traveled to Western Michigan and dropped a 42-7 decision in which it committed nine turnovers and gave up seven field goals to Broncos' kicker Mike Prindle, an NCAA record that still stands. The schedule's second attractive feature – in the form of an open date – helped boost Marshall's fortunes after the two straight losses.

With bruised egos and bodies, the Herd had two weeks to prepare for Homecoming against Appalachian State and it made the most of the time. Surratt, a 5-foot, 185-pounder and now the Herd's lead running back, shone as brightly as the sun on the warm October afternoon as he hauled in four touchdown passes from Fodor and ran for another score to lead the Herd to a 35-7 rout of the outmanned Mountaineers. His five-touchdown effort broke a Southern Conference record, and the four TD catches snapped a Marshall mark and tied one for the SC.

"It was one of those games you dream about, but never think you'll have," Surratt said. "I couldn't have asked for more. It seemed like every time I touched the ball, something great happened. What a feeling."

Now, only two victories stood between the Herd and its magic number. But to get them, Marshall would have to win at least one game on the road. Its first attempt came against The Citadel in Charleston, South Carolina. The Bulldogs spotted Marshall a 7-0 lead less than three minutes into the game when Fodor ended a 74-yard march with a 1-yard dive. He spent much of the rest of the day, however, running backward from a relentless pass rush that recorded five sacks totaling 58 yards and led to three interceptions, one that was returned for a touchdown. Never was Parrish's earlier statement that Fodor's performance would dictate that of his team more profound. In the face of a heavy rush and multiple coverages, Fodor had his worst day of the season connecting on 10 of 28 passes for 171 yards with 69 of the total coming on one completion as the Bulldogs took a 28-17 victory.

Marshall returned to Fairfield to face UT-Chattanooga in its final home game of the season. With road games remaining at Western Carolina, Illinois State and East Tennessee State, a first-ever victory over UTC appeared to be imperative for the Herd to retain any hopes of a winning season. A win over the hated Mocs was not far from the realm of possibility, however. Marshall, despite a decided disadvantage in talent, had a history of playing well against UTC. This year would be no different.

Although Fodor wound up throwing for 304 yards, and the Mocs had 331 yards total, defense punctuated the action that took place on an Indian Summer afternoon that saw the temperature climb into the 80s. There were nine turnovers in the game with all but one coming deep in the opposition's territory. Fittingly, the teams traded field goals for a 3-3 deadlock at halftime. Running back Artis Edwards put the Mocs ahead with a 1-yard drive to end the first possession of the second half. Backup kicker Kevin Gault, filling in for Latulipe, who was hurt on the second-half kickoff, got the Herd within 10-6 late in the third quarter with a 30-yard field goal.

After two solid stands by its defense, Marshall's offense took over with 6:19 left in the game, but 95 yards from a go-ahead score. On this march, however, Fodor guided his teammates across the distance in a fashion that made it look more like 95 feet. His sixth straight completion found Surratt circling out of the backfield for an 11-yard touchdown with 2:50 remaining, and the crowd of 12,211 erupted with a sense of victory.

The fans were still buzzing as Gault lined up for a second kickoff after the Herd was offside on its first attempt. A few seconds later, backup running back Jonathan Parker silenced those cheers with a 93-yard return for a touchdown. On the first play after the

Mocs' kickoff, Fodor was intercepted. UTC easily disposed of the final 2:13 on the clock and with it most felt, Marshall's hopes for a winner.

Doubt even crept into the Marshall locker room for the first time. Player after player wondered if it was meant to be.

"The same old Marshall," Swisher said as he sat in his cubicle amid silent teammates. "It was right there for us then it was gone."

Parrish, though devastated himself, was having none of his players' "snake-bitten" attitude.

"We've come back before and I expect that we'll do it again," he said afterward. "It'll take a lot of intestinal fortitude."

For all Parrish's hopes, however, his team failed to show much of anything in Cullowhee, North Carolina, where Western Carolina methodically defeated the uninspired Herd, 30-0. The only spark Marshall showed came in a bench-clearing altercation after Fodor threw an interception. There were words and shoves exchanged. Parrish felt so strongly that a few of the assistant coaches for Western's Bob Waters had fueled the fracas with taunting words that he didn't shake hands with his counterpart at game's end. In fact, Waters literally chased Parrish off the field trying to secure the handshake. Waters discovered Parrish's displeasure only after keeping the Marshall bus inside the confines of Whitmire Stadium until Parrish would step off the bus and talk to him. The loss left Marshall with a 4-5 record and plenty of doubts about its future.

"Right after that game, in the first few minutes was honestly the first time I thought we wouldn't do it," Hynus recalled. "Two games on the road you've got to win. That's tough. Then the coaches came in and pumped us up. We did still have two games and that's what we needed. It was down to character at that point."

Assistant coach Mark Deal had to give one of the uplifting talks.

"I remember Rob Bowers coming up to me after that game and asking what the hell had gone wrong," Deal said. "He had that questioning look in his eyes, like it was over, we can't do it. I told him we'd just been beaten by a Top 10 team. I said, 'We've still got two games left, don't we? That's how many we need to win isn't it? We're gonna do it. You've gotta believe it.' He said, 'Right, we are gonna do it.' "

That outlook aside, Parrish later would admit that during the long bus ride home even he had started to doubt if his team could reach its goal. And history was not in

Marshall's corner in its quest to win the final two away from home. The last time Marshall had won road games on successive weekends came at the start of the 1958 season.

In Illinois State, the Herd faced a team that possessed superior speed, quickness, size and strength. In fact, with more or less the same team in the season before, the Redbirds had pounded Marshall, 27-3 at Fairfield, flying in just a few hours before the 7 p.m. kickoff, administering the beating and departing for home before midnight. The Herd was a two-touchdown underdog this time around.

"Nobody's giving us much of a chance are they?" Parrish asked as his team prepared for its final full workout the day before flying to Normal, Illinois. Given an honest answer, he nodded his head and replied with confident firmness: "We're gonna surprise some people." He then started his customary quick gait back to his team. Whether this was the knowledge of an experienced coach surfacing or the attitude of one who was clinging optimistically to fading hope, Parrish sensed something in his team.

With a lot of help from the unpredictable Midwestern weather, the Herd proved Parrish a prophet. The mild, breezy morning that greeted the team at breakfast turned into a blustery afternoon of freezing rain and hail that saw the wind gust to 40 mph and the temperature plunge into the 20s as a tornado passed within 10 miles of Hancock Stadium. After the teams ran through their pre-game workout, the field was cleared and the 2:30 p.m. kickoff delayed. There was even discussion of postponing the game until the next day. But within 30 minutes, the precipitation had stopped and the game was on.

With a steady wind blowing 25 mph from the north, it was evident from the outset the team that could control field position would have a great advantage. Marshall won the toss and elected to defend the north goal, which put the wind in the Redbirds' faces. Although the Herd was unable to generate much offense, punter Mike Salmons kept Illinois State pinned deep with two good kicks, the second stopping at the Redbirds' 3-yard line. Marshall forced a punt and took over on the ISU 31. On the first play, Fodor hit Surratt on a circle route out of the backfield and he raced home for the touchdown. Gault added the conversion. That, as it turned out, was all the points the Herd needed.

Illinois State had the wind in the second period, but took over deep in its own territory. The Redbirds failed to score after having one pass intercepted and losing two fumbles. Paul Politi got the Redbirds on the board in the third quarter with a 23-yard field goal, but that was all they could gain with the wind. Gault added a 27-yard field goal for insurance with 10 minutes left in the game and the combination of wind and Herd defense halted any hope of the Redbirds coming back.

"What did I tell you?" Parrish said as he emerged from a joyous dressing room after the 10-3 win. "Nobody gave us a Chinaman's chance to come in here and win, but we did it. You don't know how proud I am of these kids. Their backs were against the wall. They really showed something. They want to win."

Although the next game at East Tennessee was to provide the clinching win, it was the victory at Illinois State that really handed Marshall the winner. There was no way the Herd would be denied against the Buccaneers, who already had assured themselves of a winning season and had little motivation for the game other than to be a spoiler.

"After coming through at Illinois State, everybody knew we'd win the last one," Hynus said. "We had great practices, everybody was up. We just knew it was coming."

The Herd's enthusiasm carried over to Huntington. Numerous businesses hung up "6" in their windows. The team was given a parade send-off Friday morning as it left for Johnson City, Tennessee, and was greeted by some 2,500 fans when it took the field in Memorial Center.

"We came out and saw all that green," Fodor said later. "We weren't going to lose in front of all those people."

Deal believed the same thing.

"Swisher came in after warm-up and said, 'Did you see all those fans. It's just like home,' " Deal recalled. "I said, 'We can't lose. Those people aren't gonna let us.' "

Fodor, who completed 25 of 51 passes for 329 yards in the game, ended Marshall's first possession with a 6-yard touchdown run off an option play less than four minutes into the game. East Tennessee matched that when Robbie White hit Jerry Butler with a 7-yard scoring pass. Fodor hit Lewis with a 7-yard touchdown pass midway through the second quarter only to see White tie it with a 6-yarder to Mark Neely just 22 seconds before the half. White, who would finish 20-of-43 for 234 yards, connected with Mark Murphy on a 72-yard bomb with 10:40 left in the third period and Marshall's hopes began to flicker. LaTulipe countered for the Herd with a 44-yard field goal on the ensuing possession and that seemed to pump some life back into Marshall.

The Herd's defense forced an ETSU punt on the next series, but All-American punter George Cimadevilla put the Herd in a hole by dropping his boot just outside the goal line where it was downed. Surratt and Randy Clarkson combined for three carries and a first down at the 13-yard line. That set up the Herd's longest play of the season and it couldn't have come at a better time. Fodor faked a handoff to Clarkson, which drew up the Bucs' secondary, dropped a step and found Swisher wide open on a post pattern from his split end slot. The speedy receiver caught the ball in stride and raced untouched to the end zone to give the Herd the lead and send the Marshall fans into a frenzy.

The Herd's coaches spotted the opening on Surratt's carry the previous play and brought split end Hynus inside to Swisher's flanker spot and moved the faster Swisher outside hoping he could score off the play.

"The coaches figured it would be so wide open, they wanted to have every chance we'd score," Hynus laughed. "That's why 'Swish' and I traded."

That was all the boost the Herd needed as it later overcame a Cimadevilla punt that pinned it on the 4-yard line to cover the 96 yards in 15 plays with Clarkson diving over from a yard for what proved to be the clinching score with 12:59 remaining.

The Bucs, though, struck back with 5:23 left when Butler scampered 9 yards for a score. ETSU stopped the Herd on its next possession to get one more shot at the victory with 3:41 remaining. After three plays, the Bucs had gained just two yards and lined up in punt formation. But Cimadevilla had no intention of punting this time as he took the snap and threw a pass to tight end Tom Dodd that gained 17 yards. With about two minutes left, ETSU still was alive. Marshall needed a big play, and less than 30 seconds later, it came. On a second-and-7 at the ETSU 37, White hit Butler with a swing pass and the talented tailback danced away from a crowd into the open field and appeared headed for a big gain. MU's Tony Lellie recovered, however, to make a hit and Butler fumbled. For what seemed like an eternity, the ball rolled free, before Herd cornerback Leon Simms finally pulled it in at the Bucs' 49.

There was just 1:29 left on the clock.

East Tennessee still had two timeouts, which meant Marshall had to have a first down if it was to run out the clock. Clarkson, who ran for 105 yards on 28 carries in the game, took care of that on the first two plays with gains of 2 and 8 yards.

Finally, it was over. Marshall had its winning season. The nation's longest active streak of non-winning and losing seasons no longer belonged to Marshall. The distinction passed to Columbia.

Marshall quarterback Carl Fodor confers with offensive assistant coach Mark Deal, left, and head coach Stan Parrish during a timeout with 1:29 left in the final game of the season against Southern Conference rival East Tennessee State on November 17, 1984. The three discussed the best way to secure a first down on the ensuing play in order to maintain possession and run out the clock to turn a 31-28 lead against the Buccaneers into the Herd's sixth victory of the season, thus ending the longest active streak of losing seasons in NCAA Division I football. Marshall picked up the first down on the next play sending the estimated 2,500 Herd fans who'd traveled to the game into a frenzy with the school's first non-losing season since a 5-5 mark in 1965. (Photo courtesy of The Herald-Dispatch)

"All you had to do was look in that locker room," Parrish recalled years later. "That was all the story you needed. It told it all. No questions, no words, just a look at those kids. They had 20 years worth of teams and players in there with them. I'll remember that scene as long as I live. I don't think I'll ever be a part of something that meant so much to so many people."

As many had feared, producing the school's first winner in two decades made Parrish an attractive property for schools seeking a new coach. His name was connected with a handful of openings around the country, but only surfaced as a candidate for the job at Tulsa where John Cooper had left for Arizona State. Just as he had when he was hired, Parrish maintained he wouldn't actively seek any other job while at Marshall, but owed it to himself and his family to pursue opportunities when he was contacted. He interviewed for the Tulsa post early in 1985, but withdrew his name from consideration shortly after the contact. Don Morton subsequently was hired to replace Cooper.

With the coaching rumors put to rest, Parrish's task for 1985 was proving that the previous year was not a fluke. Although the element of surprise provided the year before by the passing game now was gone, Parrish had a trick or two to use for the defense in his quest to bring Marshall its first back-to-back winners since 1963-64. The fact that he had eight starters returning on both offense and defense also was a promising sign. And the schedule again was in the Herd's favor. Four of its first six games were at home. Its second game at Morehead would be the Eagles' opener and its third contest against Ohio would be the Bobcats' initial outing. The fourth game at Eastern Kentucky would be the Colonels' second game after an off week following their opener.

"Our schedule again is conducive to a good start," Parrish said in preseason. "That's always a big key for any team."

Just as the season before, the Herd rode Fodor's passing to easy wins over West Virginia Tech, Morehead and Ohio. Although the numbers weren't as prolific – mainly because he was throwing against seven and eight-man coverages – Fodor was equally as effective. And, for the first time, the defense was matching the offense in consistency.

"We went hand in hand," said senior linebacker John Ceglie of the solid all-around play after the win over Ohio. "One picked up where the other left off on the field. The game just carried over that way all night. You know, we won last year, but I don't think we played like winners until now."

While 1984's early-season test came against Furman, this season it was highly regarded Eastern Kentucky at Hangar Field in Richmond where the Colonels had won 36 straight games. EKU long had been a benchmark for I-AA excellence under veteran coach Roy Kidd and this season promised to be no different. Eastern again was picked to win the Ohio Valley Conference and ranked sixth by Sports Illustrated in its pre-season poll. Against that backdrop, Parrish knew this would be the game that could capture more of the I-AA spotlight Marshall had slipped into by last year's winning season.

"There are games that mean a lot more than the one win or loss that goes in the book," Parrish recalled. "Eastern was one of those games for our program."

Marshall linebacker John Spellacy, then a freshman starter, pointed to the game as the key to the Herd's success the remainder of his career.

"We'd heard we didn't belong on the same field (with Eastern). We took the attitude we had nothing to lose. We played our hearts out. That game, I think, established Marshall as a program to be reckoned with."

Despite both teams possessing potent offenses – Marshall's via the pass and Eastern's off a ball-control running attack – defense dominated before a crowd of 14,200, including 2,500 MU fans, on the hot, sunny afternoon. John Mitchell's 44-yard field goal with four seconds left in the first half handed Marshall a 3-0 lead. After stopping Eastern Kentucky on the first possession of the second half, the Herd extended the lead to 10-0 when Fodor hit a sliding Abercrombie with an 11-yard touchdown pass with about five minutes gone in the third period. With its defense disrupting the Colonels' offense play after play, that was all the points the Herd needed to pull the biggest upset since the win over Miami in 1976. Mitchell added a 41-yard field goal later in the third period to make it 13-0 before the Colonels' averted the shutout with a touchdown on the game's final play. More than a fourth of the 318 yards the Colonels gained came on the late touchdown drive.

"Our defense was superb," Parrish said. "Again, it bent, but didn't break. They got after it on every play."

Kidd was equally impressed.

"I give all the credit in the world to Marshall," the coach said afterward. "Their defense was outstanding; they kept us off guard all day. A good team beat us."

Marshall was rewarded for its best start since 1965 by being ranked third in the first I-AA poll of the season. At the time, it was the highest ranking for any Marshall athletic team in the school history.

The Herd ran its winning streak to five straight at Fairfield with a lackluster 17-14 win over The Citadel. Marshall won despite four turnovers, nine penalties and numerous mental mistakes. Fodor hit Swisher with a 24-yard touchdown pass less than 30 seconds into the final quarter to bring MU back from a 14-10 deficit. Marshall's defense again utilized the blitz to stop the Bulldogs cold on their final four possessions to preserve the win.

"It was a case of the defense getting it done there or we lose," Parrish said. "I don't know why we made all those mistakes and didn't play well, but we won in spite of it all."

Next came the game that generated as much controversy as excitement during any in Parrish's two seasons. It came as a result of a 10-10 tie with Western Carolina, which brought a share of the No. 12 ranking to Huntington for the game against the No. 3 Herd. After leading 3-0 at the half, Marshall found itself down 10-3 with just 3:22 remaining as Western placekicker Kirk Roach lined up for a 39-yard field goal that could clinch the win. The sophomore all-conference selection, though, missed – his first ever inside 40 yards – to give Marshall another shot. It was his third miss for the game, something he would never repeat in an All-American career. The Herd fumbled that chance away two plays later. Marshall's defense, however, forced a Catamounts' punt, giving the offense another opportunity with 1:14 remaining at its own 17.

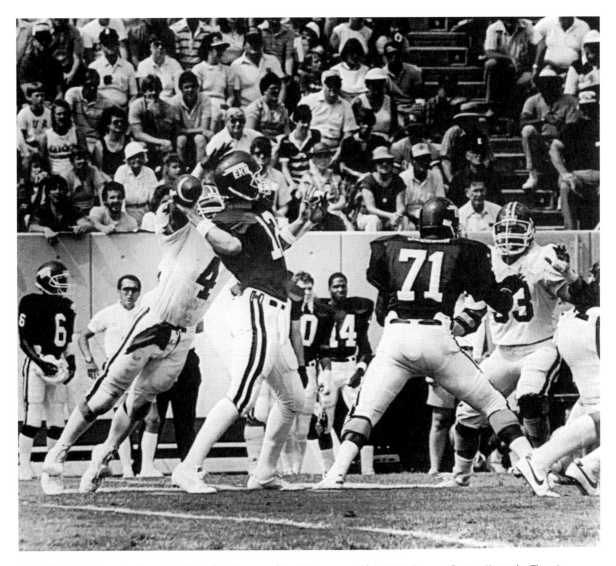

Marshall gained the national spotlight in the fourth game of the 1985 season with its 13-7 victory at Eastern Kentucky. The win snapped the Colonels' 36-game winning streak at Hangar Field, ranked first in most NCAA Division I-AA pre-season polls. Defense, like the blitzing pass rush of linebacker Jerome Hazard on quarterback Mike Whitaker, was the key for the Herd. Marshall limited the Colonels to 318 yards, more than a fourth of which came on a drive in the final minutes that ended in a meaningless touchdown on the game's final play. The win earned Marshall a No. 3 ranking in the first I-AA poll of the regular season, the school's highest ranking in any sport at the time. (Photo by Lee Bernard)

Fodor misfired on three straight passes before sophomore Keith Baxter made a leaping grab between a pair of Western defenders down the middle for a 37-yard gain. After three more Fodor misses, the Herd again was forced to convert on fourth down. This time Fodor found Bob Ulliman alone across the front side of the Cats' zone for a first down at the

Versatility was the trademark of running back Randy Clarkson. As a junior in 1984, Clarkson led Marshall in rushing with 467 yards. Used more as a receiver out of the backfield in 1985, the Columbus, Ohio, player led the Herd in pass receptions with 49 and touchdowns with seven. (Photo by Tim Grobe)

Western 6-yard line with just 16 seconds remaining. On first down, Fodor rifled a pass to a sliding Abercrombie across the middle of the end zone for the touchdown. Abercrombie had told Fodor in the huddle he did not want to be thrown the ball, but after the team reached the line of scrimmage, both Fodor and Abercrombie saw an opening in the Western coverage that led to the pass.

"I was scared, I didn't want him to throw me that ball," Abercrombie recalled. "I didn't want to be the one to mess it up. But when I got to the line, I saw the way they had set the coverage and I looked in at Carl. He looked at me and kind of nodded and I knew he was going to throw it to me."

Now, the decision – take the tie or go for the win? Without hesitation, Parrish sent on Mitchell, who added the tying point.

"There wasn't a decision," Parrish said. "I'm tickled to death with a tie."

He was, however, mildly criticized by media and some fans. "If we'd already lost in the conference, then I'd have gone for two points," Parrish added later in defense of his strategy. "But (a tie) was a circumstance that's a win for us in every way but the record. We're undefeated in the conference and the rankings and still have a chance at the conference championship."

Those hopes were lost, though, as No. 9 Furman drubbed the No. 7 Herd, 34-3 the next week in Greenville, South Carolina. Displaying nearly flawless defensive and offensive execution, the Paladins dominated the Herd from the outset. And to add insult to the defeat, the Herd's dressing room was broken into during the contest. Many players and coaches lost money and other valuables. With the chance for the league title gone and hopes for a playoff berth slim at best, a winning season was all the Herd had to cling to as it entered the season's final four games.

It clinched the winner in a 21-16 decision against VMI during Homecoming. The victory, however, wasn't assured until the Keydets were stopped by the clock at the Herd's 7-yard line when quarterback Al Comer, not knowing his team was out of timeouts, was tackled on a desperation scramble from the pocket. After a week off, the Herd saw its hopes for the playoffs end in a 38-7 drubbing at Tennessee-Chattanooga. The swarming Mocs defense held the Herd to just 125 total yards. It was so bad that Marshall had to resort to trickery to get on the board – a play that saw Fodor hand off to Clarkson on a sweep left with the running back stopping before he reached the line, wheeling and throwing a pass across the field to Fodor in the back of the end zone.

Back home, Marshall drubbed East Tennessee 34-21 in what proved to be Fodor's finest day of the season. By completing 23 of 47 passes for 330 yards and three touchdowns, Fodor moved to the top of the SC's career passing yardage list and Marshall exceeded its victory total of the season before. Parrish, still insisting his team had a shot at the playoffs, warned he would not be satisfied with just bettering 1984 and predicted a top effort in the season finale at Appalachian State, also a playoff contender.

"We've got one left to play and I think you'll see these kids play their hearts out in Boone," Parrish said hoping to publicly pump up his team. He would later admit, though, he sensed his team would prefer to pack it in and not go to Boone.

His fears were confirmed as the fired-up Mountaineers routed the uninspired Herd, 40-0, holding it to a Parrish-era low 74 yards of total offense.

"It was over for them after beating East Tennessee," Parrish said. "They'd won the seventh game to beat last year, didn't lose at home and Carl got the big record. In their minds, it should've ended right there."

No sooner had the season ended than Parrish was again in the line for another coaching job. This time it was Kansas State that came calling. In fact, Parrish was in Kansas two days after the defeat at Appalachian, canceling a scheduled question-and-answer session with The Herald-Dispatch on November 18, to talk with Wildcats' officials. The coach later revealed that K-State had contacted him more than a month before the Herd season had ended, but he put them off until after the final game.

In K-State, Parrish found much the same situation he had at Marshall only at the I-A level. Undeterred by the fact that only five winning seasons had been produced by coaches at the Manhattan, Kansas, school in more than half a century, Parrish accepted the challenge with the same vigor he displayed in taking the Marshall post two years before.

Although extremely proud of his stay at Marshall ("You can't put a price on the accomplishments," he said.), Parrish was quick to spread the credit around.

"I was the right guy at the right time," he said reflecting on his tenure. "The players were here, they just needed a little different direction to bring the talent together. That's what I gave them. It's like building a house. Sonny laid the foundation and I came in to put up the walls and the roof."

Parrish never found the same success with the Wildcats as he did with the Herd. He went 2-30-1 in three seasons in "The Little Apple." He currently is an assistant coach at Ball State following stops at Rutgers, Michigan and with the Tampa Bay Buccaneers.

Chapter seven

The tactician takes over

Here comes this guy, he's down to earth – a working stiff. He's an honest guy, he's a family guy with no pretense about him. A little chubby guy and he turns out to be a hard-nosed son of a gun and everybody loves him. I've never seen anything like it. The chemistry seemed to be perfect for this guy. I think George Chaump brought a new dimension to coaching here that I have never seen before. It almost becomes an image of that school. It's like a perfect marriage. As a writer for 57 years, I've never seen Huntington turned on to the football team the way it was during the last four weeks of the 1987 season. The only thing that came close was the 1947-48 basketball team when it won the NAIB title. I've seen other manifestations of it – the NIT bid in 1967, the NCAA basketball team of 1971-72. But for football, this was a first. I just don't remember it. The wave and all that nonsense, people going crazy – it was incredible. The stuff George Chaump did, I didn't believe could ever happen at Marshall. I'm still not sure how he did it.

– Ernie Salvatore

It was mid-December 1985 and for the seventh time in 18 years Marshall University again found itself in need of a football coach. This time, however, the

---

George Chaump brought an impressive coaching resume to Marshall when he was hired shortly before Christmas in 1985 from NCAA Division II Indiana (Pa.) University. The native of Harrisburg, Pa., had been Woody Hayes' chief offensive assistant at Ohio State for a number of years, and then moved to the NFL where he served in a similar capacity for John McKay with the Tampa Bay Buccaneers. While with the Bucs, Chaump coached quarterback Doug Williams, who got the long-suffering club to within a victory of a Super Bowl berth in the mid-1980s. Asked later to describe Chaump, Williams said: "Talk to me about George Chaump as a coach and I put him in a category with only two other people I've played for — Eddie Robinson and Joe Gibbs." Williams was an all-American for Robinson at Grambling, and won a Super Bowl with the Washington Redskins under Gibbs. (Photo by Michael Malone)

departing coach was not a victim of a firing or resignation. Rather, he was hired away for his success. Miracle worker Stan Parrish had completed two amazing years – 6-5 and 7-3-1 for the university's first consecutive winning seasons in 21 years – and moved on to an even greater challenge at Kansas State, a member of the high-profile Big 12 Conference.

Marshall Athletic Director Dave Braine, who had taken over after Lynn Snyder moved to Oregon State just a few months earlier, conducted a wide-ranging search for Parrish's replacement. One name bandied about prominently was Bill Kelly of West Texas State, who happened to be Braine's good friend. Another to pop up was Gerry Faust, who had resigned at Notre Dame after five trying seasons. The belief around Marshall was that Faust's name – regardless of his rocky tenure with the Irish – would give the Thundering Herd instant notoriety. Faust visited Huntington and was a guest at the home of Marshall President Dale F. Nitzschke, who paraded an array of Huntington area business and community leaders in and out of the posh Ritter Park president's residence for audiences with the former Irish coach. Faust turned down the job and accepted the head coaching position at Akron the next week.

Waiting quietly and unassumingly in the background was a head coach at a NCAA Division II school in Pennsylvania. His name was George Chaump. Few people in Huntington knew much about him. He had spent 11 successful years at Ohio State as an offensive assistant to the legendary Woody Hayes, and three more as backfield coach for John McKay with the National Football League's Tampa Bay Buccaneers. And in four seasons at tiny Indiana University, Chaump turned the Big Indians from doormat to powerhouse in the Pennsylvania State Athletic Conference. His overall record was 24-16-1, including an 8-2-1 mark and Western Conference championship in 1985. Chaump's credentials obviously were enough to impress Marshall officials and the 51-year-old came on board as head coach on December 20, 1985.

"It didn't bother me people were saying 'George who?' " Chaump said. "I've never lost confidence in my ability as a coach. I won't take a back seat to anyone. I credit the administration for its foresight. The AD was under a lot of pressure, but he did what he thought was right. That's what leadership is all about."

Braine's observation: "George Chaump has been a winner at every level of football. I know that he'll continue Marshall's football progress."

Chaump understood this stop would be like all the rest. He would have to prove himself to the Thundering Herd fans.

"Football – George Chaump-style – is exciting football," Braine said in introducing the coach. "Under his direction, I can see a Southern Conference championship and a berth in the NCAA Division I-AA playoffs in the future for Marshall University."

Chaump made Braine a prophet in just one season. But not without being smiled upon by the football gods — the first time on a rainy evening on October 10, 1987, in Louisville, Kentucky, during a game against Division I member University of Louisville.

If the football hits the ground, Marshall's record dips to 2-4. Winning season? Doubtful. The I-AA playoffs? Forget it. National recognition? No way. Just another in the long line of shattered dream years to which Marshall had become accustomed instead of the one that would unfold after fate intervened.

That's when the football didn't hit the ground.

The Hail Mary pass thrown by quarterback Tony Petersen landed in the hands of the Thundering Herd's Keith Baxter in the end zone as time expired at Louisville's Cardinal Stadium, and gave Marshall a shocking 34-31 victory. The Herd's dream season likely never would have materialized had Petersen and Baxter not teamed for their fantastic finish in Louisville. After all, a 2-4 record with five games to play is nothing to get excited about. But Marshall now was 3-3 and very excited.

"This could be the turning point," Petersen said of that victory. But while the strong-armed quarterback's statement was accurate, it may have been a bit tardy. For when Marshall's historic success of 1987 is recounted, the pivotal point of the campaign actually may have occurred the season before – on September 20, 1986. It was on that evening, in a game against Eastern Kentucky at Fairfield Stadium, that Petersen assumed the duties as Marshall's starting quarterback. His rise to the position turned a promising, but struggling, team into one that in the span

George Chaump left Marshall after four seasons to become head coach at the Naval Academy. He was hired to coach the Midshipmen by former Marshall coach Jack Lengyel, who was the athletic director in Annapolis, Md.

of 15 months would reach heights never before dreamed by even the staunchest of school supporters.

The Thundering Herd still was trying to establish an identity under Chaump as it prepared for its biggest test to date on that warm fall evening. Chaump made an impressive debut three weeks earlier, leading Marshall to a 42-0 whipping of overmatched West Virginia Tech. The next week, however, the Herd was upset 19-10 by Morehead State. Marshall bounced back for a 21-7 victory against I-A rival Ohio University, but despite the 2-1 mark, Chaump was anything but satisfied with his club. Granted, there had been solid play both offensively and defensively. John Gregory, a sophomore quarterback who transferred from Southeast Louisiana when that school dropped football, had directed the offense capably, but the 23-year-old former professional baseball player still seemed uncomfortable with the system. The defense had a shutout, but it, too, had proved spotty in many situations.

It was consistency that Chaump was looking for against Eastern, again the favorite to win the Ohio Valley Conference. Consistency, however, was the farthest thing from Chaump's mind as Gregory was being carried off the field in the third quarter after injuring a knee. The coach was plotting a way to protect a 13-3 lead with an untested quarterback he had recruited from San Joaquin Delta Junior College in Stockton, California, through only telephone calls. Had it not been for Dale Dawson's 52-yard field goal late in the fourth quarter, Marshall would have escaped with better than the 13-13 tie with which it was saddled that night.

Petersen threw only two passes after taking over for Gregory, who'd beaten out his Lodi, California, counterpart in the spring. One of his passes was complete – to a Colonels' defender. Once it was discovered that Gregory would be sidelined for at least two weeks, the Marshall fans hoped Petersen's short, ineffective relief stint was the result of nothing more than previous inactivity and the pressure of the situation. Chaump, in a manner that would quickly become a trademark, showed no signs of panic. If there was one thing Chaump had come to know in his two decades of coaching, it was talent in a quarterback. He saw it in the films he had watched of Petersen's games at San Joaquin and in the statistics the player compiled – 283 completions in 541 attempts for 3,516 yards and 20 touchdowns in 20 games. Firm in his belief that Petersen would be able to run his team, Chaump never wavered in his confidence.

"Tony Petersen will be a fine quarterback for us," the coach said. "He's proven he has the ability to lead a team and I have every confidence that he'll do the job for us."

Even Chaump, as astute as any in judging quarterbacks, could not have predicted the success Petersen would have in the next 22 games in which he started for the Herd.

Not unlike other athletic feats that advance to legendary proportions before they are finished, Petersen's got off to a rocky beginning. On a rainy right against perennial Southern Conference power Furman, the 6-foot-1, 200-pound quarterback completed 12 of 26 passes for only 112 yards with two interceptions. The Paladins departed with a 38-10 victory leaving Marshall at a break-even point after five games.

Although unspectacular, it was apparent that Petersen did, in fact, have the tools. Work was all that was needed to fit them into Chaump's system. Petersen followed up the defeat in his starting debut by guiding the Herd to four straight victories in impressive fashion. Marshall dispatched VMI 16-9 as Petersen completed 14 of 27 passes for 210 yards. A 21-for-39 effort for 394 yards and two scores followed in a 34-19 win at East Tennessee State. He was 12-for-19 for 123 yards and a TD while splitting time with a now-healed Gregory as Marshall pounded outmanned Davidson, 63-14, a week later.

Although Gregory had fully recovered, Chaump had no designs on breaking up a winning combination. Petersen proved the move a sound one the next week against Tennessee-Chattanooga. Facing a team that had never known defeat against Marshall, largely because its defense was so dominating, Petersen ended the Herd's frustration by passing for 339 yards and three touchdowns in a 41-20 victory. The win assured Marshall of its third straight winning season, a first for the school since the 1941 team finished off a string of six straight winners.

It was, however, Marshall's final success of the year. A steady rain and a strong defense slowed Petersen and the Herd the next week as Appalachian State escaped with a 27-17 victory to end the Herd's hopes of a first-ever SC championship. Marshall closed the season at Western Carolina and, displaying little motivation, fell 33-20.

Although not elated with the results of the year, Chaump believed his first season was a good foundation on which to build. Especially since he had the majority of his starters returning, including Petersen, who was named second-team all-Southern Conference after completing 100 of 209 passes for 1,599 yards and eight touchdowns in his seven games. Those statistics, while respectable, wouldn't come close to the numbers Petersen would register upon his return.

Free safety Mark Snyder, here forcing a fumble by East Tennessee State running back George Searcy, was an example of George Chaump's coaching genius. Snyder came to Marshall from junior college as a quarterback, but shortly found himself the odd man out at the position with fellow transfers Tony Petersen and John Gregory. Chaump, though, knew Snyder needed to be on the field somewhere because of his overall athletic ability and figured the secondary was the place. Snyder had played defensive back as an All-Ohio player at Ironton High School and Chaump thought the player's knowledge of offenses from years at quarterback would be an asset on the other side of the ball. It often seemed Snyder knew exactly what the offense was going to do as he intercepted 10 passes in 1987 to set a single-season record. Snyder became Marshall's head coach in 2005. (Photo by Mindy Schauer)

With nine starters back on both offense and defense, Marshall entered practice in the fall of 1987 with very few question marks. Its 6-4-1 record in 1986 had earned it a measure of respect from its conference brethren. The Herd was picked to finish in the middle of the pack in the league, which, by most standards, would be satisfactory in view of Marshall's past poll placements. Chaump, though, was upset. He felt his club had proven it could play with the best in the league. Publicly, the coach tempered his view on the ranking. Privately, however, there was no mistaking his anger. Proving the pollsters wrong became a prime motivating factor.

The Herd's first chance came at home against Morehead State. The game, played in the rain at Fairfield Stadium, was scoreless in the first quarter, but Marshall managed to take a 10-0 lead at the half. Petersen was intercepted four times in all, with three of the turnovers in the first quarter.

The game still was in doubt until late in the third quarter when Petersen hit speedy split end Mike Barber for an 80-yard touchdown to give Marshall a 16-0 lead. Barber beat his one-on-one coverage and Petersen – as would become his trademark in 1987 – put the ball right on target. It capped the first of three 80-yard scoring drives in the second half. Marshall scored twice more in the fourth quarter and its defense stuffed the Eagles the rest of the way. The Herd finished with 519 yards while Morehead had only 255.

"I hope we got all the mistakes (six turnovers) out of our system for the year," Chaump said. "We wasted a lot of opportunities to score in the first half. It was uncharacteristic of us, I hope."

The next Saturday proved, however, to be the most uncharacteristic of the season for Marshall. It was a bad day, maybe the worst of the year, on a soggy afternoon in Athens, Ohio, where rival Ohio University would pin a 23-15 loss on the sloppy Herd. It was the Bobcats' lone victory of the year. Marshall's defense was at the center of the defeat, time and again, letting runners off the hook after making initial hits.

"We tackled poorly," Chaump said simply.

OU rushed for 292 yards, including 137 by tailback John Caldwell and 75 by freshman quarterback Anthony Thornton.

The next week against Eastern Kentucky, Marshall received a dose of heartbreak on top of the humility it had swallowed against Ohio. Rarely, if ever, in MU football history has a Thundering Herd team gone on the road and moved the ball as well as this one did against the Colonels, particularly in the first half. Incredibly, Marshall rolled up 417 total yards in the first two quarters, taking a 28-7 lead in the process.

But in the second half, with most of the record home-opening crowd of 22,400 at Hangar Field chanting "EKU," Marshall's lead slipped away. The cushion stood at a seemingly safe 34-17 on the first play of the fourth quarter when Petersen threw a yard to big, strong junior tight end Sean Doctor for a score. But the momentum shifted to EKU only seconds later when the Colonels' Danny Copeland returned the ensuing kickoff 83 yards to the Herd 6-yard line. Two plays later, EKU scored to make it 34-24.

After a Petersen interception, the Colonels drove 35 yards to score, cutting the deficit to 34-31. And, finally, EKU tied the score at 34-34 with 6:23 left on James Campbell's 30-yard field goal. Another interception of a Petersen pass set up Campbell's game-winning, 20-yard field goal with 1:04 to play.

"I don't feel quite right. Our kids were set to play a great game because we knew we would have to," Chaump said. "We gave the game to them with all the turnovers. It just seems we're fighting against all the odds. I would go to war with this team."

As it turned out, the Herd played one great half and one poor half. The result was a demoralizing defeat that dropped its record to 1-2, despite 397 yards passing by Petersen, 180 yards in receptions by Barber and 138 yards rushing by tailback Ron Darby.

Chaump knew his team should be 3-0 rather than 1-2. The talent was there, but where were the wins?

The momentum began to swing Marshall's way in a 38-13 win over Youngstown State. Returning home to Fairfield was just what the Herd needed. It was an easy win, really, even though MU's quick-strike offense was taken away by design. "They did exactly what we thought so we changed our plan and went for the more sustained drive," Chaump said. "They were determined to do one thing – take away the home run. It cut down on our stats passing-wise, but the important stat is the final score."

Despite the bitter defeat a week earlier at Eastern Kentucky, Marshall still remembered its offensive success against the Colonels. And Youngstown paid for the Herd's well-learned lesson. Petersen passed for 203 yards and one touchdown and Darby rushed for 63 yards and a pair of touchdowns. "The idea was ball control," Darby said.

Defensively, Marshall improved, holding the Penguins and star quarterback Trenton Lykes to 206 total yards. They had just 12 first downs and were forced to punt seven times. Youngstown coach Jim Tressel was impressed. "Marshall played harder than we did today," said Tressel, the current head coach at Ohio State University. "They played like a team that was unhappy and had something to prove."

It was time now to prove to the Southern Conference that the Herd had arrived. In 10

Nick McKnight was a key figure in a Marshall defense that stuffed Appalachian State in the 1987 I-AA semifinals in Boone, N.C. The Herd limited the Mountaineers to just 30 yards rushing on 29 attempts and intercepted three passes to key a 24-10 victory that avenged a 17-10 loss to ASU during the regular season in Boone. Appalachian carried an 18-game winning streak at home into the contest. (Photo by Lee Bernard)

previous seasons in the league, Marshall tried to show it could compete with the best in the SC. Now it wanted to prove it could beat the best. With a trip to Greenville, South Carolina, for a date with powerful Furman up next, the Herd wouldn't have to wait long to see where it stood.

The Paladins, who had never lost to Marshall in 10 league meetings and 11 in the all-time series, appeared more vulnerable this year than in the past. But as the conference had learned, Furman was never as weak on the field as it seemed on paper. Marshall received another painful reminder of that fact on a warm October afternoon in Paladin Stadium

Quarterback Tony Petersen (17) and tailback Ron Darby were just two of the handful of offensive weapons for the Herd in its memorable run to the 1987 NCAA Division I-AA championship game against Northeast Louisiana in Pocatello, Idaho. Petersen was a junior college transfer from California who passed for a title game-record 447 yards in Marshall's 43-42 loss to NLU. Petersen finished with 6,501 yards passing in just 22 games to fall 154 yards short of the school and Southern Conference marks of former Herd star Carl Fodor. Darby, who stood just 5-foot-7 and weighed only 170 pounds, became Marshall's first 1,000-yard rusher since Ron Lear in 1979 with his then school-record 1,506 yards on 313 attempts in 1987. (Photo by Lee Bernard)

when Furman rallied for two touchdowns in the final 6:45 to pull out a 42-36 victory over the shocked Herd, which could not help but see a repeat of the debacle at Eastern, but in more damaging proportions.

"What can I say?" a bewildered Chaump asked after the heartbreaking loss. "We were prepared. I felt confident we could beat them. I never thought we'd do so many bonehead things at crucial times. We lost our own ballgame. This was worse than EKU because it was Furman."

Marshall, now 2-3 overall and 0-1 in the league, rolled up 552 yards of offense, including 386 passing by Petersen, but Furman was close behind with 444 yards. Furman junior tailback John Bagwell rushed 27 times for 213 yards and four touchdowns, including the game-winner with 53 seconds left. For Marshall, Barber and Doctor displayed their one-two receiving punch with a combined 14 catches for 271 yards. But the big offensive show was not enough to enable MU to overcome its other mistakes.

"We did so many things wrong in the kicking game. You can't be erratic in the kicking game and win," Chaump said. "We gave up two touchdowns set up by kickoff return coverage breakdowns. We missed two field goals and an extra point. We fumbled a punt and we made a bad decision on a return out of the end zone."

And, yet, the Herd lost by just six points – on the road and to Furman of all teams. Things absolutely had to get better, Chaump thought.

But the veteran coach knew that games such as the one his team had just experienced could be particularly damaging. Enough so that it could carry on through the rest of the year. Marshall had to experience some success — in dramatic fashion if possible — to counteract the last-minute loss and leave a deep impression on its psyche. It had to come soon, in the next game at Louisville, if possible. The headline "A prayer answered" in The Herald-Dispatch on October 11, 1987, revealed that it did.

Marshall finally got its long-awaited break when Petersen connected with Baxter for a 31-yard touchdown pass with no time

Mike Barber caught nine passes for 195 yards in the 1987 championship game against Northeast Louisiana to cap a season that saw the junior receiver finish with 106 receptions for 1,757 yards and 11 touchdowns. The fleet, fearless receiver's reception and yardage totals led the nation in I-AA and were school and Southern Conference records. Barber was a consensus All-American and went on to a successful career in the NFL with the Cincinnati Bengals and is a member of the College Football Hall of Fame. (Photo by Michael Malone)

left to give the Herd the victory over the Cardinals. Somehow, MU seemed destined to lose this one just as it had lost to Eastern Kentucky and Furman. The pattern of blowing leads continued in the Bluegrass State as Louisville wiped out a 28-10 halftime deficit and was in perfect position to pull out the victory. But it was Marshall's night, one that would stamp its season as special.

"The free safety let me behind him," Baxter said of the touchdown, which came after the final horn. "He was off balance and I was set so that gave me the whole advantage. (The ball) was catchable the whole way."

Petersen took the final snap from center with only two seconds showing on the clock. He had been sacked on the previous play and the seconds continued to tick away as the Herd scrambled to the line. Petersen lofted a high pass toward the end zone, hoping to hit wide receiver Bruce Hammond. "I thought I'd overthrown him," Petersen said. "I was hoping maybe he could tip it up, then K.B. (Baxter) came into the picture."

The realization that Marshall had beaten the Cardinals touched off a wild celebration in the end zone while the stunned Cardinals just dropped to their knees, shocked by the turn of events. "It's not over 'til it's over," Chaump said. "Never say quit. I've had so many of them go the other way so many times and I guess it was our turn."

Convinced his team was of championship caliber, Chaump felt it was about time it started playing like it. Unfortunately for East Tennessee State, that time arrived as Marshall hung a 27-7 defeat on the Buccaneers to celebrate Homecoming.

"I've been around long enough to know what a lot of championship teams do," Chaump said after the win. "I saw many elements of a championship team out there. I haven't seen a championship team that doesn't have a good defense. Once we stopped messing around, we played good today. I haven't seen a championship team that hasn't been able to run the ball. We ran the ball when we had to. Although our passing stats may be a letdown to some people, our overall game was much better. At times, it didn't look pretty, but the rest of the time the game was beautiful."

Offensively, Petersen was 24 of 43 passing for 286 yards. Doctor had eight receptions and Barber six, and Darby rushed 20 times for 97 yards. On defense, linebacker Rondell Wannamaker intercepted two passes. With the victory, Marshall jumped over the .500 mark at 4-3. Chaump talked about the Herd being a championship-caliber team and suddenly interest in the Herd was on the rise.

Virginia Military, boasting the league's No. 1 defense, offered the next test. It was a test in name only as the Keydets' top-ranked defense looked defenseless in the face of Marshall's 42-7 victory. Petersen completed 9 of 10 passes for 147 yards and two touchdowns in the first quarter alone as the Thundering Herd stunned the Keydets in taking a 21-0 lead at Fairfield Stadium. By halftime it was 35-7, and Marshall's third straight win was secure.

"We took it as a challenge to do something no one else had done," Chaump said. "We have confidence we can throw. A challenge like that arouses the competitive spirit. They tried everything on us, but I haven't seen anything that could really shut us down this season."

Petersen completed 19 of 31 passes for 294 yards, pushing his season total to 2,496 yards with 16 touchdowns. It seemed certain that Petersen eventually would break Carl Fodor's single-season yardage record of 2,888, set in 1984. Marshall now was 5-3, but the schedule was not in its favor. Trips to always-tough Tennessee-Chattanooga and Appalachian State awaited the Herd and would play a major factor in MU's quest for another winning season.

Marshall and Chattanooga took the field on Halloween night, and when it was over, the Herd had escaped with a 28-26 victory. Petersen had another big night with 294 yards passing, but uncharacteristically threw five interceptions. The Herd, displaying its fast-start ability again, jumped to a 21-0 lead in the first quarter then held on to improve its record to 6-3. It was MU's fourth straight win and its first ever at UTC's ancient Chamberlain Field.

"After the first quarter it was Halloween night, trick or treat," Chaump said. "We gave away the treats."

In all, Marshall committed a season-high eight turnovers. Or, as Chaump said, "enough mistakes to last for a year." But the Herd still won, thanks to a late defensive stand. Marshall's defenders held UTC on downs after it had recovered an onside kick at the Herd 49 with 1:49 left in the game and the Mocs trailing. Actually, UTC had a chance to tie the game with 1:49 left in the fourth quarter after Steve Colwell's 7-yard touchdown run, but Marshall's Reggie Giles batted down the two-point conversion pass.

The Herd was rewarded by being ranked No. 18 in the weekly NCAA Division I-AA poll. The ranking by a panel of four athletic directors carried with it playoff implications since playoff participants are determined in part by their rankings. Not only would the

Southern Conference lead be on the line in the next game, but so would two rankings. Appalachian, as it had been for much of the year, entered the game ranked second.

Appalachian billed games in Boone, North Carolina, "Black Saturday" and the Mountaineers made the label ring darkly true for the Herd by ending Marshall's four-game winning streak with a 17-10 decision. Not only was the streak over, but so was MU's chance of winning the conference championship. Appalachian, in fact, wrapped up the title with the win and improved its league record to 5-0. Marshall, now 6-4 overall, dropped to 3-2 in the league.

"I guess you could give Appy State some credit for playing well in a game that meant the championship," Chaump said.

Defensively, Marshall held Appalachian in check. The difference was two Mountaineers' pass completions that resulted in a touchdown and set up a field goal.

"I thought we defended Appalachian pretty well," Chaump said.

After all, the hosts managed just 222 total yards before 14,306 fans on the sunny afternoon. Marshall dominated the statistics, gaining 332 yards and compiling 18 first downs to ASU's 13. Petersen, his powerful right arm busy as usual, completed 22 of 48 passes for 258 yards and a touchdown. The Mountaineers, though, pressured Petersen all day, recording seven sacks and intercepting three passes.

Again, however, the Herd earned respect from a strong opponent.

"Marshall's a great team. If you relax on one play they can hurt you. They have the potential to score from anywhere on the field," said Appalachian's All-SC defensive end Anthony Downs.

Just how great the Herd was had really not yet been seen. Though only one regular-season game remained, the best was yet to come. The Herd, which dropped to 20th in the ratings after the loss, went into its season-finale against Western Carolina hoping this game wouldn't be the last. A victory, Marshall figured, should earn it an at-large berth in the I-AA playoffs. A record-smashing, dominating, crushing win, it gathered, would further enhance its chances. And that's just what the 14,423 fans at Fairfield Stadium saw – a thrashing. Marshall whipped the Catamounts, 47-16, locking up second place in the SC with a 4-2 record.

"In my heart, I think we merit it," Chaump said of a playoff berth.

The Herd shredded Western's defense for a then school record 642 yards, one of an

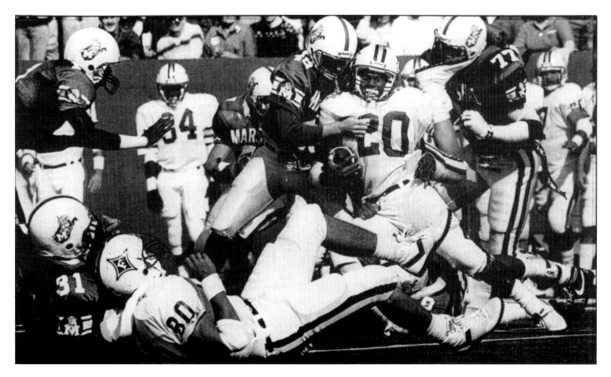

Marshall made its first victory against perennial Southern Conference kingpin Furman a memorable one, stuffing all-conference running back Bobby Daugherty and the Paladins 24-10 on October 8, 1988, before a Fairfield Stadium record crowd of 19,371. Unfortunately for the Herd, Furman avenged the loss a little more than two months later by eliminating the Herd from the NCAA Division I-AA playoffs with a 13-9 win in the semifinals. The win spurred the Paladins to a 17-12 victory against Georgia Southern for the national championship. (Photo by Tony Jones)

---

incredible 41 marks that were either equaled or broken as the Herd completed a 7-4 season. For example:

- Petersen completed 34 of 68 passes for 481 yards and three touchdowns.
- Barber, a junior, caught 14 passes for 180 yards, giving him a then SC record 1,237 yards for the season.
- Barber and Doctor bettered Barber's single-season reception record of 64, set in 1986. By game's end, Barber had 78 catches, Doctor 70.

  Now, the season was over. Or was it? The victory pushed Marshall back to No. 18 in the poll. With many teams ranked ahead of Marshall still with a game to play, all the Herd could do was wait a week and see if the selection committee was convinced the team belonged in the playoffs. It was, as it turned out, well worth the wait.

  All Marshall wanted was a chance. And it got it, at home no less. The Thundering

Herd and its high-powered offense were granted their wish when the I-AA selection committee included MU in the playoffs. The Herd, which moved to 14th in the final poll, would play No. 8 James Madison and the result was an overwhelming win for Marshall. The Thundering Herd rolled up 499 yards total offense against the No. 17 defense in I-AA while its defense limited the ground-oriented Dukes to just 281 yards on a beautiful fall afternoon at Fairfield Stadium. The 41-17 result was very much indicative of the difference between the two teams.

"I think we put up," Chaump said. "I was afraid we'd be overlooked, but I just knew we were better than some of those teams if we were given the chance to prove ourselves. We did."

The Herd, 8-4 and seeded 11th in the 16-team field, had blitzed James Madison with an attack that resulted in the most points and yardage against the Dukes all year. Petersen riddled their secondary for 387 yards and four touchdowns while JMU's potent Wing-T offense managed just 115 yards rushing. Marshall led 10-0 after one quarter, 24-0 at halftime and 27-0 after three quarters. Free safety Mark Snyder, who would later figure prominently in Marshall football, established a school record with his ninth interception of the year.

The game was never in doubt. And neither, now, was the Herd's ability, as the near-perfect performance against James Madison proved.

"If we played our game with no turnovers and no mistakes, I thought we'd be all right," Chaump said. "We really scrutinized their games. I felt it would be tough to move on our scheme. We held them in check."

One down and three to go. But as easy as the first game seemed, it could not match the second against the Big Sky Conference's Weber State. The Wildcats of Ogden, Utah, were a direct opposite of James Madison, relying on a controlled passing attack and a series of draws and delays for a running game. Although noted for a big offense, Weber was no match for Marshall in the quarterfinals on the brisk early December afternoon at Fairfield. Even though the Herd scored 51 points against the Wildcats, it was the defense that shone the brightest in the 51-23 romp. Weber had an offensive reputation when it came to Huntington, but left town wondering what happened.

"We were in control in all phases of the game," Chaump said. "You never predict what you can do to somebody, but we felt our defensive game plan would be great, or they'd pick it up and burn us."

The Herd defense finished with a school record seven interceptions and sacked Weber quarterback Jeff Carlson six times.

"That was a pretty good whipping," said then-Wildcats coach Mike Price, the current head coach at the University of Texas-El Paso. "They outplayed us in most every department."

Petersen threw four touchdown passes and even Barber threw a pair from his split end position. The Herd also managed to block a couple of punts.

Again, the Herd was not challenged. It was becoming more and more clear that this Marshall team was indeed special. It was on a mission. And it wouldn't stop until that mission — which two months earlier seemed an impossibility — was accomplished. But first, a rematch with Appalachian in Boone, was in order.

In a year of abundant offense, it was the Thundering Herd's defense that excelled when it visited the Mountaineers for the second time in five weeks. Appalachian, seeded No. 1 in the field, managed just 149 total yards and only nine first downs as Marshall won 24-10 to advance to the I-AA championship game in Pocatello, Idaho, six days before Christmas. The victory was especially satisfying for the Herd's 3,500 green-clad fans who had followed their team to the game.

"Congratulations to Marshall," said Appalachian coach Sparky Woods. "Coach Chaump had a good game plan. They came after us early and stayed after us all afternoon."

Marshall used an adjusted defensive set that stymied the Mountaineers to the tune of 30 net yards rushing on 29 attempts. The Herd also intercepted three passes. MU showed Appalachian an eight-man front as usual, but in a different set. Instead of an extra lineman, linebacker John Spellacy filled the role on the line while free safety Ken Green moved closer to the line.

"Our defense deserves a lot of credit," Chaump said. "They really didn't score on our defense. We kept them off balance. The coaches got the players to execute."

And Marshall handled Appalachian State's pass rush well, allowing just one sack compared to seven the first time the two met.

"We changed our blocking scheme," the coach said.

Technicalities aside, Marshall simply whipped the Mountaineers to cap a brilliant three-week span of post-season play.

"There's no greater thing that went on in America today than this game," Chaump said. "It's very satisfying and it manifests everything we do."

Petersen passed for 261 yards, surpassing 200 yards for the 14th straight week, at the time, a NCAA record in all divisions.

The loss ended Appalachian's 18-game unbeaten streak against conference opponents and ended its season with an 11-3 record. For Marshall, now 10-4, there was still one more week to go. The Herd was Pocatello-bound to meet No. 3 Northeast Louisiana at Idaho State University's 12,000-seat Holt Arena. For years, Marshall had struggled to gain respectability, to even be considered on the same level as its conference mates. Now, in an incredible surge upward, the Thundering Herd would be playing for a national championship.

It wasn't too many years ago that 10-game seasons were the rule in college football. And 10 games were more than enough in Huntington, where Marshall failed from 1965 through 1983 to win more than it lost. But this was 1987. And here was Marshall University, a perennial loser until 1984, playing Game No. 15. And here was Marshall University, still without a Southern Conference title, playing for a national championship. It boggled the minds of even the most ardent Herd fans.

Although it was December 19, the weather for the title game was not a factor. Marshall and Northeast traveled into the Rocky Mountains to meet in a facility commonly known as the Minidome. Amazingly, 1,000 or so Thundering Herd fans also made the trip. Even Young Thundering Herd Coach Jack Lengyel was among them. He talked with the players before the game and declared, "Marshall deserves a winner." Those who couldn't go to Pocatello gathered around their televisions for a late-night extravaganza on ESPN, fully expecting Marshall to pull off one more miracle. But it did not happen. The teams combined for 1,146 total yards, 56 first downs and 85 points. Marshall, however, only had 42 points of the total.

Northeast entered the game with a 12-2 record, having beaten North Texas State, 30-9, Eastern Kentucky, 33-32 and Northern Iowa, 44-41 in overtime, in its three playoff games. Obviously, the Indians' defense was anything but invincible. But, just as obvious, the offense was powerful. Quarterback Stan Humphries, who would go on to lead the San Diego Chargers to Super Bowl XXIX in 1994, ranked fourth in the nation with 276.8 yards a game. He had completed 244 of 455 passes for 3,583 yards and 26 touchdowns before the title game. So, it was fairly evident that a Petersen vs. Humphries showdown would decide the outcome. And it came off. In Pocatello, Humphries was 26-of-43 for 436 yards and three touchdowns with no interceptions. Petersen went 28-for-54 for 474 yards and four touchdowns with three interceptions. It was quite a show. But it did not last long enough for Marshall.

NLU started the scoring on its first possession, driving 63 yards in seven plays. Tailback Cisco Richard went 15 yards on a draw play with 11:24 left in the opening quarter, and Teddy Garcia kicked the extra point for a 7-0 lead. Marshall, though, wasn't fazed. In just 3:05, the Thundering Herd drove 64 yards in nine plays to score on Brian Mitchell's 33-yard field goal to make it 7-3. NLU, almost routinely, came back with a big drive, moving from its 30 to Marshall's 15 in only three plays. But after an incomplete pass, Humphries was sacked by the Herd's Shawn Finnan, fumbled and Cecil Fletcher recovered for Marshall at the 26, ending the threat. The quarter ended with Northeast on top but the lead was to be short lived. Late in the first quarter, Wannamaker pounced on a fumble by Tommy Minvielle at the NLU 25 and six plays later Petersen passed 9 yards to Baxter for the go-ahead score. Mitchell's kick gave Marshall a 10-7 lead with 14:23 to play in the first half. And so it went … offense and lots of it.

Northeast regained the lead at 14-10 on Richard's 7-yard run with 9:25 left in the half, but Marshall pulled within one on Mitchell's 31-yard field goal at 1:17 of the quarter. Then came what Chaump considered the most demoralizing score of the night. After a roughing-the-kicker penalty on Marshall, the Indians retained possession at their own 43. On second-and-10, Humphries hit Kenneth Burton for a 52-yard gain to the Herd's 5. On the next play – and with only 15 seconds to go in the half – Humphries passed to Mike Manzullo, giving Northeast a 21-13 halftime lead.

"We shouldn't have given them the score before the half," Chaump said. "There's no way they should've scored with such a little amount of time left."

Again, though, Marshall fought back. Petersen passed 9 yards to Barber for a touchdown with just 2:02 gone in the third quarter. A two-point conversion pass failed, but the Herd had regained the momentum. Just three minutes later, after a fumble recovery by Green, Marshall took the lead as Petersen hit Baxter with a 29-yard touchdown pass. Petersen then passed to Hammond for the two-point conversion, and Marshall led 27-21. And the incredible onslaught of offense continued.

On its next possession, Northeast used just 3:08 of the clock in driving 78 yards to score. Humphries connected with senior Chris Jones from 9 yards for the touchdown, and Garcia booted the extra point for a 28-27 NLU lead. And the third quarter was barely half

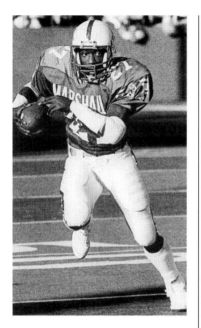

What Ron Darby lacked in size, he certainly made up in heart, becoming Marshall's career rushing leader in an offense that emphasized the pass by gaining 3,903 yards before he departed in 1989. (Photo by Tony Jones)

over. Marshall followed the kickoff with a blazing 80-yard, seven-play drive that took only 1:58. The key play was a 40-yard pass from Petersen to Baxter to the Indians' 17. The touchdown came on the next play – a pass to Hammond with still 4:49 to go in the third quarter. Petersen passed to Doctor for two points and a 35-28 lead.

Northeast was stopped on its next possession as Minvielle fumbled and Finnan recovered at midfield. Eight plays later, Darby went 8 yards around right end to score, giving MU a 41-28 lead. Mitchell added the extra point, and the Herd had a 42-28 lead with 36 seconds left in the third quarter. Chaump felt good, as did the Herd fans and players.

"I didn't expect them to score 43 points," the Marshall coach would say later. "I figured we'd score about 42 and hold them to 20."

But for one of the few times in the historic season, Chaump was wrong. By the time the fourth quarter was half over, Northeast had regained the lead at 43-42. Humphries passed 10 yards to Kenneth Johnson for a score with 13:34 to play, then NLU followed a Marshall punt with an impressive 80-yard, 11-play drive to take the lead. Humphries scored on a 3-yard keeper, and Garcia kicked the extra point for a 43-42 lead with 7:19 to go. There was still plenty of time for the Herd's quick-strike offense.

Marshall took the kickoff and drove steadily down field. When Darby broke loose for a 13-yard gain to the Indians' 22, the Herd had a first down with three-plus minutes remaining. A national championship was that near. The Herd already was in field goal range, so Chaump called for safe handoffs to Darby. The shifty 5-foot-7 sophomore gained a yard on a run to the right, then tried the middle on second down. There was plenty of room and Darby found it. He scooted for good yardage, but then he went down at the 17 and the ball came loose. Northeast's Richard

Green recovered the bounding ball at the 7 and elation turned to depression along the Herd sideline, which felt the fumble came as a result of contact with the ground.

"I thought my knees were down when I fumbled," Darby said later.

But Marshall was not conceding defeat. The Herd forced NLU to punt and regained the ball with 1:22 to play at the Indians' 39 thanks to a 14-yard return by Snyder. Hopes were revived. With Marshall's big-play offense, field goal range was just a couple of short Petersen completions away. But the Indians' defense, at the time when it counted most, held. On first down, Petersen's long pass was just inches out of the reach of a diving Hammond at the goal line. On second down, NLU tackle Rodney Young dropped Petersen for a 14-yard loss. The Herd called a timeout, then Petersen tried to pass again on third-and-24, but the Indians' Perry Harper intercepted at his own 40 and Marshall's hopes were shattered, two points shy of achieving its dream.

Dejected, Chaump and his team accepted the runner-up trophy. Marshall's effort, albeit in defeat, was appreciated by its fans. The team was greeted at Tri-State Airport upon its return from the game the next afternoon. Several thousand more fans waited in Henderson Center, Marshall's basketball arena, to voice their support in an appreciation rally.

"I dreamed, I hoped, but I never really realized anything like this," Chaump recalled of his expectations for the historic season. "I was just so grateful to have played a small part in the great success that did so much for the community. Our winning helped lift a spirit at Marshall and in Huntington that had been dormant for so many years. Marshall showed a spirit to the whole country that represents what being involved in athletics is all about. People interested in athletics now associate Marshall with more than just the team that lost everybody in the plane crash."

The Herd had fallen short of its championship goal, but that could not diminish the magnitude of a season that spanned far more than the schedule of games from September through December. The season had far exceeded the limits of the 1987 calendar.

It began with the ignominy of the recruiting scandal nearly two decades before, then moved to a rain-swept Wayne County hillside on November 14, 1970, when the plane crash temporarily robbed Marshall of a football program that was well on the way to recovering from the scandal's stigma. But the school fought back, fielding a team less than 10 months later. And, although that team had little more than heart, luck and support of a devastated community on its side, it somehow won two games to prove that even the worst of tragedies could not overcome the determination to keep Marshall football alive.

But the struggle did not end with that first crucial season of 1971. It continued through two more coaches and 13 more years before the program realized the success that seemed destined for the team that had perished. And the success endured. The first taste of victory in nearly two decades in 1984 only whetted the appetite for more. Victory followed again and again, to put the program on a plateau that previously had existed only in the imaginations of those closest to Marshall. Where once there was only hope of respectable performances and scant possibility of victory came now a thirst for championships. Marshall football truly had come full circle.

"George Chaump achieved the dream everybody before him was taking Marshall toward," said Lengyel, then the athletics director at the Naval Academy. "We began the journey back after the crash and I'm glad to be a part of the tapestry. When George took the Marshall job, I knew he'd take them a long way. The story of Marshall is what athletics is all about. No matter the circumstances, quality leadership, administration and students came together to achieve an impossible dream like a phoenix rising from the ashes."

Marshall was on the national stage for all the right reasons now, and Chaump was determined to keep it there. Many of the key components of the '87 team were returning for '88, and the coach pulled no punches when evaluating his squad. It was going to be a contender for the Southern Conference and I-AA championships from the first day of pre-season practice. Eight games into the season, the Herd was undefeated and ranked first in the nation. It stumbled in the ninth game, however, losing 20-3 at The Citadel. The loss, though, wasn't enough to cost Marshall at least a share of the conference championship. After two more wins, the Herd and Furman split the title and because Marshall had beaten the Paladins in the regular season, it earned the league's automatic bid to the playoffs.

Chaump, believing he had an even better team for the '88 playoffs than the one in '87, privately said his team was the one to beat in the 16-team field. The Herd opened with a 7-0 win against North Texas at home to earn a home date with Furman, which had lost 24-10 to the Herd in the regular season before, at the time, the largest crowd in Fairfield Stadium history. Helped by a desperation pass at the end of the first half that resulted in a touchdown and seven controversial calls by Southern Conference officials, Furman hung on for a 13-9 victory to end MU's title hopes and boost its own. Two weeks later, the Paladins defeated Georgia Southern 17-12 for the national championship.

With his success, Chaump became a target for coaching vacancies around the country. He interviewed for openings at Ohio State, Missouri and South Carolina., and although among the last couple of candidates for each, the jobs went to others. After a mediocre — by recent Marshall standards — 6-5 record in 1989, Chaump answered Lengyel's summons from the U.S. Naval Academy and took over the Midshipmens program.

So, a second straight Marshall coach had been hired away by a I-A school. Again, Herd fans wondered if the winning would continue.

Chapter eight

Won for all

Jim Donnan's strongest point was recruiting. He brought probably the best talent the school had seen to campus and knew what to do with it. Jim was successful here, but for some reason he didn't quite ignite the town like you'd have thought with his winning ballclubs and that national championship. He was an efficient and productive coach, but there's more to coaching than a winning team. You also have to connect to the community and for some reason he never did other than with a select few. Jim never really captured the imagination of the community, I think, because he was a difficult guy to get close to. Despite that, he had and still has a strong emotional tie to the community. He truly liked Marshall and didn't really want to leave, but he had to accept the offer to go (to Georgia) because it was just too good. When Donnan left, there was disappointment, but not the kind of reaction you'd think for a coach who'd accomplished what he did. That'll always be puzzling.

– Ernie Salvatore

Marshall's football program was at a crossroads and so was Jim Donnan's coaching career. That they combined for a journey that ended at a destination never before visited by any Thundering Herd team was far more than mere coincidence. It was Donnan's plan and also that of Lee Moon, the Marshall athletics director who hired him.

Marshall now was a household name in college football, but no longer for losing. It was among the elite programs in NCAA Division I-AA both on the field and

With the scoreboard telling the story, Marshall fans celebrated the victory against Youngstown State on December 19, 1992, by storming the field and bringing down the goalpost in the south end zone of Marshall Stadium. (Photo by Rick Haye)

Marshall kicker Dewey Klein (10) heads to the sidelines for congratulations along with holder Andy Bowen (35) and blocker Mark Mason after Klein's field goal defeated Western Carolina 27-24 in triple overtime in 1991. Klein finished his career that season as the career scoring leader in Marshall and Southern Conference history. (Photo by Mike Kennedy)

off. However, it was missing the crown jewel for every sports entity of consequence — a championship.

Donnan was in a similar situation. He had become a well-respected assistant coach following a stellar playing career as a quarterback at North Carolina State. He was among the brightest offensive minds in college football, most recently coordinating the high-powered Wishbone at Oklahoma. But he now was a year into working for Gary Gibbs, a former colleague.

Gibbs had been Donnan's defensive counterpart with the Sooners when Gibbs was named to replace Barry Switzer, the school's legendary head coach. Switzer had resigned at the end of the 1988 season and was the man who hired Donnan five years earlier. Donnan had no problem with Gibbs' elevation to the top job, especially given the fact Gibbs was an OU graduate.

"But at the same time, I didn't really think there was near the future for me at Oklahoma as there was when Switzer was there," Donnan recalled. Enter Moon, who had coached against Donnan before he entered athletic administration. "The reason I contacted him was I'd always been impressed with him as a coach," said Moon, now an assistant athletics director at UAB. "I didn't know him personally, but he coached on offense and I was always on defense. His offenses had always been successful and he'd been with successful programs."

Moon pitched the program to Donnan during a meeting in Dallas. Donnan, despite knowing very little about Marshall other than the plane crash of 1970, and even less about Huntington or West Virginia, liked what Moon said about the future of the program, with its solid fan base, state-of-the-art stadium under construction and its place in the Southern Conference and I-AA. He was in a pool of candidates that included Larry Blakeney, Rip Scherer and Bill Clay, each with a resume similar to Donnan's and each seeking a step up the coaching ladder to direct his own program.

Donnan, though, was the one who got the call from Marshall, being introduced at a January 19, 1990, press conference as the replacement for George Chaump. When word on Donnan's background with the Wishbone hit the media, visions of a return to run-favoring coaches like Frank Ellwood and Sonny Randle were prominent in the minds of the now pass-favoring Herd fans.

Donnan quickly perished those thoughts by saying the football would be in the air as much as, if not more often than, it had been under either Stan Parrish or Chaump. His promise looked like a curse when during the spring he found a team that lacked an experienced quarterback and overall team speed. However, through position changes and some confidence building, Donnan and his staff were able to reach their goal of putting the best 22 players on the field, and the result was a seventh-straight winning season for the Herd.

The 6-5 record could have been better with a break in two games in particular — a 17-14 loss to defending I-AA champion Georgia Southern and a 15-12 defeat to perennial I-AA power Eastern Kentucky. The Herd led both ranked teams — GSU was 20th and EKU

Michael Payton went from a raw uncertain quarterback as a sophomore in 1990 to earning the distinction as the best player in NCAA Division I-AA two seasons later as the Walter Payton award winner. The native of Harrisburg, Pa., left Marshall as the NCAA leader in single-season and career passing efficiency with a rating of 149.15 for regular-season games. He combined to run and pass for 82 touchdowns, school and Southern Conference records when he finished. (Photo by Charlotte Parsons)

Defenders chasing Troy Brown, as on this 71-yard punt return for a touchdown against Eastern Kentucky in the first round of the 1992 I-AA playoffs, were a familiar sight during the do-everything, junior college transfer's two seasons with the Thundering Herd. Brown not only was a threat receiving, running reverses and returning kicks, but he also played in the secondary. In addition to this scoring return against EKU, Brown caught 10 passes for 188 yards and two touchdowns in the Herd's 44-0 rout. (Photo by Brian Ferguson)

No. 1 — with fewer than seven minutes left in the game before falling at home. The loss to Eastern came in the final game at Fairfield Stadium and enabled the Colonels to stay undefeated on the season.

To the Herd's credit, it shook off the loss to Eastern and kept the school's record streak of winning seasons alive with a 42-14 romp at Western Carolina the next week. Donnan had laid the foundation of his program. Now, he knew it was time to begin building toward that championship. He and his staff didn't waste any time.

The Herd qualified for the I-AA playoffs with an 8-3 mark in 1991. The losses came

A Marshall record crowd of 33,116 packed new Marshall Stadium on September 7, 1991, for the Herd's inaugural game at its new facility. MU sent the crowd home happy by holding off New Hampshire 24-23.

in the opener at Appalachian State, which went on to win the Southern Conference title, at N.C. State when the Wolfpack scored two touchdowns in the final two minutes with the help of a pair of controversial calls and suspect time keeping, and against Tennessee-Chattanooga. The Herd played without starting quarterback Michael Payton, who was sidelined with a stomach ailment, when it faced UTC a week after the stinging defeat at N.C. State, which went on to play in the Peach Bowl.

The majority of the wins came in memorable fashion. The first came in a 24-23 decision against New Hampshire before a then-school record attendance of 33,116 at Marshall's new stadium, which debuted without a name. The Herd's offense was in high gear the next two weeks, blasting Morehead State 70-11 and Brown 46-0. Marshall then earned its first conference win of the season at Furman, dropping the Paladins 38-35 for the school's first win ever in the state of South Carolina.

After the back-to-back losses to N.C. State and UT-Chattanooga, Marshall outlasted Western Carolina at home 27-24 in three overtimes with the help of Donnan's son, Todd, a freshman who was filling in for the still-sidelined Payton. The younger Donnan threw a fourth-down touchdown pass to force the game's second overtime on the way to the win that kept the Herd's playoff hopes alive. MU rallied to defeat The Citadel 37-31 the

Tight end Mike Bartrum celebrates one of the nine touchdown passes he caught during the 1992 season with wide receiver Will Brown. Bartrum was named an All-American after catching 62 passes for 680 yards during the championship season. In addition to playing tight end, Bartrum also served as the Herd's center for punts, extra points and field goals. His ability as a long snapper led to an NFL career that is still alive in 2006 and included stops in Kansas City, Green Bay, New England and Philadelphia. (Photo courtesy of The Herald-Dispatch)

following week, before leaving no doubt about its playoff worth by closing the season with romps of 61-0 against Virginia Military and 63-9 against East Tennessee State.

Playing at home in the playoffs, the Herd disposed of the two representatives from the Gateway Conference and an old rival to earn a shot at the championship. Dewey Klein kicked a 28-yard field goal in overtime to push Marshall past Western Illinois 20-17 before the Herd romped Gateway champion Northern Iowa 41-13. That set up a semifinal date with annual title challenger Eastern Kentucky, which saw its season end at Marshall Stadium in a 14-7 loss.

So, for the second time in five seasons, Marshall was going to play for a national championship, and Herd fans were confident the outcome in this game against Youngstown State would be different than the one in 1987 against Northeast Louisiana. The Penguins were considered by many — including some Herd coaches — the weakest of the four playoff teams Marshall had to face. Youngstown State hadn't distinguished itself in the playoffs, needing a last-second field goal to beat Villanova 17-16 before upsetting top-ranked Nevada 30-28. The Penguins' 10-0 win against Samford in the semifinals did little to dispel

Orlando Hatchett and the other Thundering Herd running backs knew when they were behind guard Phil Ratliff they were well protected. Recruited as a defensive tackle, Ratliff was switched to offense early in his freshman season and finished as an All-American who became the first Marshall lineman to win the Jacobs Blocking Trophy as the best lineman in the Southern Conference. Ratliff is now an assistant coach at Marshall. Hatchett was the Herd's go-to back whether as a runner or receiver. He finished his career in 1992 with 2,143 yards rushing and 1,082 yards receiving. He also led the Herd with 12 touchdowns in its championship season. (Photo courtesy of The Herald-Dispatch)

thoughts that a Herd victory awaited the Saturday before Christmas at Georgia Southern's Paulson Stadium in Statesboro, Georgia.

Before a crowd of 12,667 fans, including nearly 10,000 green-clad Herd backers, Youngstown squeezed out a 3-0 halftime edge on a windy day that made kicking, punting and passing — Marshall's primary weapon — difficult. Klein uncharacteristically missed

Marshall's defense held Eastern Kentucky running back Markus Thomas, who would finish his career as the leading rusher in I-AA history, to a career-low minus-4 yards in a 44-0 romp in the first round of the 1992 playoffs. (Photo courtesy of The Herald-Dispatch)

field goals of 30 and 36 yards into the wind.

Marshall, however, had the wind at its back in the third quarter and put up 17 points while limiting the run-oriented Penguins to another field goal. Marshall was 15 minutes away from its first national title, but had to play defense into the wind.

It proved too tough a task as the Penguins deftly mixed play-action passes out of running formations to riddle the Herd defense. Four of Youngstown's completions in the quarter ranged from 26 to 55 yards with a 33-yarder going for a touchdown. Two of the others helped set up two short touchdown runs that handed the Penguins a 25-17 victory.

"When you're up 17-6 in the fourth quarter you expect to win," Donnan said. "This was a tough one (to lose)."

The coach vowed that if another chance came — and he expected it would come quickly — another loss wouldn't happen again. Donnan would wind up being right on both counts.

Marshall's goal of playing for the championship again received a boost on Feb. 10, 1992, when the NCAA announced that the Huntington Sports Committee had been chosen to host the 1992 and '93 I-AA championship games at Marshall Stadium with an option for '94. The HSC proposal had easily topped one offered by Statesboro/Savannah to return the game to Paulson Stadium.

"I'd been to four site proposal presentations, and without a doubt that was the best proposal I'd ever seen since I became part of the championships," Benny Hollis, athletics director at Northeast Louisiana and chairman of the I-AA championship committee, said in awarding the game to Huntington. "The planning was the major point in the proposal. The events, the timing, the sales, the promotion, it was all laid out for you. We'd never seen anything like that. Every angle of everything was covered."

The news elated those involved with the MU program, but it also put pressure on the Herd to reach the title game again to cover a financial guarantee well in excess of $200,000 the committee had offered the NCAA in its bid. If the pollsters were correct, the HSC had no worry. Marshall was ranked No. 1 in nearly every preseason poll, and no worse than the top three in the others. And the Herd didn't discount the faith of others. "There are a lot of expectations and it's time to put them to rest," senior defensive tackle Keenan Rhodes said. "It's time to get it on."

The Herd wasted no time in doing that, cruising to victories over Morehead State, Eastern Illinois and VMI in its first three games. That start coupled with Youngstown State's 52-49 loss to James Madison pushed Marshall into the No. 1 spot in the I-AA poll. The Herd celebrated the top ranking during an off week before visiting then Big 8 Conference member Missouri.

The Tigers and coach Bob Stull entered the game in need of a win after starting with losses to Illinois, Texas A&M and Indiana and facing their conference opener against Colorado five days after meeting Marshall. It was beat the Herd or likely start the season 0-5. Playing every bit like the desperate team it was, Missouri riddled Marshall's normally steady secondary for 387 passing yards while its defense limited Marshall to only 267 total yards for a 44-21 spanking. Donnan called Marshall's effort "the poorest performance by a college football team that I've ever been associated with."

The Herd quickly regrouped with impressive efforts the next two weeks against its

Byran Litton came to Marshall from Parkersburg (West Virginia) South High School as a 6-foot-4, 190-pound quarterback and departed as a 6-6, 256-pound All-Southern Conference defensive tackle who led the 1992 team in tackles for losses with 16 and quarterback sacks with 9 . (Photo by Brian Ferguson)

Southern Conference rivals from South Carolina. First, Marshall blistered long-time league measuring stick Furman 48-6 before cruising at The Citadel 34-13. MU backed those wins with a 52-23 romp at home against Tennessee-Chattanooga.

The Herd led 52-7 before turning things over to the reserves prompting UTC coach Buddy Nix to say, "We've played against Georgia Southern's three national championship teams, and Furman's national championship team, but I believe that's the best Southern Conference team I've ever seen." Nix's opinion evidently never reached the state of North Carolina, where Marshall's next two opponents resided because neither Western Carolina nor Appalachian State were in awe of the Herd.

The Catamounts always were a tough mark for Marshall, and with three Herd starters already out with injuries before kickoff, and another three going down in the first half, an upset was at hand. Western exploited the Herd's holes for a 38-30 win that Donnan called "a nightmare." An encore was just a week away as Appalachian handed a crippled Herd its first loss in its new stadium. The Mountaineers scored the clinching touchdown in their 37-34 win with only eight seconds remaining. ASU was motivated by a comment

Coach Jim Donnan used a cup commemorating Youngstown State's 1991 championship victory against Marshall as a motivator for his team in 1992. The cup sat outside the Herd's locker room door at the start of pre-season practice as a reminder each time the players took the field. Equipment manager Woody Woodrum put the cup on display again when the team began preparing for the '92 playoffs. A piece of the cup was chipped away with a hammer after each of the first three wins, then smashed it with the baseball bat after defeating the Penguins for the title.

Donnan made following ASU's ugly 9-3 win the previous season in Boone, North Carolina. "I don't think Appalachian's offense could score if we left the field," Donnan had said.

It was the Mountaineers' turn to talk after this game, in which Payton threw for 432 yards and five touchdowns to be the Herd's lone bright spot and earn national player of the week honors. "Marshall's got an offense, but they won't win a national championship because they don't have a defense," ASU senior receiver Anthony Smith predicted. With its league title hopes gone, and playoff life on the edge of extinction, Marshall was headed toward elevating Smith to prophet status unless something changed — and in a hurry. "Our confidence level had really slipped at that point," Donnan recalled. "We needed something good to happen."

Luckily, a non-conference game with Tennessee Tech was up next, and the now 10th-ranked Herd capitalized in its home finale on the 22nd anniversary of the plane crash with a 52-14 rout. Its confidence restored and starting units from earlier in the season healthy again, MU rolled into Johnson City, Tennessee, and left with a 49-10 romp of East Tennessee State as well as that coveted playoff berth. The Herd's performance was reminiscent of its mid-season streak of dominance against Furman, The Citadel — which ended up winning the SoCon title — and UTC.

"At that point, we were a team you wouldn't want to play," Donnan later said while reflecting on that season's historic playoff run. "We were healthy, but the most important thing was we were focused — everybody — on one thing."

Old rival Eastern Kentucky was the first to see just how focused. Despite owning a higher ranking and better record, and having I-AA's career rushing leader in Markus Thomas, the Colonels were no match for the Herd at Marshall Stadium. Payton, I-AA's top passer, threw for 353 yards and two touchdowns, both to wide receiver Troy Brown. The mercurial Brown, who would go on to a Pro Bowl career with the New England Patriots, caught 10 passes for 188 yards and the two scores, and also returned three punts for 95 yards, one covering 71 yards for a touchdown.

The Herd's defense limited EKU to just 192 total yards. Thomas, who finished as I-AA's all-time rushing leader, had a career-low minus-4 yards. Although the Colonels, including coach Roy Kidd, engaged in a fair share of pre-game rhetoric, they were gracious in defeat. "For every poison, they had an antidote," Thomas said. "It's one of those situations when you can't make excuses. We went out and played. They just played better."

Middle Tennessee, which had whipped EKU 38-7 for the Ohio Valley Conference title, was next for the Herd after disposing of Appalachian 35-10 in the first round. The Blue Raiders, in the estimation of ASU coach Jerry Moore, were better than any team in the Southern Conference. "Jim asked him if (Moore and his staff) thought we could win the game, and Jerry said 'no,'" recalled Herd defensive coordinator Mickey Matthews, who would later become head coach at James Madison where he won the I-AA title in 2004. "And in all honesty, after we looked at them on film, we couldn't say he wasn't going to be right."

Moore was no prophet, thanks in large part to the work of Donnan's son. The sophomore came in midway through the first quarter when Payton went out with a knee injury to pass for 246 yards and three touchdowns in leading the Herd to a 35-21 win. Brown was again the main target, catching eight passes for 189 yards and all the touchdowns. Veteran MTSU coach Boots Donnelly had believed in the week leading to the game that I-AA's best two teams were meeting in this matchup. He had no doubt afterward who stood alone. "The score was not even remotely indicative of how well they controlled our team," he said. "They manhandled us and beat us in every phase of the game."

The result was much the same in the semifinals against Delaware. The Blue Hens, who had won 41-18 at top-ranked Northeast Louisiana in the quarterfinals, scored a touchdown on their first possession, but nothing more as the Herd cruised 28-7 to get another shot at Youngstown State for the championship. The Penguins, in their usual

Jim Donnan was a highly respected assistant at the NCAA Division I-A level who sold himself to Marshall athletic director Lee Moon and the school's search committee with a promise to bring the kind of athletes to campus who could win a championship and be a credit to the school off the field. Donnan assumed the reins of Marshall's program on January 9, 1990, leaving his job as offensive coordinator at Oklahoma. (Photo courtesy of The Herald-Dispatch)

workmanlike fashion, had eliminated Northern Iowa 19-7 in the other semifinal, and the top two programs in I-AA would again decide the title.

This time, however, the game was in Huntington where 31,304 showed up on the windy, but sunny Saturday before Christmas. For Marshall, it was more than a game. It was a mission. The Herd players not only were playing for themselves, but for all the players and fans who'd ever been associated with Marshall. They were playing for those who died in the crash and their survivors. The pressure was immense but the Herd appeared unfazed, leading 14-0 at halftime and 28-0 midway through the third quarter.

Youngstown, however, wasn't about to give up its title quite that easily. After the Penguins finally got on the board, their defense followed with stop after stop. And just as quickly as Marshall had run up its lead, the visitors had wiped it out to tie the score 28-28 with 2:23 to play. The Herd offense took over on its 19-yard line after the kickoff knowing that it likely needed to score points or lose the game given the fact its tired defense probably wasn't going to be able to stop Youngstown if the Penguins got the ball again with much time left.

Willy Merrick's dramatic game-winning field goal with 22 seconds left in the 1992 I-AA championship game against Youngstown State capped a masterful drive by the Marshall offense after the Penguins had scored the last of their 28 unanswered points to tie the game. The Herd drove 81 yards in 14 plays after the kickoff, with Orlando Hatchett's 8-yard run moving the ball to the middle of the field for the first field goal attempt of Merrick's life. The senior from Worthington, Ohio, who came to Marshall on a soccer scholarship, popped the ball up over the crossbar and through the uprights to give the Herd the title. Merrick had been the Herd's primary kickoff man throughout the season, but was pressed into extra point and field goal duty for the title game when his younger brother David was suspended for missing a practice earlier in the week. (Photo by Frank Altizer)

Payton, who earlier in the week was named winner of the Walter Payton Award, I-AA's version of the Heisman Trophy, performed in the following two minutes like the best player at his level. Mixing pinpoint passes with delayed running plays that made finding seams in the Youngstown defense easier, Payton guided the Herd down the field to a first down at the 5-yard line with only 14 seconds remaining.

While the offense was working its way through the Penguins, Willy Merrick, who had never kicked a field goal in a game in his life, stood on the sideline almost oblivious to how the game would be decided. Merrick, a senior on a soccer scholarship who'd served

Marshall senior Willy Merrick was at the center of the post-game celebration after kicking the game-winning field goal with just 10 seconds remaining to lift the Thundering Herd to a 31-28 victory against Youngstown State. (Photo by John Baldwin)

as the Herd's kickoff man, only got the call for extra points and field goals for this game after younger brother David had been suspended for missing a 9 a.m. practice earlier in the week.

"Everyone kept coming up to me and telling me it was going to come down to a field goal," Merrick recalled. "I thought, 'Really?' I couldn't believe it. It was like something I watched on TV."

Donnan didn't want to chance anything going wrong with another snap to Payton so he summoned Merrick on first down. With the crowd eerily quiet as Pete Woods snapped the ball to holder Andy Bowen, Merrick stepped, whipped his left leg forward and kicked 22 years of Marshall's agony over the crossbar and through the uprights. Youngstown had one play after the kickoff, but Brown, playing in the secondary as he would later do in his NFL career to help the Patriots win three Super Bowls, intercepted the Penguins' desperation pass to end the game.

Marshall stood atop a mountain nobody thought it could ever climb. The school that had known only heartbreak had no equal on this day. One word mentioned in passing by one man who was there simply tells in the most explicit way how Marshall's fans felt on that December 19.

"Euphoria," Rev. R.F. Smith, retired minister of Fifth Avenue Baptist Church in Huntington, said before his death in 2003. Asked to recall Marshall's 31-28 victory, the former chaplain for Thundering Herd football teams paused for a moment to reflect and at first referred to the win as "totally indescribable." Then he described it. He recalled that he felt weak, and shouted, and saw people all around him in Marshall Stadium crying once victory was realized. "And then we just sat there for a moment and remembered in spirit the men who were there before," Smith said in a voice that grew softer with each word. Euphoria.

Chris Parker came to Marshall as a defensive back, but his move to offense was among the smartest moves coach Jim Donnan and his staff made in their time at Marshall. Parker left as the school's all-time rushing leader and played three seasons in the NFL with the Jacksonville Jaguars before a knee injury ended his career. (Photo courtesy of The Herald-Dispatch)

How different the reasons were for the tears that fell on that cold rainy November 14 night in 1970, and those shed after this game. Many of the same people, some closer to the crash victims than others, cried both nights and for days after each historical event. The relatives, the friends, the companions, will likely never fully get over the tragedy that left them pained and empty. "They're functioning," Smith said. "But you always walk with a limp."

The hope is that Marshall's win against Youngstown State somehow made that limp a little less noticeable. Perhaps now, and until the end of time, the hurt will ease enough so that each person will be able to get through each day without wondering aloud or silently, why? Some will, some won't.

Nate Ruffin, a junior member of the 1970 team, wasn't aboard the DC-9 that crashed. The win helped ease some of the pain he suffered from losing teammates, coaches and supporters. He said he was coping well before the championship, but the victory was the final dose of medication needed to complete his healing process.

Ruffin, who died in 2001 of cancer, was working as Human Resources Director at the Clarion Ledger newspaper in Jackson, Mississippi, at the time of the Herd's playoff run in 1992, yet he didn't miss a game. He had driven all night from Jackson to get to the championship game.

"I don't have those negative thoughts, those nightmares anymore," he said reflecting on that historic win. "There was like an unfinished chapter. It was still not finished. Even when we became a winner, when we went 6-5 (1984) then it was like, 'hey, the story hasn't ended.' We can't just be a winner. We need something more. That win over Youngstown was the pinnacle. It brought an end to something that was a long time coming. Now, everything's OK. I've seen the mountaintop, and I was part of it."

So much ecstasy, so much relief, so many memories stirred.

"As I told the congregation on that Sunday, the day after the game, that game was not about football, it was about whether a team and a city so devastated could rise again from the ashes," Smith recalled. "That game said, 'yes.'"

Debbie Morehouse of Huntington was nine years old when she lost her parents, Dr. Ray Hagley and his wife, Shirley, in the crash. Debbie's husband, Keith, lost his father, Herd play-by-play man Gene Morehouse, in the crash. To them, the victory was the highest of highs.

"It's the biggest thrill of my life," Debbie said. "I've had a baby, married Keith ... but this was just wonderful. We've been waiting for them to build it to where that (1970) team would've been. Now, it's like, 'OK, they did it. They did what needed to be done.'"

Like his wife, Keith was nine years old at the time of the crash. He knows his father would've been there cheering on the Herd in the title game, unless of course he wasn't still broadcasting. "I think for most people in the community, they can put it all behind them now," said Keith, sports director at WSAZ-TV in Huntington. "But quite honestly, it's impossible for me and Debbie. Nobody could do that with their parents. We'll never be able to do that."

William "Red" Dawson, an assistant coach for the 1970 team who missed the plane in order to continue a recruiting trip, echoed Keith Morehouse's sentiments on the healing process. Dawson, a Valdosta, Georgia, native who's in the Florida State

Todd Donnan, the son of Marshall coach Jim Donnan, proved a capable back-up to Michael Payton before taking over as the starter in 1993 and leading the Thundering Herd to two more championship game appearances. The younger Donnan wasn't as prolific as some of his Marshall predecessors, but he was just as effective and productive in terms of victories. (Photo by Brian Ferguson)

Marshall coach Jim Donnan's friendship with NFL coach Bill Parcells helped get Troy Brown started on a professional career. Brown, who averaged a touchdown every seven times he touched the ball on offense for the Herd, was drafted in the eighth round of the 1993 NFL Draft by the New England Patriots and began his 14th season with the club in 2006. During his tenure, Brown has helped the team win three Super Bowls with the same talents he displayed at Marshall as a receiver, punt returner, and even defensive back. (Photo by Brian Ferguson)

University hall of fame following a stellar career as a tight end with the Seminoles in the early 1960s, recruited many of the players who died in the crash. "The healing will never end," he said. "I will never forget, nor do I want to forget, the people taken from the Marshall athletic department. Not one do I want to forget."

Dawson said he found many similarities to the 1970 team and the 1992 national champions. The most obvious was the talent level. Each team, at its time, was a collection of the best players to ever come to campus.

"We didn't have a I-AA, so it would've been hard to win a national championship," he said. "But I think we could've had a winning program if that plane hadn't crashed. We had the personnel and we had an outstanding coaching staff. But we never had the chance. It was taken away."

Debbie Morehouse was happy just knowing Marshall finally attained a goal her parents so desired to see in their lifetime. "If somebody had told them Marshall's going to win a national championship, it would've been hard for them to imagine."

As dramatic and rewarding as Marshall's 1992 season was, Donnan and his staff likely did their finest job in the successive three seasons. The Herd didn't win another championship, but it managed to play for two others in the face of the loss of the best talent to play for the school in its history.

Coming off a national championship, fans' expectations were high — maybe too high, Donnan thought. "I never used the word 'rebuilding,' but that's what we were doing," Donnan said. "We didn't just lose a lot of players, we lost so many impact players."

When the first NCAA Division I-AA poll came out in 1993 with Marshall ranked No. 1, Donnan was speechless. The coach believed he had capable replacements on defense, but he and his staff had to reconstruct a unit responsible for 42 points and nearly 500 yards per game a year earlier. While Brown was the team's most valuable player, Donnan viewed Payton as the toughest to replace. The veteran coach turned to his own son, Todd, to handle the job. Being the starting quarterback at Marshall was pressure enough. Doing it while also being the head coach's son added monumental scrutiny from fans.

The younger Donnan, though, wasn't without experience, having completed 92 of 165 passes for 1,340 yards and 15 touchdowns while backing Payton. Donnan lacked Payton's athleticism and he didn't have the arm of a Tony Petersen or John Gregory. Yet, he was a combination of all of those players. He threw the deep ball effectively, was athletic enough to run the option and was efficient. Most of all, Todd Donnan was intelligent.

"I didn't expect Todd to do what Payton did," the coach said. "He had plenty enough skills, but he was different than Payton." Payton realized that, too. In the preseason, Payton, who would play in both the NFL and CFL, took his successor aside and offered some advice. "I told Todd not to try to be me or anybody else," Payton said. "I told him to be who he was and to do what he was capable of doing."

Marshall set out to rely more on the running game, reflected by the fact that in 1993 the Herd didn't have a quarterback pass for 300 yards in a game for the first time since 1983. Glenn Pedro was a workhorse senior and sophomore Chris Parker was a potential big-play back. It didn't take long for Parker to prove it, running for 160 yards on just 12 carries in a 29-3 victory against Murray State in the season's second game.

"I knew Parker could be big for us," Jim Donnan said. "He had the ability to take it all the way every time he touched the ball. We'd never had a back like that before."

Marshall's defense noticed that a year earlier in practice. Recruited out of Virginia as a defensive back, when Parker moved to running back no one much noticed until he began

Under Lee Moon's guidance Marshall's football program became the standard for the rest of NCAA Division I-AA. He oversaw the planning and construction of Marshall Stadium and chaired the Huntington Sports Committee that secured the host role for the national championship game from 1992 to 1996. (Photo courtesy of The Herald-Dispatch)

making people miss in practice. Parker was special. He went on to play three seasons in the NFL with the Jacksonville Jaguars before a knee injury ended his career.

Parker proved to be the catalyst for the Herd's offense the rest of the season on the way to earning Southern Conference Offensive Player of the Year and All-America honors. He often had 100 yards by halftime, and twice in the season scored four touchdowns in a game as the Herd finished the regular season 8-3 with one of the losses coming to N.C. State. The Herd didn't secure its spot in the playoffs until a 20-16 win against Western Carolina in the season finale.

The key to the playoff-clinching game likely didn't occur on any down in the game, but months before. Moon had bought the rights to the game, originally scheduled to be played in Western's Whitmire Stadium, so it could be moved to Marshall Stadium where the Herd was 25-1 all-time. "That was a great move by Lee," Donnan said. "We'd take any edge we could get."

Marshall's I-AA bid process, its contract with the NCAA to host the championship game again, and a little luck in the outcome of other games enabled the Herd to stay at home throughout the playoffs. It took full advantage by running through Howard, Delaware and Troy State on the way to finals where it met Youngstown State, which had eliminated Georgia Southern in its semifinal. Las Vegas oddsmakers calculated that the chance of the same two teams meeting for the national title three years in a row were a million to one.

Where Marshall had lost most of its stars from its 1992 championship team, the Penguins returned a wealth of talent. Youngstown needed just two plays to score a touchdown, which proved to be all the points it would need. Marshall managed just a field goal and a safety as the Penguins reclaimed the title with a 17-5 victory. "Of the three times we played Youngstown, the only time I went into the game really thinking they were better than us was in 1993," Donnan said. "They had a great football team."

As pessimistic as Donnan was before the '93 season, he approached the '94 optimistically. Heading the list of experienced players returning were Parker and Todd Donnan as well as defensive backs Roger Johnson, who joined Parker as an All-American, and Shannon Morrison.

"Even before the '93 season I'd been looking to '94 as a year when I thought we could be really good," the coach admitted later. "I knew we'd have a lot of players back and I felt like we could be a good football team."

So did the poll voters, who placed Marshall atop the preseason rankings. The Herd lived up to its lofty expectations, rolling through its first seven opponents by averaging 46.5 points per game built on routs of 71-7 against Morehead State and 62-21 against Tennessee-Chattanooga. The eighth game at Appalachian State, however, was a puzzle as Marshall could do nothing right in falling 24-14.

Order was restored the next week as Todd Donnan, who later was voted the Southern Conference Offensive Player of Year, passed for a career-best 302 yards in a 42-30 victory against The Citadel that began a three-game winning streak to close the season and give the Herd a piece of its second Southern Conference championship. A 35-14 drubbing of Furman at home in the season-finale secured Marshall's share of the title and another playoff trip.

The Herd whipped Middle Tennessee 41-14 in the playoff opener, then slipped by James Madison 28-21 in overtime. Cornerback Melvin Cunningham had a school-record 100-yard interception return for a touchdown in the victory over JMU that put MU at Boise State for its first road playoff game since the loss in the '91 title game. It also was the Herd's first playoff game on an opponent's home field since the 24-10 semifinal victory against Appalachian in 1987.

But it didn't look as though the location would make any difference as Marshall scored on its first four possessions on the snowy, blue artificial surface at Broncos Stadium on the way to a 24-7 halftime cushion. Youngstown State already had won in the other semifinal so Penguins-Herd IV looked like a certainty for the following weekend at Marshall Stadium.

The Broncos, though, had other ideas, taking advantage of blown coverages in the Marshall secondary to come back strong. The Herd, meanwhile, struggled. Parker suddenly began losing his footing, frequently slipping on the turf before getting out of the backfield. The Herd defense unraveled and Boise State claimed a 28-24 win that put it opposite the Penguins the following week at Marshall Stadium.

"That was one of the toughest losses I've ever had as a player or coach," Donnan recalled. "Everything was sitting right there for us, and we couldn't finish it. That one was frustrating."

Despite the loss of his son at quarterback, Donnan was just as optimistic for the 1995 season, which would be his last with the Herd. The heir apparent at quarterback was Larry Harris, a speedy, elusive youngster from Georgia. The 6-foot, 185-pounder was far different from his predecessors of the recent past in that he wasn't a dropback passer. Harris, though, was a hiccup quick, a mobile player with a strong arm. Donnan loved Harris' versatility and the youngster's potential.

Harris, however, had the misfortune of playing his first college game at North Carolina State. He threw only six passes, completing four for 34 yards and an interception in a 33-16 loss. And just when it appeared he was ready to live up to Donnan's confidence, he suffered a career-ending knee injury in the home opener the next week against Tennessee Tech. Harris had completed 12 of 19 passes for 230 yards before suffering the injury, which came when he was tackled on an option play in the third quarter. All the preparation the Herd put in for Harris' multiple talents was pretty much wasted because his backup, Ohio State transfer and Huntington native Mark Zban, was a classic dropback passer.

Zban, whose father, Bill, had played quarterback at Marshall in the 1950s, was a highly intelligent player with a big arm, but not much mobility. And he had no better luck than Harris on the field. After finishing off the 45-14 win against Tennessee Tech, Zban joined Harris on the sideline early in a 37-7 romp of Georgia Southern forcing Marshall to make the quarterback who began the season third on the depth chart its starter for the first time since 1983.

That season, Carl Fodor took over for ineffective Tim Carpenter and Dan Patterson at midseason to lay a foundation for a record-setting final two seasons that turned Marshall into a school known for its quarterbacks. Nobody expected the scrawny true freshman from Knoxville, Tennessee, who would step in after Harris and Zban, would one day be a finalist for the Heisman Trophy and then play professionally in the bright lights of the media capital of the world with the New York Jets. His name? Chad Pennington.

Pennington was a lightly recruited player from tiny Webb School. He had no

NCAA Division I scholarship offers, except from Marshall. Tennessee had offered him an opportunity to walk on, but the Volunteers figured their future was secure in a young passer named Peyton Manning. Pennington had turned up at the Herd's football camp one summer and caught the coaches' attention.

"You could see right away Chad was special," recalled assistant coach Mark Gale, who coordinated the Herd's recruiting. "He was very intelligent. He had no trouble picking things up."

One thing Pennington hadn't picked up very often was weights. He stood 6-foot-3, but weighed only about 170 pounds. Pennington was able to finish off the win against Georgia Southern by handing off to his running backs. He wouldn't have that luxury the following week at Tennessee-Chattanooga. He had to throw the ball and the Moccasins knew it. The result was six interceptions by UTC, but a 35-32 victory for the Herd.

"Six interceptions, but it didn't faze him," Donnan recalled of the future first-round draft pick.

Thus, a legend was born. Pennington steadily gained confidence as each week passed and the coaching staff did its best to maximize his strengths while taking advantage of runners Erik Thomas and Parker. The result was a 9-2 regular season that ended with a four-game winning streak and put the Herd in the playoffs for a fifth straight season.

Marshall had little trouble in disposing of Jackson State 38-8 and Northern Iowa 41-24 in the first two rounds at home. The latter win put the Herd in the semifinals for a playoff-record fifth straight season, but it was again on the road. Not only on the road but it was going to Lake Charles, Louisiana, to take on unbeaten and top-ranked McNeese State.

When Marshall arrived on Friday, the temperature was in the 70s and skies were sunny. By game time Saturday afternoon, the temperature had dropped into the low 40s and a stiff breeze put the chill factor 10 degrees colder. McNeese State fans bundled up and rang cowbells almost incessantly, encouraging their beloved Cowboys to a 7-0 lead. This wasn't the first rodeo, though, for the playoff-tested Herd. Pennington, who rapidly had developed into a top-shelf quarterback, played his best game of the season, throwing for 245 yards and a pair of touchdowns in the 25-13 victory.

McNeese State football coach Bobby Keasler was impressed with Marshall, not just on that Saturday, but overall. "People don't realize what they've done at Marshall," Keasler said. "It's amazing. Where they came from to where they are, it's incredible."

With No. 1 taken care of, many Marshall fans figured a national championship was

Coach Jim Donnan holds the NCAA Division I-AA championship trophy aloft for the thousands of celebrating fans on the Marshall Stadium field after Marshalls's 31-28 victory against Youngstown State in 1992. Donnan also put three runner-up trophies in Marshall's case before departing on Christmas Day in 1995 to become head coach at Georgia. (Photo by Rick Haye)

all but assured. Montana had other ideas. The Big Sky Conference champion came to Huntington with a veteran, playoff-tested team led by Dave Dickenson, the I-AA player of the year who went on to a successful career in the CFL.

Montana led most of the game until Parker broke loose for a 26-yard touchdown run against a tired Grizzlies defense with just less than five minutes to play. Tim Openlander's extra point gave the Herd a 20-19 lead and placed the onus on the stingy Marshall defense. One stop was all that Marshall needed to secure its second national championship in four years. Dickenson, though, picked apart the Herd defense, completing a key fourth-down pass to keep alive a four-minute, 12-play drive that ended in a 25-yard field goal with 39 seconds left for a 22-20 win that left the Herd watching an opponent celebrate a national championship for the fourth time since 1987.

The suspense of that championship game, however, couldn't match the drama that was about to begin for Marshall. The University of Georgia had hired Kansas football coach Glen Mason to replace the fired Ray Goff, but Mason had a change of heart and decided to return to the Jayhawks. Very early on Christmas morning, and not long after hearing from Mason, now the coach at Minnesota, Georgia athletics director Vince Dooley turned to Donnan.

Donnan had longed to be a head coach at a major college power. He had come close many times, at North Carolina, at Oklahoma, at N.C. State, at West Virginia and at Wisconsin. Now, Georgia, a jewel of the powerful Southeastern Conference, was calling. On the surface, the decision appeared easy. Georgia was a program where a coach could win a national championship at the highest level. Even though MU was moving to I-A in 1997, it could never match the lure of Georgia and the SEC. While Marshall paid as well as many I-A jobs, it couldn't compare to Georgia.

Donnan, though, struggled with the decision. He had

taken a solid Marshall program and turned it into the most powerful in I-AA, compiling a 64-21 record that was the best in school history. If he stayed in Huntington his entire career, the school likely would have named the stadium for him some day. He had developed deep friendships in his six years in Huntington.

Donnan met early Christmas morning with Moon, telling him of his decision, maybe half-hoping that Moon would talk him into staying. They reminisced about the glory days of Marshall football and talked of how special Huntington was. Donnan was a no-nonsense coach, but also a deeply caring man. Huntington had become home for the Burlington, North Carolina, native and leaving wasn't easy.

"I had to take this job," Donnan said that Christmas day, almost apologetic. "Can you blame me?"

No one really could. Marshall had been here before, having lost Parrish to Kansas State and Chaump to Navy, but neither of those programs compared to Georgia. While Herd fans wondered about the future of their proud football program, they wished Donnan well then turned their attention to finding the man to replace him. Little did they know that the success they had experienced under Donnan merely was a block in the foundation of even greater glory to come.

Chapter nine

Rolling Thunder

People remembered Bobby Pruett as a hard-core football guy with a heck of a coaching background in high school and as a college assistant. He was a Cam Henderson-Charlie Snyder pupil who was a very good ballplayer and a very popular ballplayer here in Snyder's winning years in the 1960s. All throughout his background he said he was always preparing himself for the day he could come back to Marshall and everything fell into place for him. There was this personable guy, a West Virginia and Marshall guy connecting with the people. He's got them excited even before they start playing football. Then they go through a 15-game schedule and win every game and the national championship with this transfer (Eric) Kresser at quarterback. And the wayward son of West Virginia, Randy Moss, is catching a touchdown pass from him it seems like every quarter. Every thing came together for this 15-game winning streak and the championship and it had this town in an uproar. Football was back on top. Bobby Pruett was a very clever promoter. He turns on that West Virginia good ol' boy charm when he has to and all of a sudden Marshall football is an event. He also does a very careful job recruiting, and with good gamesmanship and excellent PR work, he had this town in the palm of his hand for years. Bobby Pruett put this program on a level I thought I'd never live to see.

— Ernie Salvatore

Bobby Pruett didn't have time to think about Marshall. The University of Florida

---

Being the head coach at Marshall University was Bobby Pruett's dream from the time he was a player for the Thundering Herd in the mid-1960s. The former two-way player returned to his alma mater as an assistant to Sonny Randle in 1979 to begin a trek through the college coaching ranks that would take him to Wake Forest, Mississippi, Tulane and Florida before coming back to Huntington in early 1996 with the slogan, "We play for championships." His teams backed up his claim during a nine-year tenure that saw Marshall rise to among the nation's Top 10 teams one season.

defensive coordinator was preparing the Gators' defense to face Nebraska's vaunted offense for the national championship in the 1996 Fiesta Bowl when he heard rumors that Jim Donnan would leave Marshall for the University of Georgia. Pruett, a former Thundering Herd star himself, had plenty to keep him occupied. Devising a scheme to slow Nebraska's Tommie Frazier and Lawrence Phillips, along with the task of wooing recruits to Gainesville, Florida, was more than enough to fill Pruett's days. Now, time for it or not, he had visions of a return to his alma mater on his mind.

And why not? Pruett's 20-year trek to Florida was part of his oft-adjusted master plan to place himself back at Marshall as head coach. Pruett made a quick call to Marshall Athletics Director Lee Moon to let Moon know of his interest in the job. "Marshall was my dream job," said Pruett, a two-way end with the Herd from 1962-64 and an MU assistant for Sonny Randle from 1979-82. "Being the head football coach at Marshall was a dream I'd had ever since I'd gotten into coaching."

Two days before Florida and Nebraska tangled for the national title, Moon called Pruett to arrange an interview. The native of Beckley, West Virginia, often joked that he's thankful Moon made the call before the Fiesta Bowl rather than after as Nebraska swamped Florida 62-24. That one game, however, wouldn't have eliminated Pruett from the running.

His defense had been among the top 25 in the country each of the last two seasons. He was everything Marshall was seeking in a coach — a coordinator at a major college football power, a veteran coach with an outgoing personality and a history of success. That he was a Marshall man himself made him all the more attractive to MU President J. Wade Gilley, who was tired of seeing coaches leave for higher-paying jobs at larger schools as Donnan and the two men who preceded him had done.

Pruett and Moon arranged a meeting in Charlotte, North Carolina, where the interview was conducted. Pruett left having no idea whether he would be offered the position. Also in the running was Mickey Matthews, Donnan's defensive coordinator and a popular choice among Herd fans. Matthews was outgoing and viewed as an outstanding coach and recruiter. While he wasn't a Marshall graduate, Matthews had been with the program since arriving with Donnan in 1990. Matthews had Donnan's firm recommendation. Pruett, meanwhile, had the backing of Gators' head coach Steve Spurrier.

Pruett not only didn't know if his future awaited in Huntington, he wasn't sure it was secure in Gainesville. Spurrier was mulling over an offer to coach the NFL's Tampa

Bay Buccaneers. If Pruett didn't get the Marshall job, he likely would stay with Spurrier, wherever that might be. Pruett, though, badly wanted to return to Huntington. Every move he made during his coaching career was calculated on getting back to where his college coaching career had started. And as often happens, many coaches must step back before stepping forward. That was the case when he answered Randle's call while a highly successful high school coach in Virginia.

"I took a $10,000 pay cut to come back here," Pruett said of his days on Randle's staff. "At that time, I think I was making something like $17,000. We made a major sacrifice, but I wanted to come back and I knew I probably wouldn't get the job (as Marshall's head coach) being a head high school coach so I had to get some college experience to put myself in a position to get the job. Then, after four years there, I knew I was going to have to leave to come back."

After leaving Marshall in 1982, Pruett spent six seasons at Wake Forest. When the Marshall job opened with George Chaump's departure after the 1989 season, Pruett applied, but Moon told him MU was looking for a coordinator from a major college power. Donnan, then offensive coordinator at Oklahoma, fit that description better than Pruett, who by then was defensive coordinator at Wake. Pruett realized then that to make his dream a reality he had to leave the long-time Atlantic Coast Conference also-ran.

"(Moon) told me the Marshall program was in such a position they wanted someone who'd been going to bowl games and playing on television and recognized the game as a little bit more big time than Wake Forest," Pruett recalled. "Se we then decided to leave Wake Forest, which we liked very much."

He joined Billy Brewer's staff at Mississippi as secondary coach before becoming defensive coordinator at Tulane in 1992. Neither of those posts directly would land Pruett the Marshall job, but they were building blocks for the job that would. In 1994, Spurrier hired Pruett as Florida's defensive coordinator. Pruett was charged with leading the defense that had a sole responsibility of getting the ball back for Spurrier's Fun-and-Gun offense. Pruett's defense did that magnificently, as the Gators went 22-2-1 in the two seasons Pruett was there. The roundabout trek to Florida paid off on Jan. 16, 1996, when Pruett was hired as Marshall's coach.

"All those moves were made to put ourselves in position to get the head coaching job at Marshall," Pruett said.

Pruett, talking with ESPN broadcaster Dr. Jerry Punch after one of his team's five bowl victories, finished his nine-year tenure at Marshall with a 94-23 record that included the NCAA Division I-AA national championship in 1996, two undefeated seasons, one Southern Conference and five Mid-American Conference championships. His winning percentage was the best for the first nine years of a coaching career since Pop Warner. (Photo by Rick Haye)

Marshall fans didn't know what to make of their new country boy coach. Unlike Donnan, who often appeared guarded with most everyone, Pruett never met a stranger. He poked fun at himself and came across, as Pruett himself put it, "as a dumb ole boy from East Beckley, West Virginia." Pruett was anything but dumb. He was shrewd, he loved Marshall and he was reverent toward those who died in the 1970 plane crash. Pruett's position coach while he was a Marshall player for Charlie Snyder was Charlie Kautz, the MU athletics director killed in the crash.

"I remember it like it was yesterday," Pruett said reflecting on that tragic November 14, 1970, evening. "I knew some of the people on that plane. I'll tell you something, the bottom of my heart fell out that day. I'll never forget where I was and how I felt."

Pruett graciously credits all of the men for whom he played or worked -- even

Woodrow Wilson High School coaches Jerome Van Meter and Nelson Bragg — as playing a role in shaping him as a coach. After Randle came Al Groh, currently head coach at Virginia, at Wake, then Brewer, then Buddy Teevens at Tulane, then Spurrier.

"They all in their way influenced me and I tried to take what part of them fit my personality and the way I envisioned things being done. If I didn't learn something good to do, I learned something not to do."

But it was Snyder who merited Pruett's highest admiration.

"He might be the best that ever coached at Marshall," Pruett praised. "And he did it with very little financial help. He was very organized, a very sound football coach fundamentally. He was where I got my base. He's where I learned most of my basis for football. We were second in the Mid-American Conference (in 1964) and I look back and I guess we probably didn't have anybody on the team any farther away than Wheeling (West Virginia). He had no money to recruit on. He just did a tremendous job with very few resources."

Pruett had little time to celebrate getting the Marshall job. Following Donnan was difficult enough. Inheriting a stacked team was a mixed blessing. The Herd was the consensus No. 1 pick in the NCAA Division I-AA preseason polls, but with that came extreme pressure to win.

MU fans knew their team should be good enough to win a national championship and they were going to settle for nothing less. "I probably should've been scared," Pruett recalled. "Coach Donnan had done a great job. The program had had so much success. I was amazed at how much better the players were than when I'd been there before. But I wasn't scared. I was excited to get started and see what happened."

Pruett wasn't content simply to inherit an extremely talented team, he added to it. Randy Moss, whom Pruett had recruited while at Florida, had been dismissed from the Florida State football team, giving Pruett a second chance to land possibly the country's most talented football player. The coach knew if Moss wanted to play during the 1996 season, he had to transfer down a level. Marshall, about an hour from the receiver's home in Rand, West Virginia, seemed the logical choice.

But anywhere Moss went, he'd be accompanied by lots of baggage. He had been involved in a racially charged fight at DuPont High School that landed him in legal trouble and eventually cost him a scholarship to Notre Dame when that school's officials denied his application for admission. Coach Bobby Bowden then gave him a second chance at a Division I career, with the stipulation that it would take exemplary behavior for him to be a Seminole. Moss botched that chance on a marijuana possession charge.

Wanting to play football and knowing Marshall's talent level, Moss landed in Huntington with the help of his legal advisors, who assured all that the player understood this was probably his best last chance to play college football. Other than an over-publicized incident with the mother of his one child at the time that was little more than a dispute between two parents, Moss didn't violate Marshall's trust. Satisfied that Moss could be as good off the field as he was on it, Marshall and Pruett welcomed him to campus.

"I considered Randy the best player in the country," Pruett said. "I think we didn't look at it as if we were taking a chance on Randy. I looked at it as we had an opportunity to have a great athlete, help him mature and become what he could be and be a part of Marshall University and that's what happened.

"We had a good fit and I think one of the reasons is that I genuinely liked Randy. I just think he's misunderstood. He wants to win so bad, and he gets frustrated if he's not winning championships. He won championships in high school and at Marshall. We had a great relationship when he was playing for us, and we still have a great relationship. He's come back and is giving back to Marshall University now in a big way."

As Moss would show nearly every game in his two seasons in Huntington, his talents far exceeded the bounds of Marshall's competitive level. Pruett knew, however, they couldn't be maximized without someone getting him the ball.

Chief among those players was Chad Pennington, a popular and promising sophomore who had thrown for 2,445 yards and completed 61 percent of his passes after being thrust into action early in his freshman season because of injuries at the position. But Pruett had another quarterback possibility. At Florida sat senior Eric Kresser, who was behind soon-to-be Heisman Trophy winner Danny Wuerffel on the Gators' depth chart. Knowing his playing time would be left to the chance of injury to the favorite player of Spurrier, himself a Heisman winner for the Gators, or a lop-sided score, Kresser was contemplating a transfer for his final season to enhance his chance of playing professionally. Just as in Moss case, Marshall appeared to be the perfect fit, especially with Pruett planning to run a virtual carbon copy of Florida's offense.

Kresser announced he was leaving the Gators for Marshall and immediately a quarterback controversy arose in Huntington. But Kresser's experience level and Pruett's persuasive manner quickly diffused the situation. Although Pennington had played well beyond his years in leading led the Herd to the I-AA championship game the season before, he was still under-sized physically. Even Pennington knew the value a redshirt season could have on the final three years of his career, and not only relating to his physical maturation.

"It wasn't an easy decision," Pruett remembered. "We almost went with Chad. There was a strong argument for going with Chad and I don't think we would've been wrong to do that. Eric won the job, though, and it worked out really great for us because it allowed us to redshirt Chad."

Initially, the decision to start Kresser didn't sit well with the fans, nor with many members of the Herd. After all, Pennington did lead the team to within a field goal of a national championship. "I remember thinking that this guy from Florida had better be really good," recalled running back Doug Chapman, who later played with the Minnesota Vikings as one of the host of Herd players under Pruett to play in the NFL. "He was."

And it didn't take long to see. About 10 minutes into Marshall's first game of the Pruett era on September 7 against visiting Howard, Kresser hit Moss with a pass off a post pattern that resulted in a touchdown. Moss only caught two other passes in the game, but the trio resulted in 134 yards. He also returned five kickoffs for 142 yards in the first of what would be a weekly show-stealing performance.

Marshall rolled up a 55-27 victory to start a season that would have not only opponents, but even the staunchest of the Herd's faithful shaking their heads in disbelief at the scenes on the field. Experts placed point spreads on most Marshall games between three and six touchdowns. Home games were worth a full touchdown to the Herd.

The opening performance, however, didn't do much to impress Pruett. He didn't find out much in the next either as the Herd rolled over Division II West Virginia State. The Yellow Jackets were coached by Carl Lee, an All-Southern Conference player for Randle in the early 1980s, who went on to an All-Pro career in the NFL with Minnesota and New Orleans. None of Lee's players had near his talent, and thus offered little resistance for the Herd, which took mercy on its former star's team by winning only 42-7.

Pruett and his staff figured a trip to Georgia Southern the next weekend would give them a good gauge of the Herd's potential. The Eagles were among I-AA's kingpins from the early 1980s through the early part of the 1990s, but pretty much had been relegated to

Eric Kresser stepped into the starting quarterback role in 1996 after transferring from Florida where he was mired on the bench behind future Heisman Trophy winner Danny Wuerffel. Kresser teamed with receiver Randy Moss to help the Herd to a perfect 15-0 record, the Southern Conference and NCAA Division I-AA national championships before playing in the NFL for the Cincinnati Bengals.

second fiddle in the Southern Conference and in the playoffs since Marshall became a title contender in 1987. If GSU was going to re-establish itself, now was a perfect time.

Just as it had before, Marshall put the Eagles in their place, leaving south Georgia with a 29-13 victory that was spurred by the play of some backups. Despite playing without starting tailback Erik Thomas, who had the flu, the Herd's running attack didn't miss a step as Chapman, a redshirt freshman, ran for 130 yards. Another backup, tight end Jason Wellman, caught a key touchdown pass in the victory.

Wellman enjoyed the flight home, but as the plane approached Tri-State Airport his mind turned to the same thing he nearly always thought about anytime the Herd flew home from a road game. "I grew up just one hillside away from where the plane crashed in 1970," Wellman recalled. "I'd heard about it all my life. I remember being on the plane and thinking of those guys on that plane, about what they were doing just before the crash. They probably were doing the same things we were doing — sleeping, talking, relaxing, thinking about what they were going to do when they got home. I thought about how that could've been me."

The win against Georgia Southern turned out to be Marshall's second-closest game of a season that was quickly turning into little more than a stroll toward the playoffs for the country's unanimous No. 1. Wins over Western Kentucky (37-3) and Tennessee-Chattanooga (45-0) followed before a lackluster 45-20 win at Virginia Military raised Pruett's ire.

"When we didn't play with emotion, that's when we got into trouble," Pruett recalled. "We had a lot of talent, but when you let down, anything can happen and our guys needed to know that."

The Herd responded the next week by pummeling Western Carolina 56-21. Kresser threw four touchdown passes and guided the offense to 629 yards while the defense sent the Catamounts to the sidelines after only three plays on each of their first eight possessions. At 7-0, Marshall was primed for what turned out to be its closest game of the season at dangerous Appalachian State, which was ranked 20th and the only team anyone believed could trip the Herd. The Mountaineers looked every bit the part by taking a 10-7 lead at halftime. They would score no more as the Herd dented the ASU defense for 17 points in the final two periods — the two touchdowns on Kresser passes — for a 24-10 victory.

A 56-25 romp of The Citadel in which Moss caught three touchdown passes to break Troy Brown's school record of 16 in a season followed the next week. Moss was having a season of video game numbers despite one gimmick coverage after another from defenses. East Tennessee State, with first place in the Southern Conference on the line, was the next to get an opportunity. ETSU double- and triple-teamed Moss in the Minidome in Johnson City, Tennessee, but he still caught a 72-yard touchdown pass that tied Jerry Rice's I-AA record for catching a scoring pass in 10 consecutive games. Moss' TD was little more than window dressing though, as it gave the Herd a 34-3 lead on the way to a 34-10 win and a share of the league title.

One opponent stood between Marshall and an undefeated regular season, a first for the school. And that opponent coming to Marshall Stadium was a big one. Furman had a playoff-worthy squad, too, and showed it by taking a 17-14 halftime lead after running its offense to perfection to help keep the ball away from the Herd. The Paladins, though, made a critical error on their way to the locker room at halftime that damaged their hopes for an upset.

There is no more shining example of Marshall's recruiting philosophy to quickly become competitive when it moved to NCAA Division I-A than quarterback Byron Leftwich. As a senior in high school in suburban Washington, D.C., the 6-foot-5, 240-pounder was being recruited as a tight end by most schools. Pruett told Leftwich, whose interest in Marshall was stirred by the Herd's TV exposure, he could play quarterback and the result was a record-setting career that led to a No. 1 draft selection by the Jacksonville Jaguars in 2003. (Photo by Rick Haye)

Several Marshall players said they saw Furman players punch the the goalpost padding as they left the field at halftime. "And they were yelling at us, taunting us," Kresser said. "They were yelling all kinds of stuff and it really fired us up."

The Paladins had tugged on Superman's cape and when the Herd was finished with a dominating second half, it had a 42-17 win to cap the perfect season as the SoCon champion and undisputed No. 1 team in the country entering the playoffs. "We'd accomplished one of our goals," Pruett said. "But we knew we were capable of a lot more."

The country was about to find out how much over the next four weeks as Marshall was hitting its stride at just the right time. The Herd was facing the best teams in I-AA and was playing like a Top-25 team — a I-A Top-25 team.

Familiar playoff opponent

Delaware was no match for the Herd in the first round, falling 59-14. Moss set a school, conference and playoff record with 288 receiving yards and scored three touchdowns, and Kresser threw for 449 yards. As bad as that defeat appeared, it couldn't match the domination Marshall showed the next week in a 54-0 drubbing of Furman. The Herd's 27-yard line was as close as the Paladins came to threatening the goal line while their running game managed just nine yards on 33 attempts.

The victories over Delaware and Furman were emotional. Northern Iowa, another familiar post-season foe, evoked no such emotion in the Herd. Pruett, however, did a masterful job of keeping his team's focus and the result was a 31-14 win that put MU in the championship game for the fifth time in six seasons against defending champion Montana.

While Marshall might have appeared unstoppable, Montana looked just as strong. Sensational young quarterback Brian Ah Yat and a bevy of veteran wide receivers had led the Grizzlies to a 70-7 blowout of Troy State in the semifinals. If any team was rolling as much as was Marshall, it was Montana, which entered the title game at Marshall Stadium with a 21-game winning streak.

It quickly became apparent it wouldn't reach 22 as Kresser and Moss hooked up on the Herd's first possession and Chapman added a 61-yard touchdown run shortly after to make it 14-0. It still was early, but Pruett said he thought Chapman's run was the difference maker. "Everybody talked about our passing game, but we had a running game, too," Pruett said. "When you can run the ball on somebody, it demoralizes the whole defense. When Montana realized we could run it and throw it, I think that broke their backs."

Kresser hit Moss with a 70-yard touchdown pass and the Herd bolted to a 23-6 halftime lead that was far too much for the visitors to overcome. Kresser hit Moss with a 54-yard TD pass, his league-record 35th of the year, to open the third quarter and for all purposes, the game was over. Marshall's defense was pressuring Ah Yat at will, nullifying Montana's potent air attack. The Grizzlies' defense, meanwhile, had no answer for Marshall's multiple weapons. The Herd built a 46-6 lead before settling for a 49-29 victory. Moss scored four touchdowns and caught nine passes for 220 yards. Thomas ran for 114 yards and Chapman 104.

Chad Pennington's decision to accept a redshirt season in 1996 after leading Marshall to the NCAA I-AA national championship game in 1995, was as beneficial to him as it was the Herd. His year of maturation, both physically and mentally, proved the foundation for a career that ended with him leading the Herd to a perfect season, a Top 10 ranking, while being a finalist for the Heisman Trophy and No. 1 draft pick by the New York Jets in 2000. (Photo by Rick Haye)

Randy Moss played only two seasons at Marshall, but they were as prolific as most players have in four. The wide receiver put up video games numbers against NCAA Division I-AA competition in his first season in helping Marshall to a perfect season and the national championship in 1996. The numbers weren't far off the following season when he helped the Herd to the Mid-American Conference championship in its first season before being a finalist for the Heisman Trophy and a No. 1 draft pick by the Minnesota Vikings in 1998. (Photo by Rick Haye)

The victory served to cement the belief by most who'd followed I-AA since its inception in 1978 that the '96 Herd was the greatest team in I-AA history. Appalachian State coach Jerry Moore, who began his 18th season in 2006 at ASU after the Mountaineers won the 2005 I-AA title, was among them.

"That bunch was a I-A team playing a I-AA schedule," Moore, the winningest coach in Southern Conference history, said a few years later at the league's pre-season media gathering. "How many guys on that team played in the NFL? How many are still in the NFL? Pennington, he didn't play a down that year and he almost won the Heisman Trophy a couple years later. Somebody will have to go a ways to be better than that team."

Not only was Marshall 15-0, it had outscored its opponents by 448 points. The Herd featured 10 all-Americans and 17 all-conference performers. Moss' 28 touchdown catches tied the Southern Conference career record. He set numerous other national, conference and school records. Pruett, who captured the national championship on his and wife Elsie's anniversary, was named national coach of the year.

The instant the final second ticked off the clock in the Montana game, however, everything changed at Marshall. No longer was the Herd a I-AA team, but the newest member of Division I-A and thoughts turned to the Mid-American Conference and to the 1997 season opener at West Virginia University.

Pruett, however, didn't have the luxury that the fans had. He had to get a program on more sound footing for a big step in fewer than eight months. And the footprint needed to be a large one.

"One of the biggest things we faced was that we were limited financially so I had to do a lot of fundraising to get things we needed that weren't in the budget," Pruett said. "We had to buy computers and video equipment for the coaches and then you had to constantly upgrade, and we didn't have the money for it. I had to go find it. We had $125,000 in the recruiting budget when I got there, which was very low so we had to to a lot of improvising. Winning football games is part of the job, but you also have to do the other things necessary to keep up with the competition and that usually involves money."

So no longer was Marshall the obvious dominant team — either on the field or off. Every opponent was bigger, stronger and faster than the Herd had faced before and their support system matched that superiority. The MAC was known as a league of big, strong, physical teams with tough defenses and slug-it-out running attacks. Marshall, meanwhile, was known for its passing game and speed. How the Herd would match up was the question everyone around the league was asking and the predictions were surprisingly varied.

"I knew Marshall was very good," then-Akron coach Lee Owens said. "But I wondered how would they be in November when the snow was flying and the wind was blowing. That was going to be the test."

Jim Grobe, then the coach at Ohio, had a different take. "When the MAC admitted Marshall, I knew we'd let the fox in the henhouse," said Grobe, who was on Randle's Marshall staff before a lengthy stay as a defensive coach at the Air Force Academy led to his first head coaching job with the Bobcats. "I knew how good those guys were and I knew what kind of coach Bobby Pruett was."

Grobe, now the coach at Wake Forest, knew Pruett would spare no effort in getting Marshall just as dominant in the MAC as it had been in all of I-AA. He understood Pruett's ability to recruit and sell his program.

"Bobby knew he was going to have to get more visability for Marshall to help when he went up against better-known schools for the players he was going to need to win when they left (I-AA)," said Ernie Salvatore, retired columnist for The Herald-Dispatch. "He was a great promoter. He was going anywhere in the country to talk about Marshall. By doing that, he and his staff were able to get time in homes that maybe they wouldn't otherwise.

"That, and his knack for pulling out those diamond talents like (Byron) Leftwich out of places nobody else looked, and getting great effort out of that guy just a notch below what the big schools want, was the basis for that quick success."

The fact Marshall had become a household name at the I-AA level played a key role in helping it establish a foothold in I-A, particularly in recruiting. Mark Gale, who served as Donnan's recruiting coordinator, was retained by Pruett as an assistant head coach and defensive ends coach, and saw first-hand the difference in the level, which increased the Herd's scholarship limit from 63 to 85.

"In the I-AA days, we'd recruit players who had absolutely no idea of who or where Marshall was," Gale recalled. "You'd try to tell them where Marshall was and you'd say, 'you know, it's between Ohio, Kentucky and West Virginia where they come together.'"

He said a change came when Marshall began winning playoff games and secured national TV exposure for the semifinal and championship games. "Now, I'd call a player and he'd say, 'I saw you on TV the other day.'"

This enabled the Herd to position itself, Gale said, for the move to I-A a year or two in advance by competing with the lower third of I-A schools for players despite still being a I-AA program.

"When we got into I-A, we wanted to recruit against the upper I-A schools," he said. "Once we got into the Mid-American Conference, that opened a few more doors."

Finding players who could run was the top priority as far as on-field talents.

"At all the places I coached, I'd learned the importance of speed," Pruett said. "Offensively, I'd seen the type of ball Coach Spurrier played at Florida and the problems it caused defenses. I had a vision of what we wanted to do. We wanted to be able to throw the ball around. Defensively, we wanted to attack people."

In order to get the talent Pruett knew was needed to compete at the I-A level, Marshall took some players that opponents on its schedule couldn't admit to their school, either for institution or conference mandates. When the Herd ended up beating those long-established I-A programs in high-profile conferences with those players, it wasn't praised for its rise, but chided for a part of the path it took to get there.

"I think there were a lot of guys we took chances on who for whatever reason struggled out of high school in some area or another," Pruett said. "We felt like there were a great number of guys who just needed an opportunity and we were able to provide it for them. Jonathan Goddard was a Prop 48 kid out of high school and he ended up graduating, making All-American and playing in the NFL. And there were many others.

"To get the athleticism we wanted and needed we took academic chances on a lot of kids. We took some guys who, for whatever reasons, weren't motivated enough in high school to do the job academically and we were able to motivate them and some of them graduated with over a 3.0 grade point average. You run a risk of failure, but we felt like we did our homework on these guys. We felt like we could motivate them in areas they hadn't been motivated. We did that and that was part of our success."

The coach and his staff also left few stones unturned seeking players whose overall high school talents might not look attractive to some, but showed flashes of potential that the right coaching could help win championships. Some of these rolls of the recruiting dice paid off handsomely. Leftwich, the starting quarterback with the Jacksonville Jaguars after being the team's No. 1 draft pick following his record-setting career at Marshall, proved to be the biggest score.

"For some reason, he wasn't highly recruited, and the people who were recruiting him were trying to recruit him as a tight end, " Pruett said of Leftwich, a strapping 6-foot-5, 240-pounder as a high school player in suburban Washington, D.C. "We were amazed at his ability. He played (high school) on a field that didn't even have grass. We went to that metropolitan area and pulled him out of there mainly because of Eric Kresser and Chad Pennington. He saw them on TV and liked our offense. We gave him a chance to be a quarterback and do the things he wanted to do."

Among the others who were short on the recruiting yardstick in one area or another, but wound up getting paid to play after leaving Marshall, were Steve Sciullo, James Williams, Girardie Mercer and Jason Starkey.

"There were a lot of guys like that who came in and played well for us," Pruett said. "All they needed was a chance. (Starkey) made himself a player. He was undersized, but he was big-hearted. A lot of them were like that."

That kind of recruiting during the 1996 season helped ease the transition to 1997 and the first I-A season. Although it lost a host of talent from its '96 team, the Herd had the most dangerous player in the game in Moss. Pennington returned at quarterback, 30 muscular pounds heavier and a year wiser, having benefited from watching Kresser, who now was with the Cincinnati Bengals.

"I was a lot stronger than I had been," Pennington recalled. "It wasn't so much arm strength as it was everything else, my core, my legs, my back. I could tell the difference."

Said Salvatore of Pruett convincing Pennington to sit a year: "A master stroke of genius. That was the move that allowed (Pruett) to set his foundation."

While winning the MAC was Marshall's goal, Herd fans were squarely focused on West Virginia. The teams had not met on the football field since 1923 when WVU had won 81-0. The teams' basketball rivalry was strong, but paled in comparison to the buzz surrounding their first football game in 74 years. WVU had resisted playing Marshall, seeing nothing to gain. Marshall, obviously with more to gain, had pressed for a game since the mid-1980s, pointing to the financial boost of keeping money in the state, rather than playing an opponent from outside the borders. On August 30, the game became a reality as a crowd of more than 60,000 — more than 50,000 sporting WVU's blue and gold — packed Mountaineer Field.

From the outset, Marshall's I-A debut had the look of disaster. The Mountaineers scored on a blocked punt and added two more quick touchdowns for a 21-0 lead. WVU extended the margin to 28-3 and some of its fans were calling for coach Don Nehlen to run up the score.

"Their players were faster and stronger than what we'd faced before," Marshall linebacker Andre O'Neal said.

Safety Rogers Beckett went a step further. "It definitely was a step up," he said. "What I took from that game was that I needed to get bigger and stronger to compete at that level. In that, it was good for us. It opened our eyes."

Marshall opened some eyes, too. WVU leveled off and the Herd rallied hard. Pennington threw two touchdown passes to Moss and with 12 minutes left in the game, Marshall had a stunning 31-28 lead. Mountaineer Field was eerily silent except for a corner of green-and-white-clad fans who were ecstatic. Not only did Marshall have the lead, it had the ball. But without Chapman, who was injured in the pre-game warmups, the Herd opted to throw rather than try to use the clock via the running game. Pennington was intercepted twice deep in his own territory and WVU converted the turnovers into touchdowns for a 42-31 victory.

In the end, WVU had saved face and Marshall had proven it belonged in I-A. "Our goal was to win the game," Pruett said. "I wasn't happy that we played them tough. It did show, though, that we could compete. It was a good measuring stick for us."

Just competing, though, wasn't good enough for Pruett. Marshall was accustomed to winning and win it did a week later at Army. The Herd's big-play offense overcame the Cadets' grinding wishbone rushing attack as Marshall won 35-25. Moss made national highlight reels that ran all season for his tremendous 90-yard touchdown reception. Pennington hit Moss with a slip screen, and the lanky receiver then eluded one defender, hurdled another and stiff-armed a third before sprinting into the end zone. NFL scouts at the game were awestruck by Moss' performance.

Marshall was 1-1 entering its third straight road game, the MAC opener at Kent State. While the Golden Flashes hadn't been a league power since the early 1970s, their fans gave MU a rowdy welcome, taunting the Herd during warmups with "this isn't I-AA." Marshall muffed the opening kickoff and fell on the ball at its own 7-yard line as Kent fans erupted and a charged-up Golden Flashes defense took the field.

The elation didn't last long. On the first play from scrimmage, Pennington faked the slip screen to Moss — the same play that had been replayed hundreds of times on national TV all week — and Kent's defense bit hard. Defenders rushed toward Moss, leaving wide receiver Lavorn Colclough running wide open down the sideline, 10 yards behind the nearest defender. Pennington lofted a pass to Colclough for a 93-yard touchdown and all the air went out of Kent's team and fans as Marshall rolled to a 42-17 statement-making victory.

The Herd was dominant a week later in its home opener, routing old I-AA foe Western Illinois 48-7 before hitting the road again at defending MAC champion Ball State. The Cardinals mysteriously single-covered Moss throughout the game and the result was five touchdown receptions and a two-point conversion. Pennington threw a school-record six TD passes as Marshall won 42-16. The Herd then dispensed of Akron, 52-17, at home before heading to Oxford, Ohio, for a key showdown with Miami.

The Redhawks had been tabbed as the East Division favorite, just ahead of Marshall, in the preseason. Veteran Herd fans had more disdain for Miami than for any other team. They remembered the 66-6 beating Miami gave the Young Thundering Herd in 1971 and were eager to take on the Redhawks with a high-powered team led by Moss and Pennington. Herd fans left disappointed as Miami broke from a 21-21 halftime tie for a 45-21 romp behind 203 rushing yards and four touchdowns from running back Travis Prentice.

The victory put Miami in the driver's seat in the East Division. For Marshall to win the division title and advance to the MAC championship game, the Herd had to win the rest of its games and the Redhawks had to lose twice. "I told our guys we couldn't control what Miami did," Pruett recalled. "We just had to take care of our own business."

The Herd bounced back a week later to defeat Eastern Michigan 48-25 as Pennington out-performed future NFL starter Charlie Batch in a matchup of two of the nation's premier quarterbacks. The Herd followed with a 45-17 victory at Central Michigan and returned home to blank Bowling Green 28-0. Miami, meanwhile, had been upset twice, giving the Herd the break it needed. All that stood in Marshall's way of a division title was a home game with Ohio, a team with one of the nation's better running attacks and an innate ability to overachieve, especially against Marshall.

MU played like a champion against the Bobcats, whose option attack befuddled many teams but not Marshall. Herd veterans had seen the option annually against its old Southern Conference opponents and already had disposed of it earlier this season against Army. Marshall limited Ohio to one first down in a 27-0 victory in the cold and rain as Moss caught an NCAA single-season record-tying 22nd touchdown pass.

Marshall took a 9-2 record into the MAC title game against West Division champion Toledo. At stake was a berth in the new Motor City Bowl in Pontiac, Michigan. Marshall was confident, at home and was favored, but Toledo was formidable. Coach Gary Pinkel, now the coach at Missouri, was highly regarded and the Rockets had beaten Miami, something the Herd hadn't done.

Snow covered the field by kickoff and neither team adapted well as Toledo took a 7-3 halftime lead. Rockets cornerback Clarence Love, who went on to play for the Philadelphia Eagles, had kept Moss out of the end zone. At halftime, Pruett made two key decisions. One was to challenge Love more often and throw to Moss at nearly every opportunity. The other was for his players to change shoes to something better suited for the snow.

The plan paid off as Pennington hit Moss with three touchdown passes in the second half and the Herd rolled to a 34-14 victory. Marshall was the champion of the league that had expelled it nearly 30 years earlier and Herd fans felt redeemed. Marshall was headed to the inaugural Motor City Bowl to take on Mississippi from the Southeastern Conference. The bowl was the Herd's first since the 1948 Tangerine Bowl, a 7-0 loss to Catawba. But first there was other business with which to attend. Marshall had campaigned hard for Moss' Heisman Trophy candidacy, drawing early season guffaws from some who couldn't believe a team in its first season of I-A football, playing in a lower-tier I-A conference, would be so brash.

Moss, who had won the Biletnikoff Award as the nation's best wide receiver, earned his trip to New York City. His 2,178 all-purpose yards ranked third in the nation and his 25 touchdowns nearly doubled the MAC previous single-season record set by Kent State's Eugene Baker. On December 13, Moss joined Michigan cornerback Charles Woodson, Tennessee quarterback Peyton Manning and Washington State quarterback Ryan Leaf at the Downtown Athletic Club in New York. Woodson won the Heisman and Moss finished fourth.

Mississippi (7-4) presented a monumental challenge for Marshall in the bowl game. The Rebels featured running backs John Avery and Deuce McAllister, both future NFL players. Quarterback Stewart Patridge was a veteran and personable Tommy Tuberville, now the coach at Auburn, was then an up-and-coming star. Patridge opened the game with a 44-yard pass to Grant Heard and Avery followed with a 1-yard touchdown plunge. A mere 24 seconds into the game, Ole Miss led 7-0.

The lead was shortlived as Marshall took the ball at its own 20 and a sharp-eyed Pennington spotted a single defensive back covering Moss. Pennington audibled at the line of scrimmage and hit Moss in stride with an 80-yard touchdown pass to tie the game. "Their cornerback was the SEC sprint champion and Ole Miss thought he could stay with Randy," Pruett remembered. "Randy ran by him like he wasn't even there."

The Rebels adjusted, double-covering Moss the rest of the game, and neutralized him fairly well. Pennington, though, frequently threw to Colclough and Nate Poole, another future NFL player, and finished with 337 yards. Chapman ran for another 153 yards, but in the end it wasn't enough. Ole Miss wore down the Herd in the dry heat of the Silverdome, and McAllister scored with 31 seconds left to give the Rebels a 34-31 victory.

As with the WVU loss, Pruett wasn't content. "We play for championships and this is the first one we didn't win since we've been here," Pruett said.

The loss whetted the players' appetites for more. "We really didn't believe in moral victories," Pennington said. "After the Ole Miss game, we came together and decided we weren't going to settle for anything less than winning. Getting close wasn't good enough. That game changed our mindset of how we approached everything."

While the season didn't end the way Pruett had hoped, Marshall had much with which to be pleased. The 10-3 record was the best ever by a first-year team in Division I-A. A conference championship was in hand, respect had been gained from the close contest at

WVU and Moss had brought the Herd unprecedented national attention. Marshall's initial season of I-A football was a success and a springboard to the future.

Marshall faced the 1998 season without Moss, who had left early and was a first-round draft choice of the Minnesota Vikings, but returned nearly everyone else. The Herd was the preseason favorite in the MAC, having convinced the doubters. Marshall wasn't a team to rest on the polls, however.

The season-opener was a conference game at Akron. There was no room for error and despite a less-than-dominant performance the Herd won 27-16. Marshall followed with a 42-12 victory over Troy State in the home opener, setting up a much-anticipated game at SEC member South Carolina. A crowd of 78,717, at that time the largest ever to see the Herd play, showed up at Williams-Brice Stadium.

South Carolina had opened with a win against MAC member Ball State, but Marshall wasn't the Cardinals. Still, the Gamecocks led 10-7 at halftime, thanks to a stingy Herd defense that twice stopped South Carolina inside the MU 10-yard line. Pennington hit tight end Brad Hammon early in the third quarter to give Marshall a 14-10 lead. On its next possession, the Herd stunned the Gamecocks by running a trick play Pruett called the "fumblerooskie" from the South Carolina 7. Pennington took the snap and reached between his legs to hand Chapman the football. Pennington rolled right and most of the defense followed him as Chapman raced left untouched into the end zone for a 21-10 lead.

"We liked the psychological effects of that play," Pruett said. "It gave us a big lift and it left their crowd grumbling because it made them look bad."

South Carolina rallied to tie the game 21-21 and had the ball with four minutes left, but cornerback Danny Derricott, lining up in the wrong coverage, intercepted quarterback Anthony Wright at midfield and returned the ball 32 yards. Two plays later, Billy Malashevich kicked a 32-yard field goal as time expired to give the Herd the victory, inciting an eruption of "We Are … Marshall" from the 3,000 or so MU fans in the stands. "We didn't feel like it was an upset," said Mercer, a defensive tackle. "We felt all along that we were the better team. It didn't surprise us at all that we won that game."

A week later, Marshall suffered a letdown at Eastern Michigan, but still won 26-23 after another late interception by Derricott set up another winning field goal by Malashevich. The Herd was 4-0 entering its home game with Miami. As it was in '97, this game would determine the leader of the East Division. Miami had an excellent team that featured Prentice, one of the country's better backs, but he managed only 84 yards as the Herd cruised 31-17.

The win spurred Marshall to three more easy wins that put it at 8-0 and at the doorstep of the Top 25 rankings. The Herd never made it inside, however, as charged-up Bowling Green pulled off a 34-13 shocker at home. "That's what I was talking about when I said we have to play with emotion to win," Pruett said. "We didn't for whatever reason that day and Bowling Green just beat us."

The loss was an attention-getter. Marshall bounced back with a 28-0 shutout of Central Michigan to clinch the East title, but lapsed again a week later in the regular-season finale at home against I-AA Wofford. The Herd pulled its starters after taking a 29-7 lead, but the Terriers' option-oriented offense took a toll on the reserves and with three minutes left in the game, Wofford lined up for a 29-yard field goal that could hand it the lead. Derricott, however, saved the day again, blocking the kick to preserve the victory. Derricott, who by then had earned the nickname "Lucky Charms," wasn't supposed to rush from his corner spot on the field but raced in to block the kick.

Marshall was 10-1 heading into the MAC Championship Game Dec. 4, again at Marshall Stadium. Again, the opponent was Toledo. The Herd scored early when holder Chris Hanson raced into the end zone off a fake field goal, but Toledo came back to lead 7-6 in the second quarter. It was then that the unthinkable happened. Pennington suffered a groin injury and left the game. He was replaced by Leftwich, then a seldom-used freshman who immediately threw an interception. The play wasn't by any means an indication of the stellar career that Leftwich would have, but it disheartened Herd fans and fired up the Rockets, who pushed their lead to 10-6.

Pennington returned to the game limping badly and it inspired the Herd. He promptly threw a 19-yard touchdown pass to Poole for a 13-10 lead. Derricott then returned a fumble 20 yards for a touchdown as the Herd took a 23-17 victory, sending it back to the Motor City Bowl to play Conference USA representative Louisville.

If Pruett learned anything from Marshall's loss to Ole Miss, it was that his team had to be in better condition. The Herd practiced inside its turf room, cranking up the heat to simulate conditions of the Silverdome. The players hated it. "I thought I was going to die," MU safety Larry Davis said. "But when game time came, we were ready."

The Motor City Bowl was billed as a battle of two high-powered offenses led by star quarterbacks, Louisville's Chris Redman and Marshall's Pennington. The teams battled to a 21-21 halftime tie. In the third quarter, Marshall's extra conditioning kicked in as the Herd scored on eight of its final 10 possessions for a 48-29 win that capped a 12-1 season and a spot in the final Top 25 poll.

The second half turnaround would become a Marshall trademark under Pruett. Time and again throughout his tenure, Marshall held a slim lead at halftime, or even trailed an opponent, only to win the game in a walk courtesy of a big second half. While halftime adjustments did play a role in the second-half successes, their ground work actually was laid in the game's opening minutes.

"One of the things we felt we had to do early in every ballgame was to run different motions and formations and show (opponents) different looks on defense," Pruett related. "We wanted to see what their adjustments to those were going to be and at halftime we had to adjust to that. Not only were we running plays to gain yards and score touchdowns, we wer also exploring the other team's defense and offense to see how they had prepared and how they were going to react.

"We started those adjustments in the first 10 or 15 plays of the game."

With virtually everyone returning from the 1998 team that finished the season in a flourish, Pruett knew 1999 could be exceptional. Marshall was a preseason Top 25 team and expectations hadn't been that high since 1996. "We knew we had a chance to be really special," Pennington recalled. "We talked about that a lot. We worked hard the summer before the 1999 season and we knew we had a chance to be very, very good."

Marshall discovered just how good in the opener at Clemson's Memorial Stadium. The Herd entered the game with supreme confidence, so much so that when the Tigers made their traditional trek from the locker room to touch "Howard's Rock," then sprinted down the slope to the playing field to the cheers of adoring fans, Marshall already was waiting for them at the 40-yard line. Herd players waved for Clemson to come down the hill, challenging them on their own turf.

"That was the kind of atmosphere we thrived in," Pennington said. "We weren't going to be intimidated."

The game was close throughout, but Clemson scored with seven minutes left to take a 10-6 lead. Marshall, unfazed, drove the length of the field as Pennington went 6 for 6 passing and Chapman followed a crushing block by left tackle Mike Guilliams into the end zone to give the Herd a 13-10 victory. Thanks to three questionable penalties that infuriated the Marshall staff, the Herd had to cover 118 yards to score the winning touchdown.

Unlike the previous season where the Herd was subject to letdowns after big victories, the '99 Herd was relentless in its pursuit of excellence. Marshall was virtually unchallenged in winning its next seven games by a combined score of 302-58. Included in that streak was a 38-13 victory over Toledo on Oct. 14. "Marshall was the best team I'd seen in the MAC in a decade, maybe ever," Pinkel later said.

Although the scores weren't quite so lopsided, Marshall cruised past Kent State and Western Michigan for a 10-0 record before completing the unbeaten regular season with a 34-3 rout of Ohio in the Battle for the Bell. The Bobcats gave the Herd a scare, if only briefly. Ohio led 3-0 in the second quarter before Marshall cranked up its offense and blew to another easy victory. During the game, it was announced that Pennington had been invited to the Heisman Trophy ceremony.

Marshall again was in the MAC Championship Game on December 3 and again at home. The opponent this time was Western Michigan. Marshall had dominated Western in the season's first meeting, but the Broncos drastically altered their strategy for the title game. The previously pass-oriented Western Division champions used a pounding running attack to wear down the defense. The change caught Marshall off guard and earned the Broncos a stunning 20-0 halftime cushion. The lead hit 23-0 early in the third quarter, but Pennington said the Herd never stopped believing it could rally.

Pennington got Marshall on the board with a 38-yard touchdown pass to Poole. Chapman followed with a 24-yard touchdown run to make it 23-14, getting the crowd back into the game. Cornerback Maurice Hines then intercepted a pass to set up a Pennington-to-Williams scoring pass and Marshall was within 23-20 with momentum on its side. When Chapman scored on a 2-yard run with 12:36 left, the crowd went wild. Marshall had come all the way back. Western, though, didn't fold, scoring with 7:20 left for a 30-27 lead.

Marshall got the ball back on its own 25-yard line with 3:13 remaining and the entire season at stake. The MAC had just one bowl tie-in, meaning that if Marshall lost this game it would stay home despite being 11-0 in the regular season. Facing fourth-and-6 from its 29 with 1:10 left, the Herd was one play away from seeing its dream season end dismally. But Pennington hit Williams for nine yards and a first down. One play later, Pennington scrambled for 33 yards. A late hit on the tackle added another 15 yards giving Marshall a first down at the Western 14 with 51 seconds left.

Chapman carried twice to the 6 and Pennington completed a pass to Williams at the 1. Pennington spiked the football to stop the clock, then was stopped cold on a quarterback sneak. The Herd called its final timeout with seven seconds left. Pruett called for a third-down pass, instructing Pennington to throw the ball away if the play wasn't open.

Pennington took the snap and rolled right before firing a pass to tight end Eric Pinkerton, who was wide open in the flat in the end zone. Pinkerton, better known as a power-hitting first baseman with the Herd baseball team, cradled the ball for the touchdown, the first of his college career. The improbable comeback was complete and the Herd was headed to the Motor City Bowl for a third straight season. "If that's not a Heisman candidate, I don't know what is," Pruett said of Pennington after the game.

Pennington was a Heisman finalist indeed. He joined Wisconsin running back Ron Dayne, the eventual winner, Purdue quarterback Drew Brees, Georgia Tech quarterback Joe Hamilton and Virginia Tech quarterback Michael Vick at the award ceremony. Pennington finished fifth in the voting, but as Moss had done, went on to show that he deserved to have placed much higher.

Marshall, meanwhile, was teamed against No. 25 Brigham Young University in the Motor City Bowl. The thought of coach Lavelle Edwards' pass-happy Cougars taking on Pennington and Pruett's Herd was inviting. Heralded BYU jumped to a 3-0 lead, but could get nothing else. Marshall recorded eight sacks on a trio of Cougars' quarterbacks and caused errant throws on a dozen passes with relentless pressure on the way to a surprising 21-3 decision. It was the first time BYU had been held without a touchdown in a game since 1974.

The Herd seniors left the field in unison, joining hands triumphantly after completing a 13-0 season and a 50-4 overall record in four years. Marshall ranked 10th in the final polls. Pennington, Beckett, Chapman and Williams all were chosen in the 2003 NFL Draft.

The 2000 season didn't hold as much promise as had 1999 or even '98, but Pruett wasn't about to let his team think it couldn't carry on the tradition. Still, replacing Pennington was an incredibly daunting chore, and the coach turned to the strong-armed Leftwich. Fans remembered Leftwich's bungling interception against Toledo, and had no idea the true caliber of player they had. When Pruett predicted Leftwich would break Pennington's records, fans viewed that as gentlemanly hyperbole.

Leftwich made his debut August 31 against Southeast Missouri State, coached by former MU defensive coordinator Tim Billings. Leftwich wasn't Pennington, but wasn't bad. He sat out most of the second half of a 63-7 rout after completing 13 of 25 passes for 205 yards. Game two of that season posed a more serious challenge. The Herd visited Big Ten power Michigan State.

"I remember thinking, 'Why do we have to go play Michigan State the year after we lost all those guys?' " Leftwich recalled. "That's the way it goes, though."

Marshall played the Spartans tough but couldn't stop bruising runner T.J. Duckett and fell 34-24. The Herd faced another road challenge a week later at ACC member North Carolina. Marshall led 9-6 at halftime but lost 20-15 to drop to 1-2 for the first time since 1987. The Herd righted itself in its MAC opener, drilling Buffalo 47-14 to set up a Thursday night rematch on ESPN with Western Michigan in Huntington. The Broncos still were stinging from the devastating collapse in the previous MAC Championship Game, came in inspired and cruised to a 30-10 win to end the Herd's 33-game home winning streak.

The season hit bottom nine days later in a 42-0 pasting at Toledo. With four losses in its first six games for the first time since 1983, the Herd was reeling with no end in sight. Not only did a conference championship appear out of reach, a winning season was in great doubt.

After the Toledo loss, Pruett gathered his team and offered a speech that would make or break their season. He handed each player a rubber band and then showed them how easily a single rubber band could be snapped. Pruett then platted several rubber bands together and showed how strong they were.

The coach also handed out flashlights, then turned out the lights in the team's turf room. He turned on one light that hardly made a difference. Pruett then asked his players to turn on their lights. The room brightened considerably.

"I told them if we banded together like that, we could be a good football team," Pruett remembered. "I knew we had the kind of team that could fight through adversity and could be a good team. They just needed to know it, too."

The message took root as the Herd responded with wins against Kent State and at Akron and at Bowling Green. Leftwich threw a late touchdown pass against Akron for a 31-28 win while Hines returned a punt for the game-sealing 20-13 win against Bowling Green. Now, the Herd was 5-4 entering its final two games. More important, though, winning just one of those games would give Marshall another East Division title.

Marshall had its confidence back as Miami rolled into town. The RedHawks were no match for the Herd, who won 51-31 to clinch the division championship. As improbable as it had seemed just a month earlier, Marshall was champion again and still the only team ever to win the MAC East crown.

The Herd went to Ohio for its season finale. With a victory, rumor had it, Marshall would be invited to play in the Citrus Bowl or some bowl other than the Motor City, which desired a new team from the MAC. Marshall, though, fell flat in Athens, losing 38-28. Still, the Herd was in the league Championship Game, again against Western Michigan and again in Huntington. This time, though, the MAC set up things so that Marshall officially would be the visiting team, dressing in the visitor's locker room, wearing white rather than green and working from the opposite sideline.

Marshall took a 13-0 halftime lead against the stunned Broncos, who had been so dominant against MU in the regular season. Veteran Western, however, pulled into a 14-13 lead early in the fourth quarter. But with six minutes left, Leftwich finished off a scoring drive with a touchdown pass for a 19-14 victory. Astonishingly, Marshall had rebounded from a 2-4 start and combined 72-10 losses to Toledo and Western Michigan to emerge as MAC champion a record fourth straight time and accept another Motor City bid to play Conference USA runner-up Cincinnati. The Bearcats were on a roll, having won five of their final six games, including a 30-point pounding of Miami (Ohio). Cincinnati, though, posed little problem for Leftwich and Marshall, which altered its defensive scheme and convincingly won 25-14 to finish the season 8-5.

Pruett viewed the 2001 season as having the potential to be special. Leftwich was a junior and the Herd was loaded with talent from its 2000 conference championship team. Several players had matured and developed as leaders. Just how much they had developed would be tested out of the gate.

Marshall opened the season at Florida. Marshall had faced some high-profile teams — Clemson, North Carolina, Michigan State, BYU and others — but none like Florida, which was the top-ranked team in the country in preseason. The game was no contest from the outset. Florida led 35-0 at halftime and rolled to a 49-14 victory in The Swamp.

Division I-AA Massachusetts posed a more reasonable challenge in the Herd's home opener, which Marshall won 49-20. MU then opened MAC play with a 37-31 victory against Bowling Green before the defense began to come around in a 37-15 win at Northern Illinois.

The Herd improved to 4-1 with a 34-14 win at Buffalo, then beat Central Michigan 50-33 and Akron 42-21.

Still, Pruett was concerned about his defense, which had given up 213 points in seven games. The defense was troubling again a week later in a 42-21 win over Kent State, leaving the coach to wonder if his team had enough to stop Miami on Nov. 10 in Oxford. To Pruett's delight, the defense was solid in a 27-21 Marshall victory and again a week later in a 42-18 pounding of Ohio. The victory over the Bobcats gave Marshall its fifth straight MAC East title, as well as its ninth straight victory. A season-ending 38-24 victory over tougher-than-expected Youngstown State left the Herd with a 10-1 record entering the MAC title game.

The MAC had changed its policy on the league championship game, opting to alternate it between the home of the division champions. That meant the Herd would travel to West winner Toledo. Marshall came out as strong as in any game all season. The Herd was ahead 20-0 and had the ball at the Toledo 1 when Leftwich misread a signal from the sideline. Instead of running a quarterback sneak, Leftwich called a play-action pass. The play didn't work and Marshall settled for a field goal and a seemingly comfortable 23-0 lead. The Rockets, though, bounced back, pulling within 23-10 by halftime.

Toledo roared out in the third quarter, scoring on its first four possessions, including on a beautifully executed fake field goal, for a 35-29 lead. With 12 minutes left, Leftwich hit Denero Marriott for the duo's fourth touchdown of the night to give the Herd a 36-35 lead. Toledo took a 41-36 lead before Marshall drove deep into the Rockets' territory. The potential game-winning drive stalled as Leftwich slipped when he planted to throw a pass to Josh Davis, who was open in the end zone. The ball sailed out of Davis' reach and Toledo won to end Marshall's reign as MAC champion.

The MAC, though, had secured an extra bowl bid this season and it was predetermined that regardless of the outcome of the MAC title game, Toledo was going to the Motor City Bowl and Marshall was headed to the GMAC Bowl in Mobile, Alabama, to face East Carolina. The matchup had a built-in story line. East Carolina, of course, was the last team Marshall had played prior to the 1970 plane crash. The schools had met just once since — in 1978 when the Pirates won 45-0.

Marshall, a school known for pulling off the unexpected and improbable, couldn't even imagine what was about to take place at Ladd Peebles Stadium. No one could. The

Herd hadn't completely shaken the loss at Toledo, feeling it had that game won and let it get away. In Mobile, East Carolina took advantage of Marshall's cobwebs and raced to a seemingly insurmountable 38-8 halftime lead, shocking fans on both sides of the stadium.

Hundreds of green-clad fans streamed from the stadium at halftime on the uncharacterstically chilly night while those in purple and gold celebrated. Those who left the stadium, or turned the TV or radio off from their homes, couldn't have dreamed what they missed. In the locker room, Pruett turned over a table full of cups filled with Gatorade, getting his team's attention. The last thing Pruett wanted was for his team to quit.

"You see that in bowl games a lot of times," he said. "A team gets behind and some guys start thinking about what they're going to do in the offseason. Or the seniors think about graduating. That kind of stuff. I didn't want that to happen, here."

It didn't happen, but Pruett knew it was going to take more than just a strong effort to get back in the game. Marshall had to make some big plays on defense or in the kicking game. Leftwich was confident despite the deficit. "We were only down 30 points," he said. "We knew we could score that much in a quarter."

Marshall got the defensive break it needed early in the third quarter when defensive end Ralph Street intercepted a David Garrard pass in the flat and returned it for a touchdown. The Herd offense chipped in a 9-yard scoring run from Leftwich to make it 38-22, then cornerback Terence Tarpley ran back another interception 25 yards for a score. When the third quarter ended, the Herd had cut East Carolina's lead to 41-36 and suddenly, this was anybody's game.

The Pirates added a field goal before Leftwich and Marriott teamed on a 30-yard scoring pass to pull the Herd within 44-42. East Carolina scored a touchdown and Marshall added a Curtis Head field goal to make it 51-45. Marshall then put together a drive for the ages. With no timeouts left and starting on its own 20, Marshall drove to the ECU 11 before Leftwich rifled a pass to the corner of the end zone. Darius Watts, another future NFL player, leaped above the defender, twisted in mid-air and hauled it in to tie the game at 51-51. The Herd was a mere extra point away from the most incredible comeback in bowl history. Head, though, amazingly missed the conversion to bring on overtime.

Butchie Wallace's 2-yard touchdown run in overtime gave Marshall its first lead of the night, 58-51, but the Pirates' Leonard Henry answered with a 25-yard scoring run for a second overtime. The Herd defense stiffened, holding ECU to a 37-yard field goal that gave the Pirates a 61-58 lead. Marshall, though, went to a familiar play — double-slant manbeater — the same pattern Davis had run against Toledo when Leftwich slipped and missed him in the final seconds.

This time, Leftwich didn't miss. He hit Davis from eight yards and flags flew. The penalty, though, was against East Carolina and the touchdown stood, giving Marshall an amazing 64-61 double-overtime victory. ESPN dubbed the game an "instant classic" and has replayed it dozens of times in following seasons. Leftwich finished with 576 yards passing in what remains the highest-scoring bowl game in history.

In 2002, Leftwich played well enough to become the Herd's third Heisman hopeful in six seasons. The big quarterback finished sixth in the Heisman balloting and finished his college career in style. His gritty performance in a rare loss to Akron, when he played much of the game with a fractured leg, caught the attention of the nation. Rarely since then has a televised feature story on Leftwich been told without accompanying video of his Marshall teammates carrying the hobbled quarterback to the line of scrimmage after each play.

Leftwich topped 10,000 career yards passing in leading Marshall to a 9-2 regular-season record and the East Division championship. Marshall faced Toledo at Marshall Stadium in the MAC Championship game. The Rockets were the thorn in Leftwich's flesh. He had lost twice to them since throwing an interception in relief of Pennington in 1998. This time, though, Leftwich came away with a victory, hitting Watts with the winning touchdown pass with less than one minute to play in a 49-45 triumph.

The quarterback's final game with the Herd was memorable as he threw four touchdown passes in a dominating 38-15 victory against Louisville in the GMAC Bowl. The game was a showcase for NFL scouts and Leftwich was selected by the Jacksonville Jaguars in the first round of the 2003 draft.

The following season presented a new set of challenges. Not only was Leftwich gone, the Herd faced a rugged schedule that included games at Tennessee and Kansas State, both Top 20 teams. Marshall was 1-0 when it went to Tennessee, where a crowd of 106,520 watched the gritty Herd fall 34-24. The Herd followed with a 24-17 loss to Toledo before heading to sixth-ranked Kansas State where backup quarterback Graham Gochneaur, subbing for injured Stan Hill, hit tight end Jason Rader with three minutes left to give Marshall a 27-20 upset, its first against a nationally ranked opponent.

"If you go back and look at the big wins Marshall football has, that one ranks right up there behind the Xavier victory after the airplane tragedy," Pruett said.

Marshall went on to an 8-4 record, but fell to Ben Roethlisberger and Miami in the East Division title chase. The Herd failed to receive a bowl bid for the first time since moving to NCAA Division I-A and was without a postseason game for the first time since 1990.

Marshall's 2004 season brought more challenges. After a surprising season-opening loss to Troy, the Herd faced road games with Ohio State and Georgia. Marshall played both powers tough. The Buckeyes needed a 55-yard Mike Nugent field goal on the last play of the game to beat Marshall, while the Bulldogs won only 13-3 in Athens.

The Herd rebounded from the 0-3 start to finish the regular season 6-5. That was good enough for a berth in the Fort Worth Bowl, where Marshall lost to Cincinnati 25-14. No one knew it at the time, but the game was Pruett's last as the Herd's coach. Explaining his decision to retire by saying "it's just time," Pruett left the following spring with a stellar 94-23 record that included a national championship, two undefeated seasons, six conference titles and five bowl victories.

"The problems weren't any more or less than when I got there," Pruett said later, reflecting on his decision. "I felt like some of the things were stagnant in the water, like the new (stadium) turf and weight room and academic support system and salaries for the coaches. We'd sort of come to a standstill."

None of that, however, did anything to diminish Pruett's chance to realize his coaching dream. Despite now being a motivational speaker when he decides to step back from retirement, Pruett still has a hard time verbalizing the most satisfying part of his tenure. He counts returning to coach his alma mater, having three Heisman Trophy finalists at a school the size of Marshall in such a short period of time as well as compiling the best won-loss percentage for the first nine years of a coaching career since Pop Warner as highlights.

"Probably the greatest part of it was running out at that stadium and seeing all those wonderful fans and seeing the joy we brought to southern West Virginia and Huntington," he said. "That's probably the thing that thrills me most.

"It was nine years of glory for the state of West Virginia, the city and everyone involved. This was not my football team. This was Marshall's football team."

Pruett's tenure wasn't without a brush with the NCAA. In December of 2001, Marshall was cited by the NCAA for lack of institutional control for a number of reasons, including violations involving impermissible employment of academic non-qualifiers. The school was placed on probation for four years beginning in 2002 and lost scholarships annually until the probation was lifted in 2006. Many believe the reduction in scholarships played a key role in Pruett's sub-par final season, and the early struggles of his replacement, Mark Snyder.

In hiring Snyder, Marshall held true to its formula of hiring coordinators from major college powers without abandoning its desire for a man with Marshall ties. Snyder, Ohio State's defensive coordinator, was a I-AA all-American safety with the Herd in 1987. "You never want to be the man who follows the man," Snyder said. "But I'm doing just that. Bobby Pruett is the man at Marshall."

Snyder grew up in Ironton, Ohio, and attended Herd games as a youngster. "Carl Lee was his hero," Salvatore said. "He said he never missed a game because he was afraid they might win one and he wouldn't see it. He wanted to be at Marshall some day." After a standout out career at Ironton High, Snyder returned to Marshall as a quarterback following a junior college stop, but wound up in the secondary where he intercepted a single-season school-record 10 passes.

"George told Mark, 'you think like a quarterback,'" Salvatore said when Chaump attempted to sell Snyder on the position change. "He said Mark could recognize the play developing, and with his speed — which was exceptional — could cause all kinds of problems for an offense. George saw Mark as a great defensive back and he was right."

Moving Snyder illustrated the coaching genius of Chaump, whose imprint, along with that of Ohio State's Jim Tressel, is clearly evident on the new Herd coach today.

"The match with Tressel was one made in heaven and set Mark up for this job," Salvatore said. "He's marked by those two great coaches — Chaump and Tressel. He's got a great foundation, but a tough act to follow. People want him to succeed because he's such a good guy."

Snyder's first season with the Herd was difficult. He inherited a young team that gave him a victory over William & Mary in his debut and then came within one play of knocking off Kansas State again. Overall, though, the Herd finished 4-7 for its first losing season since 1983.

Chapter ten

We Are Marshall

"Marshall's plane crash was simply a footnote in sports history for too long. The first game after the crash at Morehead State, no major writers were there. Where were Red Smith and Jim Murray? This was a national story nobody wanted. Back at Fairfield Stadium for the second game, the first home game, it was the same thing. It's a story that's been ignored. The only major writer who took an interest was Ira Berkow of The New York Times. He wasn't here for the game, but he came down after. He's the guy who took an interest in things and would write columns on the anniversary occasionally. How could this be an afterthought? The worst sports-related air tragedy in history and look how far Marshall had come. Oh, you'd get a throw-away reference to it from these guys when they'd come to do games on TV. They'd make mention of it, but never tell the dramatic story of where this school and this town had been, where it was now and how it got here. Now, we say why did you wait so long, but we're glad you're finally here. Then, the concern was Hollywood doing a Hollywood treatment. I was worried about truth and accuracy. This is a story that can stand by itself. There are a few things in the script that are kind of wacky, but the effort is sincere. They've captured the emotional ties this town and region have for Marshall and that's the heart of the story."

— Ernie Salvatore

Marshall University and Huntington, West Virginia, suffered deeply on

---

Matthew Fox, left, and Matthew McConaughey displayed great on-screen chemistry as the holdover assistant coach, who by a twist of fate wasn't on the plane coming home from the game at East Carolina, and the head coach trying to rebuild a program with a rag-tag group of players. (Photo by Rick Haye)

Warner Brothers invited members of the Tri-State Area of West Virginia, Ohio and Kentucky and Marshall community from around the country with a personal connection to the 1970 plane crash to be a part of the filming for the Memorial Fountain scene. Each year on the anniversary of the crash, a memorial to the crash victims is held at the fountain on the plaza outside Marshall's Memorial Student Center that concludes with the fountain being turned off until Spring. (Photo by Rick Haye)

November 14, 1970, when a chartered flight returning the Thundering Herd football team and supporters home from a game at East Carolina University in Greenville, North Carolina, crashed. All 75 people aboard were killed. Today, a monument at the base of the Memorial Fountain, located in the center of Marshall's campus, clearly describes what happened on that date:

"On this dark, overcast Saturday evening at 7:47 p.m., a chartered DC-9 airliner plunged through the drizzle into a hillside as it approached Tri-State Airport at Huntington, West Virginia, claiming the lives of all 75 aboard. Lost in the fiery crash were thirty-seven members of the Marshall University football team, five of their coaches, seven university staff members, twenty-one faithful supporters and five airplane crew members." And at the bottom, it reads: "They shall live on in the hearts of their families and friends forever."

Since the crash, those heartbreaking words have been repeated countless times in Huntington, a small Ohio River town by many accounts, but West Virginia's second-largest city with roughly 50,000 residents. Most often they coincide with the annual November 14 memorial service at Marshall, when surviving family members travel from near and far to join the locals at the Memorial Fountain, where they clasp hands, bow their heads and pray for the souls of the 75 who perished – and each other. Decades later, they still hurt; they still weep; they still seek peace and answers.

Yet, while the city of Huntington and the university still remember the worst sports-related disaster in history, many people across America aren't aware of the details of the crash. Many people might know, through a conversation here or an article there that the crash occurred, but just as many or more outside West Virginia do not know the incredible story of the recovery that led, ultimately, to Marshall's football success on a national level.

Until a few short years ago, Jamie Linden was one of those people. In the autumn of 2000, Linden was a senior at Florida State University in Tallahassee. A self-proclaimed "big football fan," he came across an article in Florida State's student newspaper about the 30th anniversary of the Marshall crash. Red Dawson, a Marshall assistant coach the year of the crash, had played for Florida State and was among those featured in the article. Dawson had joined the team in Greenville, North Carolina, for the game against East Carolina after a recruiting trip during the week leading up to the game. He continued the trip by car after the game, which saved his life. The story of his survival was newsworthy in Tallahassee and Linden noticed.

Today, in Huntington, hardly a soul, young or old, is without some knowledge of what happened in 1970. But Linden, living hundreds of miles to the south, had never heard of the Marshall crash until he read the article. He was struck by what he had read, and by the magnitude of the tragedy.

"It's built into the fabric of that town," Linden said, "but outside of Huntington it's sort of faded away from public consciousness." After reading the article, he kept thinking about it, over and over. Then just 20 years old, he talked to his parents about the crash and, yes, they knew about it. They had attended Florida State as well, at the same time Red Dawson and his brother, Rhett, were playing for the Seminoles. Linden, a marketing major, recalls sitting down with a notebook and jotting down some notes. "I thought about doing a paper on it … maybe a marketing paper," he said. And that's where his research on the

Matthew Fox, left, and Matthew McConaughey, right, flank the men they play in the movie. Assistant coach Red Dawson, closest to Fox, and Head coach Jack Lengyel, closest to McConaughey. (Photo by Rick Haye)

crash remained until after he graduated from FSU, when he took a trip to the West Coast with four buddies that turned a marketing paper into a major motion picture.

"I graduated in the summer of 2001 with a marketing degree and had no idea what I wanted to do," Linden said. He and his friends thought they would figure it all out in Los Angeles. They saved enough money to stay for only a week or two, but on their first day there they decided to show up at a taping of "The Price is Right."

"Normally, you have to reserve tickets months in advance, but it was a few days after 9/11 so nobody was traveling. We were able to walk right up and they let us in. I got on the show and won five grand," Linden said. "I thought, 'That's a sign, I'm staying.' " Several odd jobs followed, including one as a development assistant at a film production company. "I thought that was really interesting, especially how a story can start out on a page and end

Director McG, right, shows clips of recent movie scenes to West Virginia Gov. Joe Manchin, seated, and State Sen. Bob Plymale during a break in filming on the Marshall campus in April. (Photo by Rick Haye)

up on the screen," he said.

Linden wasn't the only person in California in the early 2000s with an uncommon interest in the Marshall plane crash. Mary Viola, an associate producer with Thunder Road Pictures in Burbank, was hooked as well. A New York native, she had heard her father and uncles talking about it years before, so she, too, did some research. When Viola joined producer Basil Iwanyk at Warner Bros. in September 2003, Iwanyk was thinking seriously about making a movie about the Manchester United football team, which lost eight players in a crash in Munich, West Germany, in 1958.

"I asked Basil to hold off," Viola recalled. "I wanted to pitch the Marshall story. I wanted to find an inspirational sports story and the Marshall story was inspirational, even if it hadn't been sports related. Basil had known about it, but not all the details. I gave him all

Former Marshall basketball player Mark Patton, left, was among a host of former athletes to perform in the movie. Patton, who was the Thundering Herd's leading scorer and rebounder during his senior season in 2005-06, portrays a basketball player who joins the football team after his eligibility in basketball has expired. (Photo by Rick Haye)

I had and we dug and dug. The more we dug, the more he bought into it."

Iwanyk clearly remembers the research. "The more we got into specifics, the more we couldn't believe the details," he said.

Linden, meanwhile, sold a comedy screenplay he'd written to Warner Bros. and got a "blind script deal" to go along with it, which essentially means that Warner Bros. bought a script sight unseen, the plot of which all parties involved would agree upon later. Linden clearly remembers the day the studio bought his screenplay. "March 4, 2004," he said. "Suddenly, I was a working screenwriter. It's all about timing and being lucky." He knew immediately what project he wanted to write for the blind deal, and he dug out those marketing notes he'd written four years before.

"Jamie was obsessed with the Marshall story also," Viola said. "His management told us we had to meet him. We met him and we knew quickly that he was definitely the guy to write the movie." Both Linden and Viola were amazed at all the true-life stories connected with the crash. Dawson's life-saving recruiting trip. A dream that saved lineman Ed Carter's life. The injuries that kept defensive back Nate Ruffin and other players at home. A soccer player-turned-kicker named Blake Smith, whose field goal helped the Young Thundering Herd to an improbable, stunning victory over Xavier in 1971. Of course, some fictitious characters

Director Joseph McGinty Nichol, who is known as McG in Hollywood, was most famous for his work in music videos and the Charlie's Angels films before taking on "We Are Marshall." The 38-year-old native of Kalamazoo, Michigan, quickly connected with the Huntington and Marshall community when he showed up at Marshall's spring game and donated $20,000 for kicking four field goals at halftime. (Photo by Rick Haye)

and creative dialogue would be added for the movie script, but for the most part there was no need to "Hollywood-ize" it. And everyone involved knew it.

Linden, Iwanyk and Viola pitched Warner Bros. the story and the studio agreed to start developing the project. Linden spent the next year-and-a-half turning his notes and research into a 120-page screenplay for "We Are Marshall." The next step was a cross-country phone call — actually, several phone calls.

The first call to Marshall University was hardly original, though it might have seemed a bit untimely. It was late summer 2005 and Iwanyk, at the urging of Viola and with Linden's draft in hand, was attempting to reach H. Keith Spears, vice president for communications and marketing at Marshall, to discuss his plan to make a movie about the Marshall plane crash. "I'd seen an article and I said, 'Let's try to get Keith Spears,' " Viola said. "He was clearly the guy we wanted to reach." Iwanyk left a message that was forwarded to Spears, who had received similar calls in previous years. At first Spears thought little about this latest one. He was involved with numerous time-consuming projects that occur each year before the start of the fall semester. "Frankly, I thought, 'Oh, boy, another one,' " Spears recalled.

Other proposed movies on the crash, though pitched with good intentions, were not

Matthew McConaughey said he knew as soon as he finished reading the script that he wanted to be a part of the movie in the role of Marshall head coach Jack Lengyel. (Photo by Rick Haye)

considered for a number of reasons. Most who called wanted Marshall to help finance their movie, but university officials long before had decided not to put any money into any movie concerning the crash. The logical way to tell this story, most concluded, was in a documentary that Marshall did support financially. "Ashes to Glory," produced by Witek & Novak Inc., in 2000 served that purpose and won rave reviews, awards and a national audience, so why get involved in a movie?

Still, Spears finally connected with and listened to Iwanyk, who explained what he had in mind. It didn't take long for Spears to realize that this proposal was different than previous ones. This one was from a major studio. And, in this case, the proposal was accompanied by Linden's script. "When Basil told me he had a script, I thought that was very significant," Spears said. Never mind that the script was written by a virtual unknown in the screen-writing business. If Warner Bros. was calling, the least Spears could do on Marshall's behalf was listen. He did closely, and with an open, if somewhat doubting, mind. "We felt the documentary did a very good job of describing the intense emotion of what the community had gone through," Spears said. "We didn't think it was necessary to have a movie."

During their first conversation, Iwanyk asked Spears to visit California at the studio's expense to talk with the Warner Bros. executives. "My reaction was no," Spears said. "At no time ever in negotiations or discussions of movies with anyone did I accept any free plane tickets or free rides or free hotel rooms. In fact, I paid for lunches so I wouldn't be beholden to anyone." Still, he and Iwanyk continued to talk by phone. Eventually, Iwanyk and Viola decided to take a cross-country trip of their own — to Huntington.

Iwanyk and Viola made it clear during that late-summer visit that they had been given great encouragement by Warner Bros. to produce the movie, whether Marshall was involved or not. "We knew that it is not imperative that the university be involved with a film about it, especially an historical event like this," Spears said. Warner Bros. could have made the movie without filming one second in Huntington or on Marshall's campus, or even speaking to Marshall. But Warner Bros. wanted Marshall's involvement and input. "We appreciate the fact that they came to us, asking us to be actively involved," Spears said, "and that they were above board about how they wanted to approach this."

To make matters more intriguing, a new twist emerged when another major studio suddenly expressed its desire to do a movie on the crash and sent a producer to Huntington to discuss the idea. That producer and Iwanyk — at different times — were introduced by Spears to the Marshall Board of Governors executive committee, including Chairman Menis Ketchum, Marshall President Stephen J. Kopp and Director of Athletics Bob Marcum, to whom they would explain what they wanted to do. "We asked for them to stay within some wide parameters," Spears said. "One, honor those who were killed on the plane and their survivors; two, respect the citizens of Huntington and West Virginia, and our Appalachian culture; and, three, guard the integrity of the university."

Ketchum had concerns at first as talks between Marshall and the studios began. "Our main concern was whether a movie company would budget enough money to do the movie justice and to get it national attention," he said. "We wanted enough money budgeted so that they could get the right movie stars, and cause a buzz across the country. We wanted to be sure the plane crash story would be told in a light favorable to the crash victims."

Eventually, the executive committee decided to cooperate with Warner Bros. In a previous meeting in California, Warner Bros.' senior management told Spears it would fund the entire project. When the board approved, and Warner Bros. OK'd the project, it was clear that production of the movie was soon to become reality. Spears' doubts began to fade. During the first week of November 2005, he was ecstatic. Those who work closely with him know Spears is happy when he "air dribbles" across the office floor, stops suddenly and exclaims, "Slam dunk!" This was the first of many "slam dunks" to come for Marshall in the next few months when cast, crew and location would be determined.

The project kicked into high gear in the next few weeks, although most of the action

Matthew Fox proved to be a perfect choice to play former Marshall assistant Red Dawson. Fox, who's gained recent acclaim for his role on the TV series "Lost," was able to develop his character after hosting Dawson in Hawaii while filming the TV show before movie filming began. (Photo by Rick Haye)

took place behind the scenes. Producers, directors and actors were hired, and scouting for places to shoot was ongoing on Marshall's campus and in the Huntington community. Through combined efforts of West Virginia Governor Joe Manchin's office, Pam Haynes of the West Virginia Film Office and Marshall, it was agreed that Warner Bros. would spend three weeks in spring 2006 filming in Huntington and on Marshall's campus before heading to Atlanta for the final two months of filming. This was a major accomplishment for the university, city and state.

As the names of the producers, director and writer became public, it was clear that Warner Bros. was hiring what seemed to be a young crew to make this inspirational film that would be shown worldwide. At a meeting with Warner Bros.' senior management, Spears brought up that point. "We wanted to make sure there was someone here with an ample amount of experience, not only in films, but experience in life where they could adequately portray the emotion and the spirit of Marshall University and the emotion that Marshall and the community went through at that time," Spears said. "There was concern that they would have the ability to capture the emotion and the trauma that took place." Senior management, acknowledging Spears' concerns as fair, asked Iwanyk to respond. Iwanyk was 35 years old at the time, Viola 28, Linden 25.

"Basil said, 'Jack Lengyel was in his mid-30s, Red Dawson was 28 and the boys on the plane were 18 through 21,' " Spears said. "He said, 'It is a young person's story and we think we can tell it from a young person's perspective and capture the emotion.' " Iwanyk was struck by all aspects of the story from the beginning. "They got kicked in the face and somehow dusted themselves off and went on," he said of the university, football program and community. "It's reality and you have to soldier through it." Again, Spears was satisfied and his concerns, like his doubts before, faded.

Over the course of time, rumors began to surface about who would star in the movie. The one most often repeated was Matthew McConaughey; "People" magazine's "Sexiest Man Alive," would have a starring role. Warner Bros. remained in touch with Marshall throughout, keeping the university abreast of some of the casting possibilities. They mentioned McConaughey as a prospect, so Spears quietly asked some folks around campus what they knew about him. "It was obvious, especially from the female sector, that Matthew McConaughey would be a good choice," Spears deadpanned.

Even before filmmaker McG, who had directed "Charlie's Angels" and "Charlie's Angels: Full Throttle," was announced on January 27, 2006, as the director of the "Untitled Marshall University Football Project," he was hard at work preparing for the challenge. He actually visited Huntington, unknown to anyone but Spears, with a couple of other people. They hung out at various bars, restaurants and other places and talked to a number of people to get their take on the crash and the ensuing recovery. McG returned to California convinced that a good portion of the film needed to be shot there. "This is a tough little town," he said later. "It's the little town that wouldn't quit."

Warner Bros. and Legendary Pictures turned the McConaughey rumor into reality on the same day it announced McG as the director: McConaughey would play Jack Lengyel, who coached the Young Thundering Herd for four years after the crash. "It's an honor to be stepping into his proverbial shoes," McConaughey said of Lengyel. "What he did was some life-affirming things."

The movie's star power from the big screen wasn't limited to Matthew McConaughey. Veteran character actor David Strathairn, who was nominated for an Academy Award for his portrayal of TV journalist Edward R. Murrow in the 2005 film, "Good Night, and Good Luck," plays Marshall interim president Donald Dedmon. (Photo by Marilyn Testerman-Haye)

McConaughey said he was inspired by the story and, like Linden, just kept thinking about it after reading the script. "Through the game of football, people, a team, a community come together and get back in the proverbial game of life and move on with memory and hope," McConaughey said. "That's what turned me on. It stayed on my mind, I knew I wanted to be a part of it. I'm honored to be a part of it."

Lengyel was among several people who met in Huntington with Iwanyk, Viola and Linden after reading a draft of the script. He was "very pleased" when he first heard the movie was going to be made. "It's a story whose time has come to be told," Lengyel said. "It's not a football story, it's about a community and a university, a community that made a commitment to those that perished in the tragic Marshall plane crash. It's a story about hope, faith, persistence and commitment." Lengyel requested that Linden include his entire coaching staff in the movie and Linden honored his request.

A scene in the movie that the general public and Marshall fans were not aware of is when Lengyel and his coaches take the team to nearby Spring Hill Cemetery where six unidentified players are buried and an obelisk bearing the names of the players, coaches, athletic administrators, staff and fans on its four sides is located. It was a very private ceremony that took place each season before the first game. And only the "Young Thundering Herd" players were present. Lengyel would tell them:

"These are your teammates that have gone on before you. ... Yours is the legacy to rebuild the Marshall football program in their honor. ... We may not have many victories on the fields of play. ... But your reward will be in knowing that you were a part of the foundation of the rebuilding of the football program. ... And you will share in the victories of the future Marshall teams."

Lengyel said he believes that McG, Iwanyk, Viola and Linden are all committed to making a movie that everyone involved will be proud of and will honor those that perished in the crash. He also said he is very impressed with McConaughey and his commitment, dedication and grasp of the Marshall story. "The list of stars in the movie is very impressive, and they and the entire crew have put their heart and soul into the making of the 'We Are Marshall' movie," Lengyel said.

Bos Johnson, news director at WSAZ, Channel 3 in Huntington at the time of the crash, met with Linden in the fall while Linden was researching script edits. Johnson said he was concerned when first hearing that a movie would be made. "I think we all were concerned," he said. "We were afraid something so traumatic and tragic as this could be played for the grisly, horror of it all. This is too deep a tragedy to be played for surface purposes." In early April, on the day a key scene was filmed near the Memorial Fountain at Marshall, Johnson bumped into Linden and simply asked, "How's it going?' Linden smiled and said, "Everything's fine."

"And, from what I can tell, it is," Johnson said.

McG said the story deserves nothing less than total devotion from everyone in the cast and crew. "We want to get this story told properly and represent the community fairly and get the story out to the world," he said. "We think it is a great story of survival and the best side of the human condition. We hope we touch the world.

"This is everything that's right with humanity. This is a snapshot of how you just keep putting one foot in front of the other. You may not feel like it today, you may not understand it today, but tomorrow it's going to coalesce, it's going to come together, and you're going to be thankful that you kept moving forward into the light."

Kopp said he fully expected to see Marshall University projected in a very positive light in the movie. "From what I've witnessed and in discussions with McG, I'm very impressed with the professionalism and sensitivity bordering on reverence that has been shown for the story," he said. Kopp described the making of the movie as "a testament

Anthony Mackie was cast in the role of Nate Ruffin, the Thundering Herd defensive back who missed the trip to East Carolina because of an injury. The senior was then asked in 1971 to blend with new teammates, many of whom were four or five years younger, while also helping the coaching staff keep this new group of players in line. (Photo by Rick Haye)

to many people and an unwavering commitment to a better future. It's a milestone in the life of a proud university and community, and reveals what can happen when we approach life with a positive attitude and expect good things to happen."

At Spears' suggestion, several others close to and familiar with the tragedy read the first draft of the script, then met with Iwanyk, Viola and Linden during their visit to Huntington to offer opinions and suggestions. Some, like Johnson, didn't read the script, but still expressed their opinions and concerns. "People like Keith Morehouse, who lost his father, Gene Morehouse, Marshall's play-by-play announcer; Ernie Salvatore, who covered the story for The Herald-Dispatch; future Marshall president Bob Hayes, who was put in charge of the bodies and handling funeral arrangements; and Sam Clagg, longtime faculty member and former Marshall coach who organized some of the services," Spears said. Allowing so many people to read the script was highly unusual, and special permission had to be granted. "They just don't like to let those things out and I understand that," Spears said. "However, it was important enough that they decided to do it."

As script tweaking continued, so did casting: Matthew Fox from ABC's "Lost" was cast to play Red Dawson; Oscar nominee David Strathairn was chosen to play Marshall's acting president Donald Dedmon; Anthony Mackie from "Million Dollar Baby" was contracted to play Marshall team captain Nate Ruffin; Kate Mara from "Brokeback Mountain" was cast to play a composite character, Marshall's head cheerleader Annie Cantrell; Ian McShane

The film's producers made certain that the action you would expect from a college football game was apparent in "We Are Marshall." The film hired numerous former high school and college players to carry out the movie's on-field scenes with all the realism of a Saturday matchup between two bitter rivals. (Photo by Grant Blankenship)

of "Deadwood" was cast to play Paul Griffin. Joining Iwanyk, who not long before had produced "Firewall," starring Harrison Ford, were Brent O'Connor, also from "Firewall," Thomas Tull and Scott Mednick from "Superman Returns," and Jeanne Allgood.

Excitement in Huntington was reaching a fever pitch. Even before most of the names of the stars were made public, Spears and Marshall University learned just how much interest there was in the movie. After WSAZ, Channel 3, broke the story about the movie shortly before Warner Bros. and Marshall made it official in late January, and reported that thousands of extras likely would be needed, the phones at Marshall lit up.

"The next morning everything was breaking here in Huntington," Spears said. "We knew we were going to have to do something, so we put in a special hotline, mainly so that I could answer my own personal phone. It was that wild. The first night after the hotline was set up, we received over 250 telephone calls. And that stayed consistent. People called

During filming in Huntington, Matthew McConaughey showed up at a Marshall spring practice in the colors of his beloved Texas Longhorns, and Thundering Herd coach Mark Snyder quickly provided green and white attire for the visitor. (Photo by Rick Haye)

because they wanted to be involved in one form or fashion, or to give us a story, or to share with us some event in their life that was associated with this plane crash disaster. They wanted to give us tips on the movie, or to be an actor, or to write a song, or to let us use their old automobile in the movie."

Marshall had three communications people working the phones full time, but it was still difficult to keep pace. So, Jan Fox, Marshall's vice president for information technology, created a Web site, allowing people to submit their information, and a data base. "Over a few weeks, we had over 2,500 people who either left their information on the telephone or on the Web site," Spears said.

On March 1, after a brief, rather impromptu news conference, McG and Iwanyk joined several other members of the production crew at a Marshall's men's basketball game with Central Florida University at Cam Henderson Center, the Thundering Herd's home arena. McG said before the game that how Herd fans performed the call-and-repeat "We Are … Marshall" cheer during that game could determine if the cheer to be used in the movie would be filmed in Huntington or Atlanta. The 4,300 fans, excited by the animated McG, cheered like never before. The "audition" was a success.

Dozens of people signed up at the game to be considered as extras. Two weeks later, an open casting session for extras attracted some 1,500 people to Marshall's Joan C. Edwards Performing Arts Center. Warner Bros. announced that filming in Huntington would begin on April 3 and run for three consecutive weeks. Local extras were called to work. Filming sites, including a home on Oakview Heights in nearby Kenova and a home on Merrill Avenue in Huntington, were selected as coaches' residences. But before it was time to shoot a movie, it was time to party.

With Warner Bros.' cooperation, Marshall originated the idea, Huntington Mayor David Felinton convened a planning committee, and Kindred Communications in Huntington followed through by organizing a block party on Fourth Avenue on Saturday, April 1, to welcome the cast and crew to town. Almost guaranteed that some of the movie's stars would take part, thousands of people jammed into the street, cameras in hand, to get a glimpse. They got what they came for.

The roar in the crowd was deafening when McConaughey, McG, Strathairn and Iwanyk emerged from a news conference inside the historic Keith-Albee Theatre and took the stage. McG, his passion for the

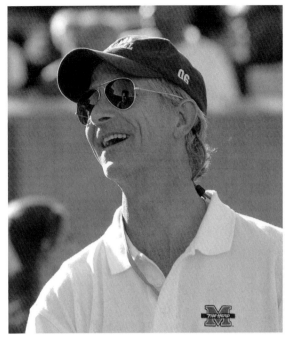

David Strathairn was among the actors who served as honorary coaches for Marshall's spring football game at which some of the movie's crowd scenes were filmed. (Photo by Rick Haye)

project unmistakable, again led the crowd in the "We Are … Marshall" chant. This time the words pierced the air, echoing from building to building up and down the central street in Huntington's downtown business district. McConaughey, too, led an enthusiastic rendition of the popular Marshall cheer.

Preparing sites in Huntington and at Marshall for shooting required many hours of tedious work in advance of the cast and crew arriving. A two-block area on Fourth Avenue in downtown, where the block party took place and some scenes were shot, looked like vintage 1970 once filming began. According to the marquee on the Keith-Albee, the featured attraction at the time was "Kelly's Heroes," starring Clint Eastwood, Telly Savalas and Carroll O'Connor, among others. The ceiling and walls of Marshall's Memorial Student Center were painted an earth-tone yellow, and old furniture replaced new to give the facility a 1970 look. Downtown storefronts were altered, and parking meters were painted gold. Buds were cut from trees on campus and leaves were added to the ground as spring was transformed into autumn.

Rex and Debby Stoler own the home at 2979 Merrill Avenue. But for one day during

Matthew McConaughey and David Strathairn rehearse a scene that appears near the end of the movie in the stands at the stadium on the campus of Morris Brown University. The school's facility, was transformed into Fairfield Stadium, Marshall's home field until the 1990s, for football scenes during filming in and around Atlanta. The transformation even included the scoreboard erected at Fairfield when the stadium was renovated before the 1970 season. (Photo by Claudia Nolte)

the filming of the Marshall movie — which by now was officially titled "We Are Marshall," it was Jack Lengyel's home. The experience was all a little surreal, Debby said, from the time the location scout first knocked on the Stolers' door to the time McConaughey spent about 20 hours in their home. "The best thing is to think that our house will forever be a part of this movie," said Debby, who grew up in the East Huntington neighborhood. "It's kind of like winning the lottery because our big old brick home is similar to all of the other ones in the neighborhood. I guess the house was in the right location."

Rex was on the front porch at 5:30 in the morning anticipating the crew's arrival, and Debby made cookies for the Hollywood guests who basically took over their home. "It was a lot of fun. We really enjoyed it," Rex said. "I really didn't believe it was going to happen until the last minute because it was hush-hush. But it was very exciting and the crew was just fantastic." Rex was a junior and Debby a sophomore at Huntington East High School when the crash occurred, which made their participation in "We Are Marshall" even more special. "The crash was so real to us," Debby said. "We lived through it like everyone in the community. When you're 15 or 16, you don't expect that kind of tragedy."

Huntington learned a lesson in filmmaking during the three-week stay by Warner Bros. McG promised that "a circus" would be coming to town, and that's just what happened. No matter where filming took place, a crowd of curious onlookers — often carrying cameras — gathered.

A couple of hundred Marshall students met near the Campus Christian Center when they heard McConaughey was doing a scene inside. He made their wait worthwhile, appearing for mere seconds after leaving the building around noon and heading to a car that whisked him away to lunch. Inquisitive students watched in amazement and took plenty of pictures, as extras, all dressed in 1970s fashion, made their way across campus to shoot a scene inside the old Morrow Library. Several members of Marshall's Board of Governors and administration took part in a scene they commonly referred to as "the board room scene," which mainly featured Strathairn and Mackie as Dedmon and Ruffin, respectively.

When lots of extras were needed for large crowd scenes, Huntington came through. More than 3,000 people, including many relatives of crash victims and MU football players from the early 1970s, showed up for a touching scene at the Memorial Fountain, and the day before about 1,200 people — mostly students — took part in a scene outside the Morrow Library.

In all, filming took place at more than a dozen sites in the Huntington area. Among them were: the home in Kenova, which was Dawson's residence in the movie; the downtown Frederick Building, where a news conference announcing Lengyel as head coach took place; the Keith-Albee; the Greyhound Bus Station; Steel of West Virginia; the lawn area in front of Old Main's west entrance; the Memorial Fountain; Buskirk Field; the Memorial Student Center; Hodges Hall; Morrow Library; a Twin Towers outdoor basketball court and Joan C. Edwards Stadium, all at Marshall; the Stolers' home; and Spring Hill Cemetery. McG had guaranteed he would treat Huntington as a character in the film, and he did just that. "The town will be treated with the greatest respect," he promised.

The cast and crew departed Huntington for Atlanta late in the afternoon on Saturday, April 22, ecstatic with the first three weeks of filming. But they didn't just exit town quietly.

Their final day in Huntington included a public event at Marshall's Joan C. Edwards Stadium that celebrated the movie and Thundering Herd football in a spectacular way. The featured event was the football team's annual Green-White game that brings spring practice to a close. The game normally attracts anywhere from 5,000 to 10,000 fans, depending on the weather and the star power of the team, but this was no ordinary spring scrimmage. Nor was this an ordinary time in the history of Marshall and Huntington. Nearly 18,000 showed up on a picture-perfect day not only for the scrimmage, but to again shout "We Are … Marshall" for the Warner Bros. cameras and microphones — and to perhaps get a glimpse of some big-time stars one more time. They got more than a glimpse.

Late in the first half of the scrimmage, McG, standing on the field with microphone in hand, once again led the cheer for which the movie is named. Again, this time he had help from McConaughey, who walked the sidelines as a volunteer assistant "coach," and from National Football League stars Randy Moss and Chad Pennington, both former Marshall standouts and Heisman Trophy finalists. The stadium shook with excitement.

The Green-White scrimmage also featured a reunion of Marshall's undefeated, NCAA Division I-AA championship team from 1996. Strathairn also "coached" during the game, but it was McG who brought the fans to their feet by kicking field goals of 20, 25, 30 and 35 yards at halftime. The fans had no idea McG had such a strong, accurate right leg. So, when he promised to donate money to the Marshall athletic department with every made kick, the fans probably had their doubts that MU would receive a penny. The final tally? $20,000.

Clearly, McConaughey was the star most movie fans clamored to see while he was in Huntington. His visits to the local Starbucks and Subway made the local news, as did his spur-of-the-moment race with some "long-legged" middle school students during a workout at the Marshall track. On the set, though, he was all business and always in character. "I challenged McConaughey. I told him, 'I need you to be better than you've ever been in this picture,' " McG said. "And I'm a huge fan of his. This is an incredible responsibility."

As the spring game approached its final seconds, McConaughey bid farewell to the crowd. He waved goodbye, gave the No. 1 sign and sprinted across the field. The "movie circus" had folded its tent and was leaving town, heading to Atlanta where the movie's remaining scenes, including the great victory over Xavier, would be shot.

Again, thousands of extras would be needed, not only to play the parts of football

Tri-State Area residents turned out for casting calls when extras were needed for filming during scenes taken in and around Huntington. They dug deep in their closets to find clothing from the early-1970s for the shoots, and some even came with vehicles from the period. (Photo by Rick Haye)

players for East Carolina, Xavier and — of course — Marshall, but to play coaches and fans. Again, Thundering Herd fans from several states in the Southeast came through. So did non-Herd fans. Even Georgia Governor Sonny Perdue, a walk-on quarterback for the University of Georgia in the 1960s, got in on the act, playing Mike McGee, who was head coach at East Carolina in 1970.

The scenes were almost eerie at Morris Brown College's Herndon Stadium, some would say later, because it looked so much like Fairfield Stadium in Huntington, where the miraculous victory over Xavier took place. Marshall fans wanted so much to be a part of telling the "We Are Marshall" story that they were willing to spend hours in temperatures in the upper 90s on June 10 to relive the game-winning touchdown over Xavier. It was, after all, one of the most incredible upsets in the history of college football, a victory that gave Marshall and all of Huntington hope. Salvatore, in a column dated Sept. 29, 1971, called the victory "the greatest achieved anywhere in any sport."

The long, scorching day in Atlanta started with a tailgate party in a Georgia Dome parking lot, located just a few blocks from Herndon Stadium. Crowd estimates varied, but at least 350 people from all over the south attended the event. Despite the temperatures, it was similar to a fall tailgate at Marshall Stadium, with Herd flags flying and banners waving, and participants wearing their green Marshall attire. Several "special" guests took part, including Lengyel and Dawson, but one of the highlights was a surprise visit from Young Thundering Herd quarterback Reggie Oliver, who had thrown the game-winning touchdown pass to Terry Gardner to defeat Xavier nearly 35 years before. The day, like the final play of the Xavier game re-created later, was a huge success.

Many tears, shed by the Marshall faithful in despair or in celebration, have fallen in Huntington since the victory against Xavier. It took the Thundering Herd 14 years after the plane crash to post a winning season. After that it won Division I-AA national championships in 1992 and 1996, then won five bowl games in six years after moving up to Division I-A. Even with all of the victories and championships on the football field, though, it's the toughness of a community that, having lost 75 people in the tragic plane crash, then seeing its population shrink from 74,000 since, caught the attention of Linden, Iwanyk, McG, McConaughey and everyone else involved in making "We Are Marshall."

"We want to capture the spirit of what it means to be young and alive and how very sad it is for a life to be taken in an untimely fashion," McG said before filming began. "There's no promise of tomorrow. I think this story embodies that better than anything we could ever imagine."

That spirit carries on to this day in Huntington where the city and the beloved Thundering Herd are one; where "We Are Marshall" has deeper meaning than most can even imagine; where 75 people died in the prime of their lives, but not in vain.

"At the end of the day, they win," Iwanyk said softly. "And you can't forget that."

"They win."

Seasons of Grief

The following was excerpted from a story that first appeared in the Chicago Tribune magazine section on Sept. 5, 1999.

I was born with the sound of a railroad whistle in my ears, the mountains at my back and the river at my feet.

That's because I was born in Huntington, West Virginia, and the city was captive to those elements. The coal was scraped out of the mountains, heaped into railroad cars, then loaded onto barges and pushed down the Ohio River. Huntington, named for railroad tycoon Collis P. Huntington, was the place where the railroad met the river.

If you lived along the Ohio River, as we did, you could stand on the bank and marvel at the great, flat coal barges sliding past like dirty black wafers. At night, their searchlights would sweep the riverbank on each side. There was something thrilling about being frisked by light as you stood on the bank, hoping your mother didn't call you inside too soon.

Things are different in Huntington these days. Rail traffic has steadily diminished. In the past three decades, Huntington's population has inched back from about 74,000 to some 50,000.

The river is still there, of course. The river and a memory.

At 7:37 p.m. on Saturday, November 14, 1970, as a cold rain pecked at the ground, a chartered jet smashed into a hillside about two miles west of Huntington's Tri-State Airport, some 30 seconds before it would have landed. Everyone aboard was killed instantly.

The crash site was a horrific mess of broken bodies, twisted plane parts and burned earth, upon which the chilly rain continued to fall, almost as if nature were trying to propagate the spot anew.

Seventy-five people died on that plane, including most members of the Marshall University football team and coaching staff, along with a contingent of Huntington residents who attended most games, home and away. The plane was returning from Greenville, North Carolina, where the Marshall Thundering Herd had lost a close game to East Carolina University.

The victims in what remains the worst sports-related disaster in U.S. history included 37 players, 12 coaches and university staff members, five flight crew members and 21 townspeople. Those deaths left 70 minor children; 18 of those children lost both parents.

Six of the dead young men could not be positively identified; their remains are buried in Huntington's Spring Hill Cemetery.

To have been born and raised in Huntington is to remember the crash, and how the city crumpled beneath the collective weight of its sorrow.

I was watching television that night with my sisters, Cathy, 14, and Lisa, 8. I had turned 13 two weeks earlier. The three of us were sprawled belly-down on the floor, chins cupped snugly in palms, faces angled at the glowing rectangle like planets toward a sun.

In the middle of the show came a local announcement: Plane down at airport. Details to come.

The National Transportation Safety Board later would determine that the plane had approached too low, too fast, skimmed some trees whose branches extended into the approach path, and exploded when it hit the ground.

My father, James Richard Keller, taught mathematics at Marshall. With so many funerals happening simultaneously, Marshall's stunned athletic department was having a difficult time finding enough university representatives to attend them all. My father volunteered to give the eulogy at the funeral of Scottie Lee Reese, a 19-year-old linebacker from Waco, Texas.

My parents loaded Cathy, Lisa and me into our family's blue and white Volkswagen bus and took off for Waco, a drive from southwestern West Virginia of about 1,000 miles. Scottie's funeral was held at Tolliver Chapel Missionary Baptist Church, about a week after the crash.

All I really can remember is looking around the church at those stricken people and their friends and wondering what they would do next. What would they do when they went home after the funeral, and the day after that, and the day after that? How would they go on?

Almost 30 years after that plane broke apart in a bleak West Virginia field, I found that I still wondered.

How did those with loved ones on the plane ever resume their lives?

"Sometimes it seems like 30 years ago," said Keith Morehouse, who was 9 when his father died in the crash, "and sometimes it seems like it happened yesterday."

Then and now, I wanted to know how people lived with such a loss, with the sudden, permanent demolition of the way they thought their world would be. Where does grief go?

Chester Reese is 71 now. He and his wife, Jimi, 72, raised six children — Ronald, Chester Jr., Scottie, William, Dwight and Cheryl — in their Waco home.

Four of their children went to Prairie View University, just outside Houston, Chester said. Scottie, though, received a football scholarship from a place they'd never heard of: Marshall University.

They heard news of the crash from a radio broadcast.

After nearly 30 years, the pain is still there, Chester said. "You don't forget it. You don't. It's something that happened and you can't do anything about it. I have to accept it.

"I have my bad moments. I do." He paused. "I get in my car and I ride. I ride out to the cemetery and visit his grave. I have a cry."

Jimi, who helps her husband run Chat 'N' Chew, a Waco restaurant they own, said Scottie's favorite hobby was singing with a Huntington gospel group called the Soul Searchers. He loved football, loved West Virginia, loved telling the folks back home about his adventures in a faraway place where the terrain was as craggy as Texas was flat, that seemed, in fact, like the exact geographical opposite of the land he knew so well.

"I think about him all the time," Jimi said. "Sometimes it seems like he's still around somewhere, like he can't be gone. When it gets round close to that day again, I start to think about it harder. Along about that time of (that) month, it gets pretty heavy.

"It ran through my mind the other day, how old he'd be, where he'd be."

Indeed, Scottie — and all of the young men on the Marshall plane — have now been dead longer than they were alive.

The first few weeks after the crash, Mary Beth Repasy recalled, she would go to Mass every day, come home and lock herself in her bedroom.

Then she would scream.

Repasy, 76, doesn't scream anymore. The wound of loss has been cauterized by time. But she remembers her son, Jack Repasy, who died at 20 aboard the Marshall plane, with a clarity that cuts through the fog of the intervening years.

He was a big, handsome young man, a receiver. He was friends with two other Marshall players, backup quarterback Bobby Harris and offensive guard Mark Andrews. The three had grown up in the same neighborhood and graduated from Cincinnati Moeller High School. They borrowed one another's clothes, wrestled on mattresses thrown on the floor, fished and kidded. They did everything together.

On November 14, 1970, they died together.

"There was one blessing. They went in a hurry," Repasy said.

She has stayed in close touch over the years with Bob and Betty Harris, 75 and 73, and Ruth Andrews, 77, Mark's widowed mother. The families have a Mass said each year on November 14 for their lost sons.

Bob Harris Sr. and Mary Beth's late husband, John Repasy Sr., did their screaming in another way: They sought answers from the NTSB about the cause of the crash, never satisfied with the answers they were given from bureaucrats. "We were both very angry," Bob said.

The Harrises had driven to North Carolina to watch their son play. They asked him to ride back with them, but he wanted to be with the team. They heard the news about the crash at a service station on their way home.

What used to hurt — remembering Bobby's smile, his laugh, the way he'd effortlessly pick her straight up off the ground — now brings her a quiet peace, Betty Harris said.

A funeral for the three boys was held at Cincinnati Moeller. As was the case for all the crash victims, the caskets were closed. Betty regrets that now, even though she knows the reason: The catastrophic nature of the accident had left the bodies scorched and torn.

"It makes you never quite believe it," she said. "You think he'll come walking along."

Ruth agreed. "We never saw Mark. It took so long to imagine him dead. You need to see him dead to accept the fact that he's not coming back."

Teddy Shoebridge was the golden boy, handsome and charming, with a big, easy grin. He was Marshall's quarterback. He came from Lyndhurst, N.J., just outside New York.

"He was a great kid. Just a great kid," said Ernie Salvatore, 77, retired sports columnist for The Herald-Dispatch in Huntington. "He was a star, no doubt about it."

When he thinks about the crash, Salvatore said, he thinks first about Ted and Yolanda Shoebridge. Of all the parents, they seemed the most devastated, the most shattered, the most inconsolable. Years later, Salvatore recalled, Yolanda still would call him at the office late at night, sobbing into the phone.

"What could I say?" Salvatore mused. "What could I tell her?"

Terry Shoebridge, 40, Teddy's brother, described the family's sorrow this way: "My parents' heart was ripped out on that day and it was never put back."

To his brothers Terry and Tommy, who still live in the Lyndhurst area, Teddy was a hero, an idol.

In the dining room of the comfortable home that Terry, an accountant, shares with his wife and two children, the Shoebridges gathered around the table to talk about their lost prince.

"I was 17 years old," said Tommy, 45, a big, powerful-looking man who coaches the Lyndhurst High School football team. He was talking about November 14, 1970, the day that changed everything. "I came home and my mother was hysterically crying. My dad was pacing in the yard. I couldn't get a straight answer out of anybody."

A frail Yolanda, 73, who would die from cancer shortly after this interview, recalled that her parish priest arrived to break the news to her and her late husband, Ted Shoebridge Sr. "In 29 years, it seems like yesterday and they're going to tell me all over again."

Terry said, "My mother lives with this every day of her life."

Yolanda and Ted Sr., who died of a heart attack several years ago, raised their remaining sons with love and care. But they never got over Teddy's death.

Dave Wellman, a reporter at The Huntington Herald-Dispatch, rested an elbow on his desk in a quiet corner of the newsroom. "It was just so long ago," he said.

He was a Marshall student when the plane went down. The first few days, he said, were "absolutely gut-wrenching." The city, like the campus, was devastated.

Store windows were draped in black. Everything seemed to be happening in slow motion.

Then time went by.

"Every year, it gets a little less emotional," Wellman said.

Morehouse, 38, was one of the six children of Gene Morehouse, the broadcast voice of Marshall athletics, who died in the crash. Keith, sports anchor for WSAZ, a Huntington television station, is the play-by-play man for Marshall football.

Over the years, he has been a frequent target for interviewers because his story is symmetrical — son picks up father's fallen microphone — but Keith never tires of such intrusions.

"Hundreds, both locally and nationally," he said, estimating the number of times he has been asked where he was on the night of the crash. "But I don't mind. For anyone who asks the question, it's the first time they've asked it. They don't know the answer."

He and his siblings were watching "The Newlywed Game" that Saturday night, Keith recalled. The phone rang. His mother answered it, shrieked — and everything changed forever.

"I remember my father as being very gentle, really nice. We'd listen to him on the radio, wrapping up the games," Keith said. On the bookshelf behind his chair is a black-and-white portrait of his father: a thin-faced, bespectacled man with a shy, earnest smile.

His mother, who died in 1989, never got over it, Keith said. She moved away from Huntington after her youngest child left home, but her memories followed her wherever she went. "She worshiped my father. She once told me that if she was in downtown Huntington and she saw him across the street, she'd still get chill bumps."

On a beach vacation after graduation from Huntington High School, Keith met a young woman who had just graduated from crosstown rival Huntington East. Her name was Debbie Hagley. She was one of the six children of Ray and Shirley Hagley, the team physician and his wife who died in the crash. She and her siblings were raised by their grandparents.

Keith and Debbie, 38, were married a few years later, after both graduated from Marshall. They are the parents of two children.

"I don't think about the crash itself," Debbie said, "but once a day, for about a split second, it pops into my mind that I really wish my parents could have seen my kids."

Her grief "took several years to get to a certain point," Debbie said. "But then, it came to a standstill. For the past 10 or 15 years, I've felt the same way. I'm OK with it. I say,

'My parents were killed in the Marshall plane crash,' and I can say it without crying."

My father never talked about the crash.

On our way home from Waco, my mother rode in the back of the van, and my sisters and I took turns up front, sitting beside my father as he drove those lonesome miles from Texas to West Virginia.

When it was my turn in the front seat, I kept hoping he would discuss the crash with me, because I would have felt so grown-up to talk about such a momentous topic. But he didn't. It was a long and quiet ride.

My father died in 1984, at 52, of lung cancer. Never, in all of the conversations I had with him during the last solemn weeks of his life, did we talk about the crash or, for that matter, about his decision as a young man to remain in Huntington, spurning job offers from other universities throughout the years.

Somehow, the two ideas seemed linked in my mind: It was as if my father, like Huntington, could never quite shake the notion that he deserved whatever happened to him, that he was powerless to resist.

Indeed, there was a kind of fatalism in my father, just as there was in West Virginia. He was an intelligent man, a gifted teacher and a troubled soul. He lived too long in the shadow of those mountains, I think, and allowed himself to forget that shadows move according to the position of the sun. They are not permanent.

When I return to Huntington to visit his grave, I am struck by how the city has transformed itself since the crash and all the sadness. Thanks to a new medical school and overflow from the consolidation of other state schools, Marshall's enrollment has almost doubled, from about 8,500 in 1970 to more than 16,000 today.

Three decades is a long time, except when it isn't.

The question that had pushed me back to the crash — whither grief? — ended up pushing me forward. "Look at the night sky," Leon Wieseltier advised in "Kaddish," his 1998 chronicle about mourning his father. "You are not seeing only the light of the stars. You are also seeing the journey of the light of the stars toward you."

I asked about the progress of grief, but I learned about the purpose of memory.

I recall quite clearly my thoughts on that Sunday morning after the crash. I tried to imagine the scene inside the plane just before it hit. Who was sitting where? Who was talking to whom? Who was thinking what?

A plane burrowing through the night sky had always seemed to me — a kid whose first flight lay some 10 years in the future — like a wonderfully snug place, a capsule that would enfold you like the warm palm of a cupped hand. I had a picture in my mind of the passengers sitting in pairs on each side of the long, low-ceilinged row, and I could almost hear the wisecracks and the big, booming laughter.

I could see the pilot and co-pilot, calmly efficient in their seats, facing a control panel decked out with lights and dials and switches, peering through the rain and fog for a glimpse of — yes, there they is — the lights of Tri-State Airport.

That was where my imagination always faltered. I didn't envision the crash. I was not interested in the crash itself, only in the moments just before.

Who was laughing, who sleeping? Who was looking out at the river?

Because it has been almost 30 years since that night, the serrated edge of grief has been, for most of those who had loved ones on the plane, rubbed by time into a smooth object. It doesn't draw blood anymore. They can carry it around with them now. They can touch it at odd moments.

They can touch it in much the same way that, perhaps 40 years ago, some might have brushed a young son's sleeping face with their fingertips, wondering what kind of man he would grow up to be, how many children he might have, what special destiny awaited him just down the road.

Julia Keller, born and raised in Huntington, West Virginia, is a Marshall University graduate. Winner of the 2005 Pulitzer Prize, she is cultural critic for the Chicago Tribune. She earned a Ph.D. at Ohio State University. She has been a Nieman Fellow at Harvard University and a visiting professor at Princeton University.

The Authors

From left: Dave Wellman, Rick Nolte, Tim Stephens, and Mickey Johnson.

Rick Nolte, sports editor of The Macon (Ga.) Telegraph since 1997, wrote and edited "The Marshall Story." The native of Huntington, West Virginia, also was a writer and editor for "Rolling Thunder" and "Won For All, "two earlier books about Marshall University football. Nolte, 51, covered Marshall football as a sportswriter for The Herald-Dispatch in Huntington from 1978to 1985, and as assistant sports editor and later sports editor from 1986 to 1993. He also has been news editor of The Herald-Dispatch, sports editor of The Chillicothe (Ohio) Gazette in Chillicothe, Ohio, and The Dominion Post in Morgantown, West Virginia, and assistant sports editor of The Times in Shreveport, Louisiana. Nolte has won numerous writing and editing awards from the Associated Press Sports Editors, Gannett Co. Inc., and sports writers associations in West Virginia and Georgia. He graduated from Marshall in 1976 with a bachelor's degree in journalism. Nolte and his wife Claudia, are the parents of adult children Mindy, Justin and twins Amy and Eric.

Mickey Johnson, executive editor of the Palladium-Item in Richmond, Indiana, since September, wrote and edited "The Marshall Story." The Huntington native also was a writer and editor for "Rolling Thunder." Johnson, 54, covered Marshall University football as sports editor of The Herald-Dispatch from 1986 to 1990. He also has been managing editor of The Herald-Dispatch, and executive editor of newspapers in Fremont and Port Clinton, Ohio, and Gainesville, Georgia. He was managing editor of the Pensacola (Florida) News Journal before moving to Richmond. He also worked as a copy editor at USA Today. Johnson has won numerous writing and editing awards from Gannett, Associated Press Sports Editors, West Virginia Sports Writers Association, and Ohio, Georgia and Florida press associations. He graduated from Marshall in 1982 with a bachelor's degree in journalism. Johnson and his wife Sheila are the parents of adult twin sons, Travis and Justin.

Dave Wellman, director of communications at Marshall since 2001, wrote "The Marshall Story." The Huntington native also was a writer for "Rolling Thunder" and "Won For All." The 54-year-old was a sports writer, assistant sports editor and sports editor at The Herald-Dispatch from 1975 to 1996, and senior reporter at the newspaper from 1996 to 2001. Wellman has won numerous writing awards from Gannett, The Associated Press and West Virginia Sports Writers Association. He graduated from Marshall in 1975 with a bachelor's degree in journalism. He is the father of an adult daughter, Kacey.

Tim Stephens, director of the Tri-State Chapter (Ohio, West Virginia and Kentucky) of the Fellowship of Christian Athletes since 2002, wrote "The Marshall Story." The Huntington native also was a writer for "Rolling Thunder" and "Won For All." The 43-year-old was a sports writer for The Herald-Dispatch from 1982 to 2002, and covered Marshall football from 1984 to 2002. Stephens has won numerous writing awards from the West Virginia Press and Sports Writers associations. He attended Marshall. Stephens lives with his wife, Emily, in Rome, Ohio.